LANGUAGES OF NATURE

LANGUAGES OF NATURE

CRITICAL ESSAYS
ON SCIENCE
AND LITERATURE

Edited by L. J. Jordanova

Foreword by Raymond Williams

Rutgers University Press
New Brunswick, New Jersey

First published in USA by
Rutgers University Press, 1986

First published in Great Britain by
Free Association Books

This collection and introduction
© L.J. Jordanova 1986

Library of Congress Cataloging-in-Publication Data

Languages of nature.
   Bibliography: p.
   Includes index.
   Contents: The eighteenth century: Nature as
ethical norm in the Enlightenment / A.E. Pilkington.
Naturalizing the family / L.J. Jordanova. Sensibility,
sympathy, benevolence / James Rodgers. The scientific
muse / Maureen McNeil – [etc.]
   1. English literature—19th century—History and
criticism. 2. English literature—18th century—History
and criticism. 3. Science in literature. 4. Nature in
literature. 5. Literature and science. 6. French
literature—History and criticism. I. Jordanova, L.J.
   PR468.S34L35   1986   820'.9'356   86-11852
   ISBN 0–8135–1194–1

Typeset by Rapidset and Design Ltd., London

Printed and bound in Great Britain by
Billing and Sons Ltd, Worcester

Contents

Contributors

GILLIAN BEER is a university lecturer in the Faculty of English at Cambridge and a Fellow of Girton College. Her book *Darwin's Plots* is now in paperback (Ark, 1985). Her research interests include the Victorian period and narrative theory and practice.

ROGER HUSS is a lecturer in French at Queen Mary College, London, with research interests in the French eighteenth- and nineteenth-century novel and popular natural history. Publications include articles on tense and on anthropocentrism and final causality in the work of Flaubert.

LUDMILLA JORDANOVA is Lecturer in History at the University of Essex. She is the author of *Lamarck* (Oxford, 1984) and of articles on science and medicine from the mid-eighteenth to the early twentieth century and on family, gender and sexuality. She is currently writing a book for Basil Blackwell on the family in eighteenth-century England and France.

MAUREEN McNEIL is a lecturer at the Centre for Contemporary Cultural Studies, University of Birmingham. She has recently completed a book on Erasmus Darwin – *Under the Banner of Science: Erasmus Darwin and his Age* (Manchester University Press, 1986). Her teaching and research interests are in gender and knowledge production and science and culture.

ANTHONY PILKINGTON was educated at Accrington Grammar School and Jesus College, Oxford, where he has been Fellow and Tutor in Modern Languages since 1966. He has published books and articles on literature and ideas in France.

JAMES RODGERS is Associate Professor of Humanities at Lawrence Institute of Technology in Southfield, Michigan. He received his doctorate from the University of East Anglia and has published papers on other aspects of *Tristram Shandy*'s relationship to science.

SALLY SHUTTLEWORTH is a lecturer in the English Department, University of Leeds. Her publications include *George Eliot and Nineteenth-Century Science: The Make-Believe of a Beginning* (Cambridge, 1984).

Editor's Preface

This book was conceived in 1978. Its long gestation has been due to a number of factors, but throughout the contributors have been patient and helpful. I thank them warmly for this and for their willingness to make changes to their pieces. I am particularly grateful to Karl Figlio and Jim Rodgers in whose company the project began.

As the Introduction explains, we hope that the volume will appeal to those with little or no previous acquaintance with science and literature as a field. The introductory material was written with such people in mind. Specialists will probably prefer to go straight to the individual contributions. Catherine Belsey and Elaine Jordan made valuable comments on the Introduction, as did the contributors. Particularly helpful were many conversations with Gillian Beer, who generously provided some material on the study of language. Several essays in this volume make clear the extent to which our subject has been influenced by the work of Raymond Williams. We are delighted he was able to make a contribution to the project.

Finally, I wish to express my appreciation of the excellent typing of Doreen Waller and Jill Scott which made the last stages of preparing the book so much easier.

L. J. Jordanova   Colchester, September 1985

FOREWORD

Raymond Williams

'I suppose the two first persons you would choose to see would be the two greatest names in English literature, Sir Isaac Newton and Mr Locke.' That is Hazlitt in 1825, reporting a conversation among his friends 'of persons one would wish to have seen'. If the use of 'literature' there is now surprising, where 'science' or 'natural philosophy' might be expected, the problem is as much ours as theirs.

There are many historical reasons for the separation of what we have learned to call 'disciplines': some of them easily defensible in local terms. But beyond these there is a much more general imposition of new categories, which offer to be mutually exclusive. 'Science' and 'Literature' are the most immediately relevant examples. It is then easy to suppose that it is from such categories that we should investigate the many different kinds of practice which, in more than one sense, they cover.

But this can be quite misleading when there are genuine problems of how different practices relate or should relate to each other, in assumptions, methods and results. People can ask, even seriously, how 'Literature' and 'Science' relate to each other, or how either relates to the very similar general category of 'Society', without noticing that versions of these relationships – given enclosures, distances, oppositions – are already inscribed in the categories themselves.

The most notorious modern example of this failure was the 'Two Cultures' controversy of the 1950s and 1960s: generous and passionate in its intended initiatives, but hopelessly confused by its enclosing categories and by its consequent omission of that whole area of practice and learning, itself reduced in shorthand to 'society', where the real and complex relationships are continually generated, tested, amended and renewed.

It is a substantial achievement of the generation which inherited that kind of misdirection that ways have been found of addressing the undoubted problems more precisely and more specifically. The essays collected in this book are in the main based on the most immediately productive of these ways: that emphasis on language as history which encourages us to look at the actual composition of ideas, arguments and theories in some of their hitherto least noticed conditions of production.

In practice this involves shifts in the analysis of language, against two strong currents of a different kind. Literary criticism, in its narrowest usage, had been moving towards a new form of isolation: that encounter of naked reader with naked text which, if accepted, excludes not only contexts but the real social and historical conditions of both reading and writing. Linguistic analysis, under its most dominant theoretical tendency, was simultaneously moving towards deliberately ahistorical and indeed anti-historical modes; interestingly with an accompanying rhetoric of the replacement of 'humanism' by 'science'. What had then to be done, in cultural studies generally, and here in this new kind of history of science, was to retrieve the effective methods of close verbal analysis which were in danger of being enclosed by these forms and to show, in practice, that any thorough verbal analysis is inevitably social and historical, unless theoretical blocks are deliberately imposed. There has been, and indeed still is, as much resis-

tance to these extended forms of analysis from hitherto dominant types of literary criticism and linguistics as from, in a more
familiar area, the simplest exponents of 'science' as a wholly
autonomous form of knowledge. Thus the appearance of these
essays, introduced from a conscious and challenging position in contemporary argument, is an event of importance: a
casebook within what is too often a loose and running controversy.

Of course what then happens, in detail, takes many different forms: analysis of the transfer, both deliberate and
unexamined, of concepts and models; analysis of metaphors
and of grammatical forms; analysis of areas of interaction between different forms of writing. Consciously historical, the
essays treat selected examples from the eighteenth and
nineteenth centuries, yet a sense of the twentieth century and of
some of its central intellectual problems comes through quite
clearly.

We can see the possibility of thinking in new ways about
such basic and in practice overlapping concepts as 'evolution',
'development' and 'progress'. We may not need alerting to
what is happening, linguistically, in such contemporary titles
as *The Selfish Gene* and *The Naked Ape*, but we need not
suppose that these are the mere wrappings of science, or of
arguments derived from it: the inclusion of models, metaphors,
transfers and allusions is a form of intellectual composition
which needs as stringent examination as the evidence which, in
apparently autonomous ways, is offered or interpreted. More
interesting, perhaps, because otherwise more easily over-
looked, are the areas of silence, absence, writing out, which
close analysis can identify, most clearly in the crucial linguistic
complex of 'Man', 'Mankind' 'man/woman', and the deeply
implicated constructions of linguistic and biological gender.
The connections between this area and new questions about
representations of the human body and then necessarily about
the nature of medicine are especially significant. Again, when

the practice of detailed analysis has been begun and is sustained, the process extends to the analytic texts themselves: I would want myself, for example, to add 'the unconscious' to the terms to be recognized as problematic.

What most matters, however, is that there is now an increasing amount of collaborative exchange between writers and scholars and scientists whose training had been defined by both practical and conceptual boundaries but who in the very energy of sustained attention to their own evidence have been led to questions which they find they have to discuss with their intellectual neighbours and, as they can, with their distant or even estranged relations. To this notable enterprise in the collaborative study of the language of science and learning can be added the less developed and methodologically less prepared collaborative study of institutions, formations, intellectual movements and schools and tendencies, which is now the most active element in the sociology of culture. Its applications to the history of science, in an open and critical rather than an enclosed form, seem certain to be productive.

Thus, in areas of great and acknowledged intellectual difficulty, and on questions which underlie many of the major disputes and decisions of our own time, new collaborative work is coming through. Much of it, necessarily, is at a research level, and for exchange between the experienced. Yet its kinds of approach offer good prospects for practical initiatives – new kinds of course and inquiry – in a more general education. What we are now trying to understand, as a way of getting and giving an education, is how different kinds of knowledge – different and related kinds – contribute to our most general kinds of understanding. What we may increasingly be finding is that some of our most general and apparently obvious ideas in turn constitute the kinds of knowledge that we can recognize, or that we use them to support the ideas.

These essays are being published at a time when there are powerful political attempts not only to reduce all educational

resources but to limit, by arbitrary assumption and preference, the full range of inquiry and research. In showing how
some of our most basic ideas, about 'nature', about 'science', about 'life' itself, are at once historically constituted and
socially changed and contested, and moreover how they can
inform or influence what seems the most 'objective' and 'fac-
tual' inquiries, this book is a significant contribution not only
to specialist studies but to our most general interest.

Introduction

L.J. JORDANOVA

SCIENCE AND LITERATURE

The distinction between science and literature is, for the contributors to this volume, a debatable one that deters rather than enhances historical understanding. Science and literature are united in their shared location within cultural history. Both fields are enriched by a more developed sense of their rootedness in a specific historical context. It has been relatively easy to place the so-called softer (i.e. biological and human) sciences in their social setting, especially in the case of theories which no longer enjoy the status of 'truth'. Regrettably, at the 'harder' and more prestigious end, attempts to give the physical sciences a full history have been less successful. Such an enterprise has often been hampered by an unfortunate polarization between 'genuine' and 'pseudo' science. This distinction led scholars to neglect the crucial connections between fields in the past because the status of the knowledge produced, judged by present-day standards, was their primary concern. A fully historical view of science is hard to attain, because virtually everything in our culture conspires to reinforce a separation between the study of science and the pursuit of the humanities, both of which are needed to understand the social and cultural history of science. So internalized has the distinction between science and the arts become that we greet any sign of a bridge between them with surprise. It thus requires conscious effort to throw off the preconceived ideas with which we approach the science and literature of the eighteenth and nineteenth centuries. Few of the institutions maintaining present-day discipline boundaries existed then. The most powerful of these is the modern professional career structure, which actively discourages people from changing fields, since to do so leads to a situation in which 'career capital' is dissipated. Interdisciplinary studies, having enjoyed a brief period of support in the 1960s and 1970s, are now coming to be seen as ideologically suspect and intellectually promiscuous, in a climate of cuts and recession. Our schools and universities cheerfully reinforce the science/arts divide. Without such institutional and ideological underpinnings the distinction crumbles. It is significant that the entire notion of a discipline is a recent one, having developed in the nineteenth century.

The essays which comprise this volume are case studies. These have a dual function. First, they present the results of research which will, we hope, be of interest both to literary critics and to historians of science. If they serve to encourage others in the field we shall be well pleased. Second, they constitute examples suited to undergraduate and graduate teaching. Essays which present the relationships between science and literature clearly and precisely seem well suited to the second task. The very situation which makes the study of science and literature compelling – their constant overlap in a setting devoid of rigid disciplinary demarcations – also leads to difficulties. It is all too easy to be overwhelmed by lengthy lists of borrowings between the two areas without a sufficiently disciplined account of the exact respects in which science and literature are related. Focused case studies should avoid such problems and display something of the cultural richness of eighteenth- and nineteenth-century thought, by avoiding the weaknesses of accounts which simply juxtapose science and literature.

'Science *and* literature', like 'science and society', is a slippery phrase. 'And' is a loose term of linkage employed in lists; it denotes miscellany and is often used in speech to get from one thought to another without spelling out exactly what the connection is. 'And' leaves much to the imagination. In science and literature, as well as in science and society, the 'ands' indicate our belief in a link, but leave its precise nature unspecified. We can imagine a number of ways in which these two areas could be related. They could be studied by the same people. They could employ the same ideas. They could each borrow from the other. They could be produced by the same cultural and social conditions.

The following essays represent interdisciplinary approaches to science and literature that owe more to methods of literary criticism than to those of history of science as traditionally conceived. This is because our primary object of study is language — that which mediates all thought, action and experience. We focus largely on the discourses common to science and literature, rather than on the literary achievements of gentlemen scientists or the 'borrowings' of writers from science. Such approaches have customarily relied heavily on notions of influence — one of the main ways in which historians of ideas have conceptualized relations between individuals. By contrast, we tend to emphasize shared cultures, contexts and even philosophical structures, since historically specific ways of knowing the natural world give rise to related modes of writing about it. Indeed, changing languages of nature go straight to the heart of shifts in scientific method. One important way forward for the study of science and literature is to seek their common ground in cultural and social history, paying close attention to original texts. Any divorce between text and context is undesirable; hence, methods and approaches from both literature and history can fruitfully be used together.

We are accustomed to think of science as composed of discrete fields. Historical reasons for the past mingling of areas we now separate are to be found in the fact that those who received any formal scientific 'training' at all did so either through general university courses, especially medical ones, or through apprenticeship, for example to an instrument maker. Medicine included anatomy, natural philosophy (i.e. physics and chemistry), *materia medica*, therapeutics, including medical botany, and what in the nineteenth century came to be defined as physiology. Medical education, which generally also included the study of classical writers, was thus very broad, and it could lead to an extremely wide range of more particular researches. Similarly, natural historians, who were often self-taught, rarely confined themselves to one small section of nature; mostly they were familiar with minerals as well as plants and animals, all of which were studied in close association with the weather and the earth. The same arguments apply to the all-encompassing character of natural philosophy. Furthermore, since only a small number of these people, at any rate in England, were entirely dependent financially, if at all, on their scientific work, there were few mechanisms for institutionalizing and reinforcing conformity to norms (cf. Morrell and Thackray, 1981). A glance at the truly miscellaneous contents of the *Philosophical Transactions* of the Royal Society of London during the eighteenth century confirms that neither the distinction between the natural sciences and the humanities, nor that between scientific disciplines, held much force.

Study of the relationships between science and literature is by no means a new enterprise but goes back to pioneering work in the history of ideas in the early part of this century. Any link between science and literature is more striking to the twentieth-century eye because we have grown up in a society which constantly reinforces and polices the boundaries between different areas of knowledge. Although scholars working in the first half of our century organized their writings thematically and explored ideas common to both fields, their researches were often predicated on the idea that literature borrowed from and popularized science (e.g. Nicolson, 1946). It is only relatively recently that scientific texts have been analysed in literary terms. Conventionally it has been a question of tracing scientific ideas and terminology, which had crept into literature, back to their original sources. Valuable though much of this work was, it tended to divorce writers from their context, paying very little attention to the conditions under which writings, literary or scientific, were produced.

Recently there has been renewed interest in science and literature as a field. No doubt this reflects significant changes which have taken place in literary studies and the history of science. There have been some important, and parallel, shifts in the ways in which science and literature are studied. For instance, both historians of science and literary critics have become aware of the dangers of constructing lists of specially privileged 'great' authors, although most departments of English literature still teach those who are defined as major writers. The same holds for history of science courses, although here the equivalent of 'heroes' have emerged in the shape of scientific institutions, societies and laboratories – the places where experimental natural science is largely done, and knowledge of nature actually produced.

But where history of science has been becoming more concrete, separating itself from its philosophical ancestry, literary studies, by contrast, have been going in the opposite direction, becoming more abstract in the wake of the impact of structuralism and psychoanalysis in the last few decades. The greater recognition of the role of the unconscious in the act of writing – an act recognized by literary commentators as being a highly complex one – inevitably drew attention to sexuality as integral to writing both from the point of view of the psyche of the author and as the subject matter of literature. This trend is clearly evident in the present volume. Social anthropologists reading the following chapters would not be surprised at the emphasis on gender, kinship and sexuality, since their subject has fully recognized that such topics provide basic models which societies use as general cultural resources. Historians of science, on the other hand, have been very slow to perceive how important sexuality has been as a model of natural relations, as in areas such as alchemy or mineralogy; how closely science meshed with other areas of human concern in exploring descent, inheritance, genealogy and family trees; how persistently natural philosophers and natural historians sought to explain sex and reproduction; and how much scientific writings are permeated by sexual language. The area of sexuality therefore serves as an example of the ways in which artificial boundaries between science and other realms of human endeavour can be broken down through greater attention to the complexities of texts and to their context of production.

THE NATURE OF TEXTS

History of science can learn much from the methods of literary critics, particularly in textual analysis. Treating scientific writings as literary texts involves, for example, asking questions about genre, about the relationship between reader and writer, about the use of linguistic devices such as metaphor, simile, and personification, about what is *not* being said, or cannot be said, and hence about the nature of conscious and unconscious constraints on writing, about the models and sources a writer employs, and about the relationship between the form and content of arguments. The end result of such investigations should be a much larger sense of how science is located in its social and cultural context.

To write is to assume a position of authority. To write as a scientist doubles the authority, because an authoritative account of reality is being established. Scientists and medical practitioners who put pen to paper are claiming to 'tell it as it really is'. Writers of fiction may do the same, as, for example, when they present their writings as 'true' stories. The act of writing does not just lead to a text, it also produces relationships between the author and the reader. Each piece of writing constructs a writer and a reader, but does not of course fully determine the nature of that relationship. It would be mistaken to assume that *any* reading of a text is possible; there are certainly limits within which it is construed. Nonetheless, the same work may be read very differently by different groups and individuals, who will select the resonances, meanings and conflicts that evoke associations for them. These associations will shift through time so that a new historical context will, in a skilled reader, produce a reading which is both conditioned by present needs and aware of past implications.

A good example of the potential for selective reading is Erasmus Darwin's scientific poetry, which could be read as poetry without constantly consulting the footnotes, or as informative description by paying particular attention to them. The two reading experiences would be markedly different. The role the reader is to play will be determined by a number of factors, among which genre, style and format are of paramount importance. A dialogue, dictionary entry, poem, letter, didactic handbook and treatise will certainly be read in radically different ways. Equally important is the language authors employ, for it is mainly by this means that they construct their authorial identity. Do they include or distance their readers, chide or flatter them, speak down to them or assume a degree of superior learning, shock or instruct them? Scientific writings can usefully be analysed in these terms which enable us to approach the question of what roles the scientific writer or the writer about nature assumes.

Those who wrote about nature in the eighteenth and nineteenth centuries negotiated through their writings not only their relationships with their readers, but also their relationships with God, and with nature itself. In relation to nature, he who

contemplates nature may be a hero who tames a feminine wildness, a seeker of Faustian powers, an intruder, a spectator, a
sympathizer, a critic, a participant, a worshipper, a man-
ipulator or a privileged confidant (Easlea, 1983; Merchant,
1980; Fox Keller, 1985). Of course, several of these can easily coexist in a single piece of writing, and even come and go in
the course of a text. These distinct positions may be tagged by
conventions of spelling and punctuation, such as the use of
capitals, by vocabulary, such as choosing between the terms
God, the Creator and the Supreme Being, by devices such as
personification, by the selection of images and metaphors,
and by many other means. They are also hinted at by such
mundane things as how the author's name is given, if at all,
and if not, the pseudonym chosen. Particularly significant
are the devices frequently employed in the eighteenth-century
novel to indicate to the reader that the contents are 'true',
deriving from genuine documents accidentally obtained, or
drawn in some way from actual events.

Authors select the genre within which they write, and the
variety of genres even within conventional scientific and
medical discourse is worth stressing, including catechisms,
Platonic dialogues, letters, case histories, encyclopaedia and
dictionary entries, *éloges* and obituaries, journal articles,
book reviews, diaries, and advice books. More recently,
when the format within which publication is accepted has considerably narrowed, an impressive amount can nonetheless be
communicated through style and rhetoric.

A number of the papers in this book argue that we must take
scientists seriously as writers, not just because some of them
were exceedingly good writers, which they were, but because
doing so provides an important range of insights which would
otherwise be lost to us. Until relatively recently, the written
word was of paramount importance in all aspects of scientific
and medical practice: medical practitioners like Erasmus Darwin were very frequently consulted by post, and much infor-

mation circulated through private correspondence. Moreover, the social status of science, and, to a lesser extent, medicine, depended on the power of the written word to reach audiences, to change their ways of thinking, to persuade people of the value of science and to legitimize the position of the practitioners. Writings by scientific and medical practitioners also revealed something of the authors' cultural background: for example, the extent to which they were steeped in the classics, and which ones, and the extent to which they were conversant with the Bible, or other languages and their literatures. Since ultimately scientific and medical writings seek to establish an authoritative view of the natural world, and often of mankind and society too, their overall persuasiveness was a crucial element in their success. For instance, there can be little doubt in the case of the evolutionary biologist Jean-Baptiste Lamarck that one element among many which contributed to his relative neglect, but nonetheless an important one, was his verbose, unpersuasive style, and his lack of descriptive precision. His prose may inform, but it certainly does not compel.

WRITERS AND READERS

The scientist, if we may use a term that only came into common parlance during the nineteenth century, is then in the eighteenth and nineteenth centuries also a writer; furthermore, scientific and fictional writers had much in common. It is equally telling that it was during this period that the idea of the writer, especially the novelist, as the scientific, i.e. accurate, recorder and observer of life, also emerged. This coming together of science and literature was greatly encouraged by the general enthusiasm for reading and writing about nature. 'Nature' included such a multitude of phenomena to be described, marvelled at and investigated, that it was inevitable that there should be considerable common ground between the areas we designate as science and literature respectively. Of course, many important pieces of writing cannot be assigned to

either category, and most people living before the late nineteenth century would have been astonished by the conviction
with which we uphold the distinction.

It is, however, not enough to write. There must be an
infrastructure of publishing and distribution if ideas are to
reach an audience wider than a tiny elite. This book covers the
period when far-reaching changes were taking place in the
publishing business, and also in education and in newspapers.
These changes brought knowledge about science and medicine
to a largely non-specialist, though predominantly middle-
class, public. Yet we must be careful in using the term 'science'
in this period; 'natural knowledge' may be more appropriate,
since it reminds us that there was no single professional elite
producing science, although France was always closer to this
situation than England. In the eighteenth and the early
nineteenth century, natural knowledge could be generated by
enthusiasts, including clergymen and medical practitioners,
travellers, merchants, farmers and craftsmen, as well as by a
privileged class which had the resources to study nature
because freed from the need to earn a living. By the mid-
nineteenth century this was no longer the case, largely because
of the belated intervention of the English state in education
and science, and also because of the new emphasis on laborat-
ory-based experimental work which entailed costs beyond the
reach of all but the most affluent amateurs. Furthermore, these
changes took place unevenly in different areas of science,
natural history being one of the last fields to professionalize.

The values of a rational, empirically based knowledge of
nature were broadcast long before the advent of state-spon-
sored science in Britain, beginning in the seventeenth century
as an integral part of larger reform movements (Webster,
1975). In the eighteenth century the sheer volume of published
material increased dramatically. The rise was in secular material, much of it directed at instructing people in social survival
skills, as the proliferation of advice books and instruction man-

uals shows. In France, where a variety of bodies operated strict censorship regulations, the situation was somewhat different, although pamphleteering was no less vigorous than in England, a situation fostered by the intense regionalism of *ancien régime* France which encouraged participation in local issues. In both countries, the new literary products were aimed at the middle classes, who were thus taking on new importance as both the producers and readers of secular materials. These new social strata were strongly committed to social progress, which meant, among other things, that a selective vision of their own environment was highly desirable. Writing for such groups therefore entailed reinforcing their ability *not* to see some things, such as poverty and the degradation of work, and to highlight others, such as the value of rationally based entrepreneurship and unostentatious lifestyles. In terms of publishing, the populace, by contrast, were catered for by traditional chapbooks (cheap, popular pocket-sized volumes) which appear to have changed very little in content, style or format during the eighteenth century.

The new secular and didactic literature was composed of many different genres of writing, some of which were classical or at least traditional in origin and innovative only with regard to ease of availability, format or price. Others, such as the novel, were distinct innovations. Contemporaries waxed eloquent about what they saw as the largely detrimental ideological power of the novel, often representing it as a woman's genre in terms of both writing and reading. For the study of science and literature the importance of the novel lay in its commitment to realism, to showing naturalistically drawn characters in an appropriate, detailed setting (Watt, 1963). Novelists made epistemological as well as literary claims. For example, Samuel Richardson, who was both an author and a publisher, presented his novels as 'true' rather than 'made up' in order to render them convincing. He also wanted to control the meanings with which readers invested them: he wished his novels to be seen as morally exemplary, and strove to eliminate any 'inappropriate' or deviant interpretations of his works (Eagleton, 1982). Those writers strongly committed to establishing a 'correct' view of nature and of human nature strove especially hard to control the ideological implications of their linguistic practices.

Writing in the wake of the scientific revolution, eighteenth-century authors could take for granted a certain optimism about the potential of scientific thought, which indicates the status attached to the names of Isaac Newton and John Locke in particular. Certain people, among them Alexander Pope, Jean-Jacques Rousseau and William Blake, were hostile to science, sometimes on religious and moral grounds that included an accusation of hubris against seekers of scientific knowledge. At the very least many people were profoundly sceptical about natural knowledge – a feeling which was generally more directed at those, such as medical practitioners, who sought to sell their knowledge as a way of earning a living. This scepticism did not necessarily touch claims to objective knowledge through observation. By the end of our period, the 1860s and 1870s, scientific institutions, the role of the specialized expert and the prestige of the natural sciences were well established. A significantly large proportion of scientific debate, however, was still conducted in the public arena, available at least to an educated upper and middle class, and indeed the audience for science, judging from the vast numbers of popular and semi-popular publications, was ever increasing. The marvels of the universe and the wonders of nature readily captured the public imagination. The ways in which non-specialist readers thought about the world around them was thus deeply influenced by the language of these publications, in just the same way as upper- and middle-class ideas in the eighteenth century were constructed out of scientific *cum* literary languages of nature.

LANGUAGE AND METHOD

The essays in this book share an interest in perceptions of nature, and especially of human nature. The phrase 'perceptions of nature' is intended to serve as a reminder that a subjective process of interpretation is necessarily involved in accounts of the natural world. Languages of nature are made and not pre-given, and they are made, furthermore, according to different rules, assumptions and aesthetic preferences, for distinct purposes by various constituencies according to their context. Galileo believed that the 'book of nature was written in mathematical figures', and that it was therefore the business of science to penetrate beneath the surface world of phenomena to the underlying structure of matter, that is, to its primary qualities and formal relations, best uncovered by those skilled in the mechanical sciences. His conviction expressed an idea that lay at the heart of the programme for the development of a mechanical philosophy – a programme which had profound religious, social and political implications and which is only comprehensible in the context of seventeenth-century European society. By contrast, for the majority of nineteenth-century intellectuals, it was the phenomenal world which alone offered legitimate insight into the workings of nature. For the physiologist Claude Bernard, for example, only our direct experience of nature could count towards scientific knowledge, and from that experience the presence of regular, determined laws of nature could be inferred (Bernard, 1957). Rather than reading nature as a set of mathematical formulae, nature's regularities were reconstructed from evidence culled from the human senses in an experimental situation. These two different epistemologies, or methods for knowing nature, led to two languages of nature, while the language that writers employ in turn reveals their epistemology, for example, through the authorities evoked, the images of knowledge employed and the value given to the different senses.

Ways of writing about nature are thus bound up with ways
of knowing about nature, and hence with questions of scientific
method. Changes necessarily take place in them in a coordinated fashion. Styles of writing and the meanings of individual
words are, of course, quite historically specific; through history new significations are continually being added while
others are falling away. Such linguistic shifts are both a cause
and a product of changing languages of nature. There is, of
course, no one privileged language at any one time, but competing ones, claiming to offer a convincing and accurate picture of the natural world. The historical changes which languages undergo can be, as the work of Raymond Williams
(1963, 1975, 1983) and John Barrell (1983) has shown,
valuable indicators of larger social transformations. The language of science is no exception. For example, what is actually
meant by nature not only depends on who is using the word
and how, since it contains a vast variety of senses at any one
time, but its meaning changes over time. Perhaps the most
important change in the idea of nature during the period
covered by this book – the eighteenth and nineteenth centuries
– is the articulation and consolidation of the idea that nature
itself is inherently historical, a product of ancient processes no
longer directly available for scrutiny. This notion was registered with particular force in the life sciences with which we
are most concerned here. The sense of the historicity of nature
not only called into question assumptions about stability and
permanence, but also raised some tricky epistemological questions about how nature's past could be known about. While
many people solved the difficulties neatly by means of the
argument generally described as uniformitarian – that the processes now observed also acted in the past, making the present
the only sure guide to the nature and rate of historical changes
– a whole host of imaginative possibilities were opened up by
the discovery of time as an agent in nature (Hooykaas, 1963).
Analogies abounded: individual life histories, the history of

the earth, of nations, tribes, races and empires, cities and families, the development of a foetus, of languages themselves. These analogies were tools of thought which generated possibilities for further investigation; they were heuristic devices indispensable for thinking (Hesse, 1966). Consequently, the antiquarian, geologist, mineralogist, biologist and psychologist had much in common.

The belief that there were profound similarities between the past and the present was the target of opposition from some quarters. People espoused uniformitarianism for a variety of reasons which are not reducible to putatively objective criteria – and many reputable figures in the early nineteenth century continued to believe in the reality of a universal deluge (Rudwick, 1972). Few people change their minds solely on empirical grounds, especially if there are strong ideological commitments underpinning their beliefs. This being the case, the language of scientific debate is crucial, for it constituted, in the eighteenth and nineteenth centuries, the most persuasive rhetorical tool available. Finding a host of appropriate analogies to natural processes and employing them to full effect was a fundamental part of scientific discourse.

Another example of the way in which changes in meaning register shifts in definitions of proper knowledge is the word 'science' itself. Originally science meant any kind of knowledge or learning, with an increasing emphasis on theoretical rather than practical knowledge, and on the ability to demonstrate the certainty of such knowledge. Gradually, science came to mean specifically knowledge of nature, that is, of the external observable world. Science was opposed to metaphysics or subjective experience, and hence the association of science with objectivity emerged (Williams, 1983, 276–80). It should be remembered, however, that this meaning developed before a structured, professionalized scientific community did. This concept of science was prominent in the eighteenth century, while modern scientific social structures appeared only in the second half of the nineteenth century. During the period this book considers, science denoted the study of nature using specific methods. In other words, it referred largely to the epistemological status of the knowledge rather than to who produced it and where; these institutional questions became of the utmost importance during the nineteenth century. Scholars may usefully designate as science anything that came under the term in the past — any attempt to apply modern evaluative criteria in order to separate past activities into genuine science and pseudo-science is profoundly unhistorical.

Changes in the meaning of key terms, such as science and nature, together with attendant alterations in notions of method and in what counts as knowledge, need to be set within a broad intellectual context. In the period with which we are concerned here, the development of positivism, as philosophical doctrine, as social theory, as scientific method, was of overwhelming importance (Kolakowski, 1972). In fact, positivism was integral to the historical changes science underwent in this period. At its core, positivism was an assertion of faith in the method of observing nature in order to infer regular, law-like patterns of phenomena. The phenomena which presented themselves to the senses of the scientist constituted reality for positivists, who were sceptical about metaphysics of any kind and hence about conventional religion. Positivism was a movement which, although firmly rooted in experimental science, had far-reaching social and political implications. Its reformist rationalism valued science as the major tool for social progress. Positivism, as it was generally received, was thus anti-theoretical, while it generated optimism about the progressive growth of reliable, objective knowledge. Its historical significance derives not merely from its being both a symptom and a cause of scientific change, but from the fact that it embodied a method that could, potentially, be applied to anything. Thus, while the actual practice of science was becoming more focused and specialized, claims about the universality of scientific method were being extended. For this reason, what started in the eighteenth century as the science of man, and developed in the nineteenth century as the moral and social sciences, was an important test case for the universal applicability of scientific method, as several of the papers in this volume indicate.

Closely bound up with debates about scientific method were debates about the nature of language itself. The late eighteenth century and the first half of the nineteenth century were in fact exceptionally fertile periods from the point of view of ideas about the relationship between language and mind, and about the history and taxonomy of specific languages (Aarsleff, 1967, 1982; Smith, 1984). Language was a part of nature, to be analysed accordingly.

A highly developed consciousness of the role of language in thought, and of the practical consequences of such a view, derived principally from the importance accorded to Locke's philosophy during the Enlightenment. Both Locke and Condillac exerted considerable influence over scientific practices (Hine, 1973). The idea that science could only advance on the correct linguistic foundations was widely held and could be applied to a variety of scientific preoccupations, from the classification of animals, plants, and inorganic bodies to the terminology used for abstract organic processes. Debates about whether and in what manner language was intrinsic to thought therefore served to heighten awareness of how language was actually being used in scientific work.

Language was increasingly seen as amenable to historical analysis. Like other parts of nature, languages changed, developed, and, most important of all, died (Foucault, 1970). Furthermore, there were relationships between languages which could be understood within a classificatory system analogous to that used for organisms. Cultures, societies and civilizations could be studied through the history of languages, leading to a concept of general cultural development, with the incipient evolutionism the word 'development' implies, such as is found in the writings of the positivist Auguste Comte.

The sense of the historicity of language is reflected in the dictionaries and encyclopaedias which characterize our period. Not only did such publications represent a codification of informal language practices, making it all the easier to discuss languages as entities, but they helped people to think about the ranges of meaning of each word, which could no longer be thought of as a simple tag for a separate idea. The uncertainty and ambiguity of language had to be confronted. This could present natural historians, natural philosophers or medical practitioners with unwelcome problems: on the one hand they were being enlisted in the service of clear, simple vocabularies, while on the other they were aware of the complexities of their own tools and objects of thought.

All these aspects of language as it was perceived in the eighteenth century must be placed in the context of the prevalence of classification as a fundamental analytical technique. Taxonomic procedures gave names to natural objects, but what was accomplished thereby was highly controversial. Debates about system, method, and the ability of names to capture natural relationships were exceedingly complex, for they encompassed questions of logic, language, epistemology and ontology (Larson, 1971).

During the period discussed in this collection, the study of language became intimately connected with new ideas of 'man's place in nature'. Two controversies in particular created connections between language theory and theories in the natural sciences. The first has already been mentioned: the origins and development of language. Closely connected with this was the second one, which had been a subject of lively debate since the seventeenth century: whether humankind uniquely possessed language and was thereby manifestly of a different order from all other living creatures. Towards the end of the eighteenth century there was a movement in the study of the history of language away from essentialist views towards the concept of language as a growing and developing medium. Linguistic change, particularly in the meaning of words, was no longer necessarily identified with decline or attrition. Instead, semantic and then grammatical and phonetic transformations came to be recognized as intrinsic to the composition of language. This historical shift was made concrete in changing lexicographical practices. The transformation of languages through time became a disciplined topic for intellectual endeavour by the beginning of the nineteenth century.

Eighteenth- and early nineteenth-century debates about language were particularly heated precisely because they were seen to have implications for such questions as the uniqueness of human beings. The sense of ideological battle was sharpened by the political and social environment which developed in France and Britain at the end of the eighteenth century. Widespread instability in both countries and the explicit conflict between different groups had a pronounced effect on intellectual debate in general and on scientific and medical controversies in particular. There was a heightened awareness of the ideological implications of intellectual positions, and most natural historians and natural philosophers understood how much hung on their words. Naturally, such writings rarely referred directly to political and social conflict but did so in a mediated way (Figlio, 1976). These conflicts were in fact largely about the nature of fundamental boundaries, like that between mind and body, human and animal, living and non-living, male and female – all of which assume central importance in this book.

BOUNDARIES AND DICHOTOMIES

In all societies, the social sciences have taught us, boundaries are integral to social structure. What they are, and precisely where they are drawn, varies enormously cross-culturally as well as between groups and individuals within a single culture. Generally these boundaries relate to the basics of existence: gender, kinship, food, work, cleanliness and personal hygiene, death and the supernatural (Douglas, 1966, 1970, 1975). Western Europe is no exception, and within science in particular it is clear that such boundaries have been of incalculable importance. Two in particular will crop up time and time again in the present volume: mind/body and living/nonliving. Through the first the distinctions between human beings and animals, and between God and mankind, were explored. On the second hinged such questions as: What is brute matter like? Can it form itself into living creatures? Hence, where the boundary between life and non-life was drawn raised queries about God's creative powers and about the uniqueness of the human race. Yet, these boundaries were rarely tackled head on. In an era of censorship, a strong church, and a state, to varying degrees, concerned to control discussion of such matters, this is perhaps not surprising. Also, the ramifications of setting these boundaries were so extensive that the underlying issues could take many different forms. It further appeared more manageable and less threatening to discuss such deep issues through other ones. Albrecht von Haller's writings on irritability and sensibility, the properties of muscles and nerves respectively, and the debates his work provoked in the eighteenth and the early nineteenth century, are a case in point. To talk of how nerves acted upon muscles was to speak about the capacity of the will to act upon the body and hence about the nature of the soul and about the relations of God and humanity. Everyone who took part in the Hallerian debates recognized this (Figlio, 1975).

Dichotomies operate at two levels. By using two separate

terms, the *difference* between them comes to the fore, while by pairing them together, the idea of a *kinship* between them is evoked. Developing the second point, we may want to inquire about the nature of the kinship, or, to put it another way, to ask what kind of a bridge exists between the two terms. This concern was particularly relevant to the living/inert and mind/body dichotomies. It was thought that places where the gap between the terms might be overcome would shed light on each element. So that in the first case both spontaneous generation and eating were considered revealing instances of how non-living matter became 'alive', while the decay consequent upon death shed light on the reverse process. In the second case, organic phenomena in which mental and bodily processes were fused, as in all aspects of sense perception, thought and speech, became especially interesting, as did madness and hypnosis, where the normal control of the mind appeared to be lacking. During the eighteenth century a number of important concepts emerged which spanned the mind/body dichotomy. Ideas like 'sensibility', 'habit' and 'organization' are examples, for they expressly defy pigeonholing as either *mental* or *bodily* concepts. Such bridging concepts were important in that, on the one hand, they constituted technical terms whose meaning had to be refined to render them precise analytical tools, while, on the other, they generated many associations leading to the sometimes hilarious free play found, for example, in *Tristram Shandy*. In being both precise and imprecise at the same time, they gave rise to productive ambiguity and a wide range of potential uses.

There are, of course, different kinds of boundaries and dichotomies. Paired terms may be contraries (black/white, up/down), continuous (hot/cold), complementary (male/female — on one reading at least), or capable of being transformed from one into the other (raw/cooked). The same binary pair can be seen at different times and by different people in a variety of ways. For example, mind/body were seen as opposites within a Cartesian frame in the sense that they had no characteristics in common: one was composed of matter and the other not. But they can also be seen as complementary in that neither can function fully without the other; furthermore, they might also be construed as two poles of an organic continuum, two distinct manifestations of the organism. Hence, the meaning of any particular dichotomy and the location of the boundary between the terms can be highly variable. Indeed, terms seen as meaningful dichotomies in one period may not appear so to another. The point is that however hard such pairs and boundaries are to pin down, they are of fundamental importance because of the consequences which flow from them.

An apposite contemporary example is the concern to define 'life' so that procedures can be established for determining 'death'. On this definition the right to use organs for transplant purposes and to turn off life-support machines depends. Similarly, 'life' and its exact meaning has been given considerable prominence in the abortion debates. Some have claimed that abortion is ethically justifiable before true 'life' begins, the problem remains that of pinning down the elusive boundary between living and non-living.

These boundaries and dichotomies focussed on three leading and closely related concepts in European thought which are repeatedly discussed in this book — nature, life and human nature. Like the bridging concepts mentioned above, each one was capable both of precise, technical definition, and of generating such a profuse variety of meanings that they spilled over into virtually every arena of intellectual debate.

NATURE

Nature is not an easy term to define (Williams, 1983, 219–24). At a banal level we might say that it is simply a word for the physical world which we understand as having an existence separate from and prior to human life. To say this immediately indicates how easily we slip into saying what nature is by showing what it is not. Nature can be that which is *un*tainted by human hands. But this definition is clearly partial: animals do not cease to be 'natural' when domesticated, even though aspects of them may change in the process. The belief that nature was somehow opposed to human artifice was widely embraced, especially in the eighteenth century. The value of such a definition was that this view of nature could be used to expose human and social *mis*behaviour. For many Enlightenment figures critical of despotism and arbitrary power, nature stood as the imagined alternative pure realm, in whose name such 'unnatural' practices as forced and arranged marriages, celibacy, inheritance and bastardy laws, war, and the Inquisition could all be condemned. Nature could thus be held in opposition to convention, law, society, arbitrariness and tyranny. It held people's belief in a world better than the one they knew, since it emanated from the essence of things and did not depend on human whims as the political and social order did.

Rousseau's thought, which invokes nature in myriad ways, is a convenient example of some of these eighteenth-century trends. He took nature as that which is prior to society – not necessarily literally, but analytically. It thus provided a conceptual yardstick against which social conventions could be measured. Generally, Rousseau found societies wanting and he roundly condemned certain aspects of 'civilization' as degrading to morals – the theatre, for example. Yet Rousseau believed in another kind of nature, which was more solid, less amenable to change. His treatment of gender, crucial to his political theory, is a case in point. For Rousseau, nature made men and women differ from each other in the whole of their beings. Not only is there a feminine nature, to which women should remain true in their conduct, but women are *of* nature in a way that men are not, in that women are bound by their natures, while men transcend theirs. Nature thus gave us the differences between the sexes in an almost providential manner. Rousseau adapts these natural roles to his own political ends, for he sees gender as one basis upon which sound societies are built (Okin, 1980; Elshtain, 1981). While it is often mistakenly assumed that he advocated a return to nature – for example, by advocating emulation of the noble savage – Rousseau does use such an idea to argue against excessive artifice in childrearing (Rousseau, 1974).

Thus, 'nature' and 'natural' are terms that can be used in virtually any context. That they have meant so many different things certainly poses problems for us. We cannot always easily discover what weight and implications a particular writer or audience attached to nature. We can, however, see that certain notions rather than others dominated in the eighteenth and nineteenth centuries. Throughout the period, the belief in some sort of natural order, lawfulness and regularity appears to have been deep and pervasive, as is amply demonstrated by the violent reactions elicited by more anarchic views of nature which developed during the eighteenth century. This sense of natural lawfulness, and the accompanying slippage between description and prescription, was greatly reinforced by the growth and dissemination of natural history and natural philosophy and by a certain empiricism associated with the popularization of both fields. Here again the developments in publishing and its market went hand in hand with conceptual developments. The refinement of taxonomies which were easier to use prompted the publication of zoological and botanical handbooks for enthusiastic amateurs. These publications in turn encouraged people to collect and study specimens themselves, thereby reinforcing their sense of an ordered nature.

Of course there were many different approaches to classification, but they all emphasized a natural order discovered by human beings. These approaches differed, however, as regards where the order is deemed to emanate from: from

God, from nature itself, or from the human mind. Popular demonstrations of natural philosophy experiments had a similar effect, expanding the market for books, instruments and teachers as well as reinforcing the lawfulness and comprehensibility of nature.

However, eighteenth- and nineteenth-century writers also questioned the unity, coherence and goodness of nature. Increasingly, nature appeared full of contradictions, tensions and ambiguities. Nature even appeared dangerous, violent and subversive, especially with respect to ethics in general and to sexual morality in particular. By the 1780s, the idea that the natural world contained unambiguous ethical prescriptions was coming to seem naive, at least in some circles. Nature was simultaneously taken as a theatre of human affairs, in a deliberate and celebratory anthropomorphism, and as containing dramas which repel or disgust the human spectator. The parallelism between human social life and the natural world could also take a more abstract form, as in the work of Saint-Simon and Comte (Manuel, 1972). Ideas like division of labour, progress and hierarchy appeared to have equal explanatory power in both realms. This raises the question of metaphor — was it that society and nature were *like* each other, that is, linked through a metaphorical language, or was it rather that they were different aspects of the *same* thing for which only one language was needed, social phenomena being merely more complex organic ones?

While naturalism came to be the dominant scientific approach during the period covered by these essays, the relationship between nature and society remained problematic. Despite claims about the foundation of a science of society, the natural and the social were seen as distinct, and from the point of view of their linguistic associations productively so. Frequently posed as a distinction between nature and culture — a juxtaposition which gave rise to many other related pairs, such as country and city — the dichotomy between the products of

laws of nature (i.e. observed nature) and the results of human
agency (i.e. culture) also had an exceptionally powerful sexual
dimension. The personification of nature as a woman, and the
associated identification of civil society, *res publica*, culture
and science with men, is an old theme (Elshtain, 1981). The
antiquity of the idea led to its vast and complex sets of associations, which have cultural histories of their own (MacCormack and Strathern, 1980).

Although the juxtaposition of culture and nature implied a
distinction between human action and laws of nature, it also
implied potential affinities between them. One of the most
important of these is that both are seen to work in our period
not by magic or supernatural powers but by naturalistic
means. We can comprehend how both nature and people produce their respective results. Hence, a science of human
nature, modelled on natural philosophy, was possible. This
version of the nature/culture pair rendered it increasingly difficult to speak of God, and related questions of the original
creation of the universe and of man, in the same terms as the
laws of nature. Yet even the phrase 'laws of nature' is misleading in that it fails to take account of fierce debates about the
relationships between the inorganic and the organic realms.
Was there a single set of laws governing both domains? If not,
what were the precise interconnections between the laws of
inert and those of animate bodies? It was through the notion of
'life' that such arguments were fought out.

LIFE

The living world, with its marvellously rich range of forms and
its unique properties, was an impressive manifestation of
nature's powers. This period saw the development of 'life' as
an abstract concept, spawning considerable interest in the
properties common to all living things and in criteria for divid-
ing plants from animals using large-scale defining characteristics (Canguilhem, 1971).

A reaction against the mechanical philosophy of the seventeenth century was certainly one powerful stimulus to the search for fresh vocabularies and methods with which to approach entities self-evidently more complex than automata. This sense of organic complexity was further fuelled by the drive to explain the mechanisms of human thought in a naturalistic way. Behaviour in general and human thought in particular focused attention on the brain and nervous system, the organic substratum of mental and sensory acts. Although self-knowledge was an important incentive to biological work, a fascination with simple animals was equally important in the life sciences of the eighteenth century. It was inevitable that this would be the case once the microscope had been focused on the organic world and revealed to the eye and the imagination thousands of previously unknown microscopic organisms. Furthermore the general intellectual climate was one in which the plenitude of living nature was frequently remarked upon (Lovejoy, 1961). This has much to do with greater travel, and more accurate observation of plants and animals at a local level. Dissection and experimental work on animals grew in the eighteenth century, and, although still highly controversial, it fed a thirst for knowledge of living nature. To this we must add the vogue for natural history and especially for botany, which the cult of nature and of gardening promoted but which would have been impossible without a growing and leisured middle and upper-middle class, an aristocracy which could afford large-scale landscape alterations, the increase in accessible natural history publications, and the development of social networks for the exchange of ideas and information.

Once life had been defined as a specific phenomenon of nature requiring attention, it was necessary to define its essential characteristics. Many eighteenth-century savants put forward ideas about what the basic organic properties were, and these were hotly debated. Many argued that organisms alone grew and replicated themselves, although claims that minerals

had the same capacities were not universally dismissed until
the early nineteenth century. Generation, i.e. reproduction,
was a central biological problem in the eighteenth century
(Roger, 1963). And the fact that gestation sometimes went
wrong, producing 'monsters', was a vivid illustration of how
nature's laws might be illuminated by occurrences which
appeared to run counter to them.

It became increasingly apparent to eighteenth-century
observers and nineteenth-century experimentalists that the
environment within which organisms existed could have a
dramatic impact on their form. It followed from this, firstly,
that one characteristic of life was its plasticity — a feature
already emphasized in relation to human beings by Locke's
sensualism — and, secondly, that there was a dialectical
relationship between organisms and their environment, another example of nature's own dynamism. This sense of the
close interweaving between life and its surroundings was
extensively explored by novelists as well as by natural historians, as several essays in this volume demonstrate.

All the intense interest in living processes inevitably provoked conceptual tensions. During the eighteenth century, liberal opinion came to ridicule the notion of direct, divine creation which certainly seemed incapable of explaining physical
abnormalities like human hermaphrodites and malformed
foetuses. The aberrations suggested that nature had its own
modes of operation independent of divine will. One implication of such a view was that the movement of matter explained
all observed phenomena, without requiring recourse to another explanatory level — will, spirit or God — to animate the
matter. Hence a dispute arose over monism versus dualism,
that is, over whether there exists only one kind of substance in
the world, or two distinct ones. The bridging concepts referred to above were frequently used to dissolve the boundaries
held firm by dualism, by implying an underlying continuity
between phenomena, like mind and body, previously kept dis-

tinct for theological and related reasons. On the one hand, then, debates about the nature of 'life' touched the heart of eighteenth-century views of nature, while on the other they were one expression of the growing interest in the scientific study of human nature.

HUMAN NATURE

A number of points already mentioned indicate the considerable attention given to human nature as a topic for systematic study: interest in the nervous system and the location of 'mind', Locke's concern with the faculties of the understanding and with the association of ideas as an explanatory device, fascination with sexuality and the feelings to which it gave rise, and widespread discussion of the mind/body problem. It has also been noted how certain observed occurrences could be used to shed light on human nature in general. Different kinds of unmanaged 'natural' experiments – madness, illnesses, malformations, monstrous events and abnormalities of all kinds, environmental variations, wolf children, variations with race, gender and climate – supplied empiricial data on the variety of manifestations of human nature. These provided an important resource for the 'science of man' – a telling phrase that reveals a commitment to apply scientific method in its widest sense to human life.

Out of this broad eclectic study the disciplines of anthropology, psychology and sociology emerged in the course of the nineteenth century, but none of these terms is appropriate in an eighteenth-century context. Interestingly, the science of man still had room for introspection as a source of knowledge – although this came to seem increasingly suspect to empiricist psychology in the nineteenth century. The development of psychology as a separate science is particularly interesting, since it partly depended on the assumption that the phenomena of mind could be studied like others in nature, that is, empirically, and were thus in a sense to be considered 'biological'.

Yet the development of psychology as a separate science also reinforced the specialness of mental phenomena. While some mental processes appeared somewhat resistant to an experimental approach, it is important to remember that much of the early work in the nineteenth century was done not by biologists and physiologists but by physicists. On the other side, there was a bridge between psychological and social phenomena so that the potential for an all-encompassing science of human life and society was present at the same time as distinct disciplines were in fact in the process of forming. Anthropology and sociology developed into very different fields in the second half of the nineteenth century, although both had arisen out of the close links between the natural, human and social sciences. Until the early twentieth century, much anthropology had a strongly biological and medical orientation.

The widespread enthusiasm for the science of man prompts us to ask whether this phrase refers to man as human, or man as male. Often those writing on the subject treated the male as the norm to which the female, a special case, should be compared. Women were a problem to be explained, and many generalizations about the human condition were deemed not to apply to them. Much writing in fact addressed itself to the nature of womanhood as a scientific and medical topic – attractive in part, no doubt, because women were easily construed as objects in nature requiring explanation. Such assumptions – that female human nature and male human nature were fundamentally different – certainly served to undermine ideas of a universal human nature, as did the growing literature on the exotic customs of so-called primitive peoples and on the variety of possible human societies.

The attraction of a universal human nature was that it could be used to underpin the idea that a general morality emanated from the human heart. This served to dispense with the arbitrary, authoritarian morals associated particularly with the Catholic Church and relocated morality in nature itself.

Nature was lawful, and thus inherently more just. The problem, and it was one that particularly preoccupied novelists, was to explain the amoral and immoral behaviour so frequently observed. Environmentalism was handy here, but not quite effective enough to dispel doubts about innate human morality. Fictional treatments are particularly revealing because they dealt openly with questions of subjectivity, character and personality which were not easily subjected to systematic empirical study. It is of course no coincidence that the period which is marked by the rise of the novel was also intensely preoccupied with subjective emotional experiences and their effect on human action. Love, desire and sympathy were of especial interest, illustrating once again the widespread concern to explain the springs of human sexuality.

Of course, the science of man contained silences too. Two obvious lacunae are class and work. Although variations in behaviour according to rank and status were often remarked upon in a literary context or in social tracts, these were rarely treated naturalistically, that is, as explainable in scientific terms. The exception was a crude environmentalism employed through such notions as lifestyle and habit, which embodied the idea that you are what you do, eat, breathe and so on. Writers in the science of man tradition frequently retained the idea of a human nature, even if it manifested itself in markedly different forms. Differences in human nature tended to be seen in terms of race, gender and environment, rather than class. Similarly, discussions in science, medicine or literature of actual work processes are notably rare in the eighteenth and the early nineteenth century, and they really only begin with the social inquiries and social surveys conducted in the wake of concern with specific industrial settings – initially large-scale textile manufacturing (Coleman, 1982). The science of man examined those aspects of human life which most interested its exponents, that is, were most compatible with their social vision: government and political structures, history, language

and education. Only in the growing field of political economy
was labour discussed. One reason for this is that writings on
human nature in the eighteenth century were, like novels, still
being produced for a largely middle-class, 'polite', learned
audience, anxious to participate in refined and general debate. By the mid-nineteenth century, class and labour were
increasingly present to the middle class because they had come
to participate more in the practical business of government,
especially at a local level, and because the problems that a
class-based industrialized society generated were part of their
immediate experience.

Historical changes were thus registered with particular
force in discourses about human nature, and a detailed
analysis of the language used reveals the complex social, political and economic issues they served to mediate. Yet it is not
enough to analyse what was written; it is also necessary to
become aware of what texts exclude.

CONCLUSION

Approaching science and literature involves working with
texts at many different levels, paying attention to their silences
as well as to their explicit content. This introduction has
sketched some of the reasons why detailed textual analysis can
be rewarding – a point which is, of course, taken for granted in
literature, but is by no means sufficiently widely appreciated
in the history of science. Naturally, there are many different
ways of studying science and literature and of conceptualizing
the multiple relationships between them. In this volume we
examine languages of nature in the eighteenth and nineteenth
centuries. We see the study of science and literature as offering
important insights into cultural history. Students of the history
of science are thereby enabled to see science within a broader
intellectual context, and to increase their awareness of the
many facets of scientific writings. Students of literature can
perceive the wide potential of critical methods and be encour-

aged to extend their reading beyond the 'great writers' into areas they may previously have imagined to hold little relevance to their field.

It is hoped that this book will prove accessible to those with no previous knowledge of the area. Hence the introduction has indicated some of the principal contours of eighteenth- and nineteenth-century culture of most relevance to the essays which follow. No attempt has been made to offer an overview of earlier work in the field, for that would be an altogether different enterprise. This introduction has, however, stressed the potential that exists for exciting new work, once the history of science and the literary study of language are brought together. The marriage of these approaches is in fact vital for our further understanding of science and medicine – activities whose full significance only emerges from historical analysis resting on a deep knowledge of original texts. The combination of general historical insights with precise textual work provides some powerful tools with which to pursue a critical evaluation of science and medicine in their cultural contexts, both then and now.

PART 1

The Eighteenth Century

'Nature' as Ethical Norm in the Enlightenment

A.E. PILKINGTON

EDITOR'S INTRODUCTION

It has become a commonplace to say that 'nature' was a key term in eighteenth-century thought. Behind such a simple statement, however, lies a complex historical situation. Pilkington shows some of the different meanings that were ascribed to nature in eighteenth-century France. These meanings had far-reaching consequences, for on them depended an understanding of the source of moral actions, of the relationships between individuals and of the nature of society as a whole. Moral and aesthetic readings of nature were thus also social and political ones. Eighteenth-century writings are permeated by these questions. Works on political economy, social theory, moral and natural philosophy, domesticity, aesthetics and religion all bear the imprint of profound shifts in how nature was understood. This is no more than we might expect.

For the most part, however, Pilkington is not discussing such works, but novels, dialogues and other imaginative writings. Many of the literary forms he discusses were new in the period, so that along with changing ideas and social contexts went innovative ways of writing. It is the relationship between these different aspects which we must examine. A convenient starting point is Ian Watt's seminal study, *The Rise of the*

Novel (1957). Although he specifically examined eighteenth-century England, his arguments have a more general application, not least because many French writers were deeply influenced by contemporary English fiction. For example Abbé Prévost, the author of *Manon Lescaut* (1731), translated, adapted and popularized Richardson's novels in France. Watt linked the growth of a middle-class reading public, the novel as a new genre, and a realist epistemology in an argument which suggests significant links between science and literature. The realism of the novel was expressed in an attention to particularity, of time, place and character, and also to environment as a detailed, specific backdrop to human action. Watt cites Richardson's use of the exact time at which letters were written as an example of the construction of an objective framework through which the content of the letters may be interpreted – a coordinate geometry for fiction. Novels written in letter form have other implications, as Pilkington and Jordanova point out, the most important one being that no privileged narrator exists, thereby showing a variety of alternative views. These developments which Watt outlined depended both on debates about the nature of human individuals and on a material infrastructure of writers, readers and publishers, i.e. a market.

It would be a mistake to assume that it follows from Watt's argument that the novel became an unproblematic mouthpiece for middle-class moralizing. Pilkington shows, in fact, the subversive elements so striking in much eighteenth-century writing. It comes, above all, through a new, explicit attention to human sexuality in secular works. Sexuality, and related questions of reproduction, kinship, genealogy and lineage, recur throughout this book. This is because they constitute a link, perhaps the major one, between nature in the sense of the 'out there', the 'wild', 'instinct', and observed human nature, and the subjective domain of feeling and sentiment that writers sought to capture. If any area of human life challenged simple, optimistic, moralistic readings of nature, it was sexuality. Its disruptive potential became ever more troublesome as the century went on, culminating in the writings of Laclos and de Sade, which Pilkington and Jordanova both discuss.

These writers had such a dramatic impact precisely because their reworking of nature as amoral has such devastating social and political implications which, in de Sade particularly, are spelled out at great length. Pilkington shows that Laclos and de Sade were not isolated freaks but that their concerns arose from decades of debate about the nature of nature. He also shows the importance of ideas about the milieu in which human action takes place. Early eighteenth-century writings frequently used the device of an imagined place, where all was good or bad, as a vehicle for a paradigmatic fable. Later writers, however, used naturalistic settings to make similar points, as Bernardin de Saint-Pierre does in *Paul et Virginie* (1788) by giving them a real tropical paradise (the Isle de France) in which to live, or as Prévost does in *Manon Lescaut* by showing his characters living most virtuously when away from France in the American colonies. And such natural environments carry their own moral values.

It is clear, then, that interpretations and reinterpretations of nature were vehicles for thoroughly exploring human preoccupations. This is all the more true since the goal of so many writers was to displace a religious view of human virtue and sin, often presented as 'artificial', and replace it with a secular, naturalistic one. Many people acknowledged, as did Voltaire, that religion might have its uses, a concession generally made in relation to the populace rather than the elite. The reference point for human nature was not God or the soul, but a material one, the empirical study of the variety of mankind, a 'science of man'. The preoccupation with developing a science of man took a number of different forms in the eighteenth century, including anthropological approaches to race and gender, philosophical inqiries into the nature of the human mind, physiological studies of the human body, and political investigations of the geographical variety of social structures.

These are the expected manifestations which have been written about extensively. To these we must add literary explorations of human subjectivity and conduct. Indeed, the realist licence given to eighteenth-century fiction positively encouraged such explorations of the hidden springs of human life. Whilst this is particularly striking in the novel, other forms of writing display the same characteristics. Pilkington discusses one of the most notable examples – Diderot's dialogue *Rameau's Nephew* (? written 1761–1774), a remarkable exploration of human nature which calls into question the possibility of generalizing about 'human nature' at all.

What Lovejoy (1961) has called the 'temporalisation of the chain of being', that is the jettisoning of the supernatural beings in the chain, in the middle of the century, not only undermined a sense of a larger cosmic order, as Pilkington points out; it also made the logical reference point the material world and the human condition rather than a spiritual realm. It is therefore consistent that attempts to find morality in nature did so increasingly by reference to human nature, rather than to a nature, created by God and dense with His rules. This was precisely the attraction of deism. It paid lip-service to the existence of a God as the ultimate Creator, yet for all practical purposes took no notice of Him at all.

In 1927 Arthur Lovejoy drew attention to the amazing variety of ways in which nature was construed as an aesthetic norm in seventeenth- and eighteenth-century thought. Pilkington has explored some of these in more detail, using largely fictional writings. The authors he discusses were not on the intellectual periphery, but were at its heart, fully participating in the reconstruction of nature. In this case it would be mistaken to see literature as passively giving voice to changes which had already taken place in another sphere of human endeavour; on the contrary, literature is one of the crucibles within which concepts of nature, and of society, are forged.

> Most errors regarding the idea of beauty arise from the mistaken
> conception of morality held by the eighteenth century. Nature at
> that time was taken to be the basis, source and type of every pos-
> sible ethical and aesthetic value. The denial of original sin
> counted for a good deal in the general blindness of that period.
> (Baudelaire, 1975, Vol. 2, 715)

Baudelaire's briskly dismissive comment on the eighteenth century, calling attention as it does to the connected uses of nature as ethical and aesthetic norm during the Enlightenment, provides a provocatively useful starting point. It is true that the idea of nature was put to work throughout the eighteenth century in a normative way: both in aesthetics, where the criterion of excellence was the solidly established neo-classic emphasis on conformity to nature, usually understood in some generalizing or idealizing sense; and in ethics, where nature was appealed to in various senses as an ethical norm. This paper will concentrate upon the second of these uses of the idea of nature.

In the period very roughly 1700–40, nature is used as a positive norm in the sense that virtue is held to be natural to man; the idea of nature provides a harmonious connection between morality and happiness. Towards the middle of the century, this equation comes to be questioned, although not rejected outright: the novels notably of Rousseau, Prévost and Diderot show nature to contain moral contradictions which make problematic its use as an unambiguous ethical norm. Finally, in roughly the last third of the century, with Diderot again, but also in the philosophy of d'Holbach and the fiction of Laclos and de Sade, a new use of the idea of nature emerges: nature is now argued or shown to be ethically neutral and blindly amoral. The aim of this paper will be to trace in more detail these shifts in meaning behind the constant appeal to the term 'nature'.

I

The question of the 'naturalness' of virtue is raised by Montesquieu (1689–1755) in the much-discussed episode of the
Troglodytes in his *Persian Letters* of 1721 (Montesquieu,
1949–51). The episode occupies Letters 11 to 14 and it is to
these that reference will be made. Usbek, one of Montesquieu's Persian travellers, is asked what he understands by his
view that men are 'born to be virtuous'. His answer takes the
form of the fable of the Troglodytes: a nation who perish
because of their lack of moral sense, but for two families whose
heads were remarkable in that they 'loved virtue'. They
refound a society based upon virtue which becomes strong and
prosperous. Notably they raise their children in the belief that
'the interest of the individual is always found in the common
interest; and that to seek to separate oneself from the common
interest is to seek to destroy oneself'. So far Montesquieu
seems to be going no further than an emphasis upon
enlightened self-interest. He appears to advance that same
equation of virtue with a recognition of the practical value of
identifying self-interest with the collective good which was
expressed in some well- known lines by his English contemporary Alexander Pope (1688–1744):

> Forc'd into virtue thus by Self-Defence,
> Ev'n kings learn'd justice and benevolence:
> Self-Love forsook the path it first pursu'd,
> And found the private in the public good.
>
> (Pope, 1966, 266)

Yet neither Montesquieu nor Pope presents the equation as a
simple matter of learned expediency. This is Pope on the state
of nature:

> Nor think, in NATURE'S STATE they blindly trod;
> The state of Nature was the reign of God:
> Self-love and Social at her birth began,
> Union the bond of all things, and of Man.
>
> (Pope, 1966, 263)

Hence men did not discover an entirely novel truth when they
recognized the identity of 'Self-love and Social'; they were not
framing a practically useful strategy but rediscovering and
reaffirming a natural principle, that 'Faith and Moral, Nature
gave before'; the sage 're-lum'd her ancient light [that is, of
nature], not kindled new'. These lines articulate what Jean
Ehrard (1963) has called the great aspiration of the eighteenth
century: a vision of man living in a harmonious relationship
with himself and with other men and *naturally* in accord with

> . . . the World's great harmony, that springs
> From Order, Union, full Consent of things.
> (Pope, 1966, 267)

In his fable, Montesquieu explores a similar vision. In the
assemblies of the Troglodytes, the common voice was that of
'simple Nature'. What establishes above all the 'philosophical' perspective of the fable is the role allowed to religion: the
Troglodytes 'learned to fear the gods' and 'religion polished
the roughness which Nature had left in manners'. Yet the connection between religion and morality remains equivocal: the
Troglodytes do not *need* to 'fear the gods' in order to behave
equitably, since they behave virtuously simply by acting in
accordance with the promptings of untutored nature. In other
words, virtue is associated not with constraint but with
euphoria: the distinction – a crucial one for our subject – is between the 'theological' view that virtue is not natural to man but
must be the result of an effort to transcend the necessarily
selfish or corrupt promptings of human nature, and the
'philosophical' view that the moral sense was inherent in
human nature and that it was possible to behave virtuously by
acting in harmonious accordance with the promptings of
nature. The distinction is between a prevalent seventeenth-
century view, somewhat pessimistic and morally rigorous; and
a view which began to gain currency in the early eighteenth
century, somewhat optimistic and morally euphoric. The

young Troglodytes thus realize that 'virtue is not something
which should demand an effort' and that it is not a 'painful burden'. The fable, however, ends on an ambiguous note, when
the people resolve to elect a king, preferring to be ruled by
authority from above rather than to continue to regulate their
lives easily and harmoniously by natural virtue. The old Troglodyte chosen to be king laments the fact that his fellows find
virtue 'oppressive' and wish to live under 'a yoke other than
that of virtue'. 'How', he asks, 'can I order a Troglodyte to do
something? Do you want him to perform some virtuous action
because I command it, when he would perform it in any case,
without me and by the simple impulse of nature?' The fable
ends thus quite literally with a question mark. Is virtue a
natural impulse or is it after all still a 'yoke'? The very
framework of the tale adds to our uncertainty: the mode of the
parable, the legendary setting, make us hesitate as to the kind
of connection which we should make between the fable and the
real world. Montesquieu himself was perhaps uncertain as to
the status of the work: a vision of a possible utopia? a glimpse
of a past golden age, nostalgically evoked? an expression of
the engaging eighteenth-century mode of the innocence of
unspoiled pastoral?

   This latter mode is marked in *Télémaque* (1699) by
Fénelon (1651–1715), where virtue as natural euphoria
rather than as self-conscious rigour is repeatedly stressed. The
hero's reaction to moral exhortation by his tutor Mentor is to
exclaim upon the happiness of men 'to whom virtue is revealed
in all its beauty' and to ask how 'virtue can be seen without
being loved and how one can love virtue without being happy'
(Book 4); he is encouraged to reveal to others 'amiable virtue'
and to make men realize 'how delightful it is to enjoy in solitude
those innocent pleasures of which nothing can deprive the
shepherd' (Book 2). To Montesquieu's fable corresponds in
Fénelon the description of the life of simplicity and virtue,
grounded in conformity with nature, led by the inhabitants of

Bétique who, by following 'sound Nature', are able to be both 'so virtuous and happy at the same time' – the now familiar 'nature-virtue- happiness' equation. Télémaque's comment, after hearing the account of this pastorally idyllic society, is to regret that, to our sophisticated minds, this 'natural simplicity' seems hardly believable and little more than a 'pleasing fable' (Book 8). The mythical framework and the heavily didactic tone are natural enough in a work written for explicitly educational reasons but leave us in something of the same uncertainty as does Montesquieu's 'pleasing fable'. Both works present images of the euphoria of natural virtue not in terms of some real connection with the contemporary world but in terms of nostalgia or aspiration. In either case, it is at one remove from the pressures and complexities of real life against which, as we shall see, novelists later in the period will test the idea of virtue as natural and euphoric.

A similar point might be made about a passage in an early work of Voltaire (1694–1778). His *Treatise on Metaphysics* was composed in 1734. Not intended for publication, it enabled Voltaire to be bolder than Montesquieu in connecting virtue exclusively with nature and in not allowing to religion even the limited moral utility role ascribed to it by Montesquieu. The new eighteenth-century philosophical view, which, as we saw above, came to challenge the established theological view, is voiced vigorously by Voltaire when he argues that 'those people who would need the support of religion in order to behave morally would be to be pitied and they would be monsters in society if they did not find within themselves the sentiments needful for social life and if they were obliged to borrow from elsewhere what ought to be present in our very nature' (Voltaire, 1937, 63).

In England one of the classic statements of the kind of optimistic view of moral nature advanced by Voltaire had been elaborated by Shaftesbury (1671–1713) in his *Characteristicks* (1711). The author's easy and urbane confidence in the inherently moral nature of man now appears very dated, and, as we shall see, it was indeed to appear dated already by the middle of the century. His essays remain, however, one of the most elegant and engaging expressions of the moral optimism and confidence in nature which define this early eighteenth-century mood:

> Sense of right and wrong therefore being as natural to us as natural affection itself, and being a first principle in our constitution and make, there is no speculative opinion, persuasion, or belief, which is capable immediately or directly to exclude or destroy it. That which is original and pure nature, nothing beside contrary habit and custom (a second nature) is able to displace. (Shaftesbury, 1900, Vol. 1, 260)

A further passage from the same essay, *Inquiry concerning Virtue and Merit*, expresses his serene conviction of the self-evident goodness of general human nature:

> 'Tis impossible to suppose a mere sensible creature originally so ill-constituted and unnatural as that, from the moment he comes to be tried by sensible objects, he should have no one good passion towards his kind, no foundation either of pity, love, kindness or social affection. 'Tis full as impossible to conceive that a rational creature coming first to be tried by rational objects, and receiving into his mind the images or representations of justice, generosity, gratitude, or other virtue, should have no liking of these or dislike of their contraries . . . (259–60)

This is the celebrated 'moral sense' which Shaftesbury, presumably generalizing from his own well-disposed and benevolent disposition, but also thinking very much in line with a whole new emphasis becoming current at the time, held to be part and parcel of universal human nature. The 'delight in beholding torments, and in viewing distress, calamity, blood, massacre and destruction, with a peculiar joy and pleasure' is therefore 'wholly and absolutely unnatural' and 'of this passion there is not any foundation in Nature' (331–2).

It is true that the kind of position outlined so far did not pass unchallenged even in the early eighteenth century. Pierre Bayle (1647–1706), influential throughout the Enlightenment, was plainly impatient with the optimistic notion of a natural moral sense when he asked:

> What, pray, is the *voice of nature*? What does it preach? Merely that one must eat and drink well . . . It is wrong to claim that it is contact with wrong-doers which inspires these passions; they are apparent not only in beasts, which simply follow natural instinct, but also in children. They exist prior to faulty education and if one did nothing to correct nature, there would be nothing more corrupt than the human soul . . . (quoted by Ehrard, 1963, vol. 1, 333)

Bayle's contention here reflects a long and influential tradition of thought: the theological belief that since the Fall, human nature is radically corrupt and that virtue can only be achieved, if at all, by transcending the promptings of nature rather than by following them. The 'voice of nature' is therefore for Bayle brute instinct. Virtue would consist not in obedience to the voice of the 'simple nature' of Montesquieu or the 'sound nature' of Fénelon but in a 'correction' of nature. In this view, moral behaviour is not that which is in euphoric accordance with nature but that which rigorously transcends nature; and at this point it is natural to mention Mandeville (1670–1733). He has much in common with Bayle and provides an English echo of Bayle's refusal to accept reassuringly settled assumptions about the goodness of nature. Much as Bayle disturbs the moral optimism of say Montesquieu and Fénelon in France, so Mandeville disturbs that of Pope and Shaftesbury in England. Both thinkers have also been the subject of scholarly attempts to define exactly where they stand.

In the case of Mandeville this is a particularly vexed question. F.B. Kaye's edition of *The Fable of the Bees* (1924) remains a classic study. He points out that Mandeville's conception of virtue allowed no action to be virtuous if it was inspired by selfish emotion; and this assumption, given that he held all natural emotion to be fundamentally selfish, entailed the rigorist view that no action was virtuous if it was dictated by natural impulse. Furthermore, like Bayle, Mandeville tends to use 'reason' in opposition to 'nature' (whereas the later Enlightenment generally seeks to bring the two terms into a harmonious relationship with each other — Rousseau would be a notable example of this) and thus to argue that no action is virtuous unless it is inspired by a rational motive; as he understands by 'rational' something antithetical to 'emotional', it follows from both strands of his thought — the rigorist and the rationalist — that all action which is dictated by natural impulse is necessarily vicious. As Mandeville himself puts it, the name of virtue should be reserved for 'every performance, by which Man, contrary to the impulse of Nature, should endeavour the benefit of others, or the conquest of his own passions out of a rational ambition of being good' (Mandeville, 1924, Vol. 1, 48–9).

II

The point has been made that the 'dilemma' of the novel in the eighteenth century sprang from the fact that here was a new genre ('new' in the sense that there were no classical models of what it might be nor any classical prescriptions as to what it ought to be) which it was extremely difficult to define in terms of the aesthetic of *la belle nature*. Excellent work has been done on the problems of the eighteenth-century critic and novelist in trying to provide a theoretical justification of the new genre, with its characteristic interest in real life in a contemporary setting, in terms of the closed critical system of neo-classical idealizing naturalism. In fact, the novel in the period can be seen to be subversive in both an aesthetic and an ethical sense: it was a new genre which was recalcitrant to the basic idealizing assumptions of the aesthetic of *la belle nature* and which at the same time, by its interest in the concrete complexities and opacities of real life, called more obliquely into question the *ethical* assumptions of the optimistic idealizing idea of moral nature adumbrated in the first part of this paper. This movement is already in evidence in the novels of Marivaux (1688–1763).

Jacob and Marianne, hero and heroine of *The Peasant Parvenu* (1734–5) and *The Life of Marianne* (1731–41) respectively, are plainly meant to embody an ideal of moral naturalness in their various encounters with social reality and enjoy the full sympathy of their creator. Yet these are no unambiguously moralizing works in the vein of Fénelon; on the contrary, they exploit ironies and moral uncertainties in a way which connects them with the emergence of the new line of the modern novel. One need only refer to the marvellously 'innocently natural' line of reflection followed by Marianne in order to justify acceptance of gifts from an older man and would-be seducer:

> After all, I said to myself, M. de Climal has not so far mentioned love; perhaps he will not even dare mention it for a long time and it is not up to me to guess the motives behind his attentions. I have been introduced to him as a man who is charitable and pious, and he has behaved charitably towards me: so much the worse for him if his intentions are not honourable; I am not obliged to read into his conscience . . . (Marivaux, 1949a, 109)

Marianne here comes across as more ingenious than naturally ingenuous. The voice of nature in all its apparent simplicity and naïvety serves to 'justify' conduct which is morally ambiguous. Similarly Jacob rebukes a young woman, Geneviève, for listening to their employer's offer to her of money in return for her favours, because as he claims 'I was naturally honourable'; but this does not prevent him from accepting money from her himself shortly afterwards although he is well aware that she has come by it through what Jacob disarmingly calls a 'slight irregularity of conduct'. However, he justifies his action by claiming that as a natural and untutored spirit, he was not used to 'subtle reflection' about things, and that in any case he went on to make good use of the money by using it to take lessons in writing and arithmetic! Here again we are struck by the gap between the natural innocence of Jacob and the dubious morality of his actual conduct. The gap is disturbingly suggested in the account which he gives of his relationship with and subsequent marriage to a wealthy and elderly spinster, where the reader is uncertain whether to see in Jacob the simple natural soul that he presents himself as being or the gigolo that his actual conduct implies.

Marivaux's theatre offers similar examples of basic ambiguities in the relationship between nature and morality. Jean Ehrard has pointed out how the apparent thematic opposition in *The Double Infidelity* (1724) between 'nature' embodied in the innocent peasants Arlequin and Silvia, and 'artifice' embodied in the courtiers — an opposition accompanied by a thematic opposition of virtue and corruption — ultimately leads nowhere, since it is precisely because of the natural innocence of their unreflective natures that Arlequin and Silvia feel no moral scruples about their 'double infidelity' to each other nor about their acceptance of the artificiality and immorality of court life into which they are both finally integrated (Marivaux, 1949b).

Remarkably similar ambiguities are present throughout the *History of the Chevalier des Grieux and Manon Lescaut* (1731) by Prévost (1697–1763). It is appropriate to call to mind the full title, usually shortened to *Manon Lescaut*, since it calls attention to the fact that it is the character and conduct of des Grieux which provide the main interest of the work. It is an interest which is relevant to our theme, since it stems from Prévost's fascination with the uncertainties in the relationship between nature and virtue. He describes his hero as 'an ambiguous character, a mixture of virtues and vices, a perpetual contrast between virtuous sentiments and vicious actions' (Prévost, 1942, 1). The Superior of Saint-Lazare, where des Grieux is for a while imprisoned, voices this sense of a puzzling contradiction between the hero's moral nature and his immoral conduct. He recognizes that des Grieux has a 'mild and amiable nature' to which the 'excessive libertinage' of his conduct seems to bear no relation (Prévost, 1942, 56). There appears, in other words, to be a lack of continuity between des Grieux's 'virtuous sentiments' which define what he naturally *is*, and the list of 'vicious actions' (eventually to include lying, swindling and murder) which are characteristic of what he *does*. The same ambiguity is apparent in the character of Manon; when deported to Louisiana they gradually incline towards 'virtuous love' and resolve to marry; of Manon, des Grieux claims that she was 'honest and natural in all her sentiments, a quality which invariably disposes people to virtue' (Prévost 1942, 137). But it is only very late in the day that Manon does become 'disposed to virtue' and then only when the move has been made away from the temptations of Paris to the bleaker setting of a convict settlement in the colonies. The novel as a whole might tend to demonstrate the exact opposite of des Grieux's claim; it might suggest that 'natural sentiments' by no means evince an invariable disposition to virtue. We are reminded here of one of the first things which des Grieux tells us about himself: he says that during his time at college before meeting Manon he acquired an excellent reputation, since he had 'a naturally mild and equable temperament', 'applied himself to study from a natural inclination' and consequently his teachers 'took to be virtues some signs of a natural aversion from vice' (Prévost, 1942, 9). A central enigma in the novel, and one which Prévost appears to have

found genuinely puzzling, is the fact that in spite of des
Grieux's 'natural aversion from vice' – which is not merely a
somewhat complacent claim made by the hero about himself
and thereby vulnerable to irony, but on the contrary generally
recognized by those who taught him to be a feature of his
character – the hero's life is marked by one deplorable action
after another. Prévost was of course a man of the Church.
This could partly explain why his view of the relationship between nature and virtue is more theological than philosophical
(using these terms as defined earlier) and thus obliquely subversive of the moral optimism about nature which was gaining
ground in the period. Or could it be that the contradictions in
des Grieux, and Prévost's clear and unsentimentalized insight
into the *problematic* equation of nature and virtue, reflect the
genuine novelistic fascination with the moral opacities of real
life? In the lines quoted above, the hero's remark that some
signs of a natural aversion from vice were counted as virtues,
raises in a delicately understated way the crucial question as to
how far virtue really does consist in a natural impulse rather
than in, for example, the 'seeds of virtue' planted in the hero's
mind by his pious friend Tiberge early in their history and
which, at the end of his story, des Grieux says, are beginning
to bear fruit, not as a result of natural moral sense but as the
consequence of bitter experience.

This conclusion had been anticipated by an earlier exchange between the two friends. Tiberge had tried to bring des
Grieux back to the path of virtue by using the kind of appeal of
which Montesquieu and Fénelon would have approved –
namely, that virtue is natural to man and that happiness is
therefore found by practising virtue, since one is thus conforming most fully and harmoniously with one's nature. This
euphoric conception is impatiently dismissed by des Grieux:

Preachers, if you would seek to bring me back to a life of
virtue, then tell me that virtue is necessary and indispensa-

ble but do not disguise from me the fact that it is severe and painful. You may establish that the pleasures of love are ephemeral or forbidden and that they will be followed by eternal torments . . . But you must admit that given the human heart as it is, they are the source of our greatest joy in this life. (Prévost, 1942, 64)

The point which Prévost puts here into des Grieux's mouth was far from being an original one. In a sense, however, the point was at the time a challenge, since it recalled attention to an ethical position which had become somewhat obscured in the context of the morally optimistic perspectives outlined in the first part of this essay. More forcefully and directly than Marivaux, Prévost calls into question the euphoric equation of nature and virtue. This question was to be explored further as a central issue, in far more sustained and elaborate terms, by Rousseau (1712–78).

The New Eloisa (1761) is one of the most complex, if not indeed tangled, masterpieces among eighteenth-century novels. On the face of it, the novel has a pleasingly clear and simple structure: the heroine, Julie, and her tutor, Saint-Preux, fall in love and embark upon an affair. They are, however, unable to marry because of the hostility of Julie's aristocratic father to the socially inferior Saint-Preux. Julie eventually agrees to defer to her father's wish that she marry an old friend of his, Wolmar, whereupon Saint-Preux spends some years in travel. This takes us to the end of the third of the six books into which the novel is divided. The second half of the novel relates the return of Saint-Preux to find Julie apparently happily married to the older Wolmar, who invites Saint-Preux to become tutor to their children and make a new life as a member of the household, whereby his relationship with Julie might survive in terms of the stable values of esteem, trust and friendship rather than in the unstable terms of their earlier passion. Julie goes so far as to claim that this new relationship would be what she would freely choose anyway, as being positively preferable to the more dynamic but unstable relationship as lovers. But tragedy arises: Julie rescues one of the children from the lake and falls ill as a result. She recognizes just before her death that she has after all continued to love Saint-Preux passionately and welcomes death as an escape from the constant temptation of adultery with him. The surface clarity and simplicity contrast strongly with the eighteenth-century preference in novels for what Rousseau rejected as 'commonplace individuals involved in extraordinary events', and it embodies his own preference for the serious novelistic treatment of social and moral issues, through characters exceptional for their sensibility who are involved in situations which are relatively unexceptional.

In marked contrast, however, with the apparent clarity of the surface structure, with its balance of the dominance of passionate love in the first half and the eulogy of settled married happiness in the second half, is a highly involved thematic structure — involved, in part at least, because of the conflicting ways in which the idea of nature is set to work at different points in the novel. Throughout the first half, until the marriage, we appear to be confronted by the somewhat familiar eighteenth-century theme of the frustrations experienced by natural man in an unnatural society. This is how Julie and Saint-Preux are described:

> These two beautiful souls were made for each other by the hand of nature itself; it is in the delight of a happy marriage that, free to exercise their moral strength and their virtues, they would have illuminated the world by their example. Why must an absurd prejudice alter the designs of Providence and disturb the harmony of thinking beings . . .? (Rousseau, 1964, Part II, Letter 2)

The harmony of nature, happiness and virtue evoked here is a recurrent theme in the first three parts. Saint-Preux praises in

Julie 'that divine harmony of virtue, love and nature' (Part I, Letter 21) and these values are opposed to the artificial social order, represented by Julie's brutal and prejudiced father, which disrupts this natural moral harmony. Julie writes to Saint-Preux to remind him of the euphoria of life lived in accordance with natural moral sense:

> Be sure that if there is a single example of happiness on earth, it is found in the man of virtue. You received from heaven that happy inclination to whatever is good and moral: listen only to your own desires, follow only your natural inclination . . . (Part II, Letter 11)

Until the marriage the book appears to be organized around the conflict between the natural mutual passion of the lovers and the artificial claims of society. However, it is in the long letter in which Julie relates to Saint-Preux her feelings during the marriage ceremony that a fundamental tension in the moral structure of the book first becomes apparent. Julie describes a radical change of heart on entering the church; she evokes an 'unknown power' which seemed to 'correct suddenly the disorder of my feelings and to reestablish them according to the law of duty and of nature' (Part III, Letter 18). 'Nature' is now abruptly invoked to sanction not the passionate love for Saint-Preux but the settled marriage with Wolmar. Julie goes on to describe lyrically the transformation which has taken place in her; she is like 'a new being just emerged from the hands of nature'. She appeals to the Supreme Being, claiming that she wishes only to devote herself to the husband whom He has given her (why the brutal prejudice of her father should now become an intention of Providential design is not explained) and claims that she wishes only for 'all that is in harmony with the order of nature'. At this point the reader is perhaps tempted to lay at Rousseau's door the charge of contradiction; the contradiction here, however, is not in Rousseau's thought but in the nature of things, wherein Rousseau sees clearly and consistently that there is inherent a fundamental tension. For Julie it is as natural to wish to obey her father as it is to be drawn to Saint-Preux; Rousseau sees clearly that it is in the nature of the personality both to experience the urge towards dynamic involvement in a relationship which engages fully the emotions, and to be drawn to a relationship based on the more static values of stability, esteem and trust which engage different but equally demanding areas of the self. A careful reading of the novel might exculpate Rousseau from accusations of muddled thinking and, on the contrary, give him credit for expressing with considerable honesty and clarity a new sense of nature as profoundly marked by inner tensions and contradictions of a kind which make it difficult to continue to enrol the idea of nature in terms of values of harmony and euphoria.

The point could be taken further to embrace the whole presentation of the static idyll of Clarens (the estate of Julie and Wolmar) in the second half of the book. Our main source of information about life at Clarens is Saint-Preux himself, through the letters which he writes describing it. What Clarens embodies essentially in the eyes of Saint-Preux (but not necessarily in the eyes of Rousseau, who by the very nature of the epistolary novel is able to remain uncommitted to the views advanced by the characters) is a 'natural order of things'; he calls it an 'order of things where nothing is conceded to mere opinion, where everything is of genuine utility and which limits itself to fulfilling the true demands of nature . . . (Part V, Letter 2). 'The voice of nature softens the wildness of our hearts,' exclaims Saint-Preux of the impression made by the simplicity of the 'natural' life of rural activity at Clarens (Part V, Letter 7); and again 'nature has ordered everything in the best possible way; but men seek to improve upon it and the result is that we spoil everything' (*ibid.*). Ultimately, however, the moral structure which so insistently engages the idea of nature, and which Saint-Preux repeatedly points to, fails to convince. His claim that there exists a natural order of things

which is morally satisfying because all things within it are reg-
ulated for the best, is contradicted by the uneasy and intermit-
tent recognition that nature contains disruptive impulses (such
as the famous episode of the storm on the lake, which functions
as a kind of metaphor for the turbulent persistence in the minds
of Julie and Saint-Preux of the disruptively passionate
impulses which they claim to have transcended) which cannot
be fitted into the rationally settled and stable, that is, supposedly natural and morally satisfying, framework of Clarens.
The novel, in short, brings out, rather as those of Marivaux
and Prévost had done, the failure of the idea of nature elaborated in the early eighteenth century to contain harmoniously
the tensions and contradictions now recognized to be present
within nature itself. The early view is still asserted, as when
Julie writes, in terms of which Pope or Shaftesbury might have
approved, that 'all contributes to the common good in the universal system. Every person has his proper place in the best
possible order of things' (Part V, Letter 3). It becomes clear,
however, that the scheme of things at Clarens, although meant
to embody this general insight, does leave a great deal out: a
scheme which is grounded in reason and nature, and where
there is consequently no scope for change or improvement
(since only what is irrational or unnatural can be improved)
and which invites the self to respond only to the limited terms of
a stable sense of completeness and settled integration – such a
scheme fails to engage those areas of the personality which are
more dynamic, restless and emotional in nature. Julie herself is
brought to a painful recogntion of this, when she admits:

> I see all around me reasons to be happy and I am not happy;
> a secret apathy invades my heart; I feel my heart to be
> empty and swollen . . . The devotion which I feel for all
> that is dear to me is insufficient to fill it; it is left with superf-
> luous energies for which it finds no use.
> (Part VI, Letter 8)

What finally emerges from the work, then, is a sense that nature, in spite of the aspirations and claims of the characters, cannot provide an unproblematic and satisfying moral scheme of the sort which they seek to establish. Nature, as Rousseau himself clearly saw, contains deep-seated and even tragic divisions. Julie's cousin, Claire, who is something of a spectator of much of the action of the book, makes the point very economically when she says that 'in this situation, whatever decision you take, nature will both authorise and condemn it' (Part II, Letter 5). A comparable sense of nature as deeply marked by unresolved divisions is apparent in the thought of Rousseau's friend and contemporary Diderot (1713–84).

It is particularly illuminating to trace in Diderot's writings the stresses to which the eighteenth-century idea of nature became more and more subject. His first published work was in fact a free translation of Shaftesbury's *Inquiry concerning Virtue and Merit*, and the appearance of this translation in 1745 was timely, serving as it did to give sharper definition to ideas on the relationship between nature, happiness and virtue which had, as we have seen, been aired in France along somewhat unsystematic lines during the first half of the century. To attempt to chart in detail the shifts in Diderot's thought would be a major task. Suffice it to recall here the basic emphases of the *Inquiry*: that there is a natural order of things, a *rerum natura* in which man's place is settled; that man is naturally sociable and benevolent; that he fulfils his nature, and thereby finds happiness, in the exercise of virtue. Then let us consider Diderot's later attitude to these optimistic assumptions as he ironically and equivocally embodies it some twenty years later in the dialogue *Rameau's Nephew*, published posthumously but thought to have engaged Diderot over the period 1761 to roughly 1775. The comparison is a very eloquent one.

The work takes the form of a debate between Rameau and an interlocutor identified only as *Moi* but whom it would be imprudent to assume to be Diderot himself. It is true that he

has much in common with Diderot, but an outright identification of the two would fail to do justice to the sense which the
work gives us of being a suggestively inconclusive series of
exchanges on topics such as nature, morality and the pursuit
of happiness. The confrontation about which the work is
organized is between *Moi*, who, broadly speaking, is armed
with moral attitudes and values characteristic of that optimistic stance held typically by Shaftesbury, and *Lui*, Rameau,
who is an amoral parasite. The tensions of the encounter
derive in large measure from the frustrations experienced by
Moi in his attempts to define and locate *Lui* in terms of his
optimistic moral scheme and from his final reluctant recognition of the impossibility of confining the disturbing phenomenon which is *Lui*, in such a scheme of explanation and value.

Moi voices from the start his discomfort in the presence of
Lui, by whom he appears to be both intrigued and disturbed:

I do not esteem eccentric characters of this kind . . . They
delay me once a year when I come across them, because
their character contrasts markedly with that of other people
and they disturb that tedious uniformity which education,
social conventions and decorum have introduced. If one
such person appears in company, he is like a grain of yeast
which ferments and restores to each and every person some
measure of his natural individuality. (Diderot, 1972, 91)

'Nature' as seen to operate in *Lui* plainly no longer provides
the basis for a settled sense of natural sociability; on the contrary, it is now associated with the anti-social, amoral individual whose 'natural' individuality challenges the 'tedious
uniformity' of the even surface of that social life which is felt to
be grounded not in nature but merely in education and conventional notions of decorum. The tensions within the work are
reflected in the ambivalent reactions of *Moi*, who is able to
recognize the artificiality of social life and moral conformism
and who is at the same time unable to feel happy in the pre-

sence of a figure who by merely being what he is calls attention
to that artificiality.

The debate widens to consider the place of man in the
scheme of things. The point is made that in terms of ideal
nature a man of genius such as Racine should have been
endowed by nature also with the virtues of the moral individual. *Moi* seeks to explain this apparent tension between
Racine's creative genius and defective moral sense by an
appeal to *Lui* to see the concrete and particular case in terms of
the general order of nature:

> Let us forget for a moment the point which we occupy in
> space and time and let us extend our view over the future
> ages, the most distant regions and over peoples still unborn.
> Let us think of the good of the whole human race. If we are
> not magnanimous enough, then let us at least pardon nature
> for having been more sagacious than we are ourselves.
> (*ibid.*, 99–100)

Moi is here appealing to the kind of intellectual position most
memorably expressed by Pope in the first part of his *Essay on
Man* (1734), where he had stressed the importance of seeing
the contingent facts of human life in the universal context of
that 'general order' which 'since the whole began' had been
'kept in Nature, and is kept in Man'. *Lui* is not persuaded to
abandon the plane of the immediate reality of actual life; he
puts a simple question to *Moi*, asking why, if nature is as powerful as it is sagacious, it did not make of a man of genius like
Racine a harmonious embodiment of both artistic talent *and*
moral goodness (*ibid.*, 100). This elicits from *Moi* no more
than a feeble restatement of his optimistic belief in the general
order of nature, of the kind which was serenely affirmed by
Shaftesbury but which is here confronted by Diderot with an
attitude, like that of Candide when faced by Pangloss, of
immediate adhesion to the concrete reality of life and which
refuses, like Candide, to subordinate man's experience of

what is morally unsatisfactory about life to any large and general scheme of explanation designed to account for it in terms of some appeal to the idea of nature as a whole.

There is a further aspect of the optimistic ethic of nature called into question by *Lui*. In response to *Moi*, who as a good *philosophe* subscribes to the idea of virtue as natural euphoria, *Lui* asks whether it is important to be moral; 'in order to be happy, certainly', replies *Moi*; 'but,' says *Lui*, 'I see around me a host of moral people who are unhappy and a host of people who are happy without being moral'. To this simple appeal to observed fact, *Moi* can only offer the weak rejoinder 'So it seems to you' (*ibid.*, 129). This brief exchange brings out the fundamental opposition between *Moi* and *Lui* which has already been noted: *Moi*, something of a philosopher in the benevolent and optimistic Shaftesburyan mould, reiterates a use of the idea of nature to connect virtue and happiness in the face of *Lui*, who does not so much *argue* a different *position* as content himself with pointing unsystematically to the undeniable truth that *Moi*'s claim does not seem to be borne out by appeal to observed fact. *Lui* goes on to talk about the facts of his own existence in terms of an idea of nature which is very unlike that of *Moi*; in other words, he takes over 'nature' as the great watchword of his interlocutor in order to subvert it: he disconnects it from the morally benevolent ethic of *Moi* in order to use it as a justification of the life lived, like his own, in terms of conforming amorally to one's individually given brute nature:

> Since I can find happiness in those vices which are natural to me, which I have acquired without work and which I retain without effort . . . it would be strange if I were to torment myself in order to change my nature . . . Virtue is praised but hated and avoided, it is frozen by cold and in this world one needs warm feet . . . Why do we so often see people of piety to be harsh, awkward and unsociable? It is

because they have taken on a task which is not natural to
them . . . And friend Rameau, if he were to begin one day
to display contempt for material fortune, women, good
food, idleness and to play at Cato, what would he be? a
hypocrite. Rameau can be no other than he is . . . (*ibid.*,
129–30)

One of the many ironies of the dialogue is that the view of
nature advanced here by the cynical *Lui* is anticipated by the
more conventional *Moi* when he suggests that the natural order
exists quite independently of any of the man-made ethical
categories in terms of which we attempt to grasp it:

Let us leave aside nature as a whole since we do not know it
sufficiently completely to praise or blame it, and since it is in
itself perhaps neither good nor bad, if it is merely necessary
as many reputable thinkers consider it to be. (*ibid.*, 101)

It is the divisions and shifts in the ways in which the idea of
nature is set to work by Diderot which make his thought particularly eloquent of the evolution of ideas in the second half of
the century. Side by side in his works are found a use of nature
as ethical norm and also a view of nature such as that suggested
by *Moi* which implies that nature is as it is by pure necessity,
that it could not be otherwise and that it is impossible to derive
from it any ethical value. The first of these positions is found in
his *Supplement to Bougainville's Voyage* (1772): the happy
inhabitants of Tahiti have remained close to 'nature's law' and
consequently their legislation is superior and their lives simpler
and happier than those of civilized nations which have
departed from nature's law:

How far have we departed from nature and happiness! The
empire of nature cannot be destroyed; men will seek in vain
to block it and oppose it but it will nonetheless endure.
(Diderot, 1953, 201)

> Do you want to know in a word the history of all our mis-
> eries? Here it is. There existed a natural man; into this man
> there was introduced an artificial man; and there arose
> within him an unending conflict which lasts through life . . .
> There are however some situations which restore man to his
> original simple state . . . In fact, what becomes then of all
> merely conventional virtues? In wretchedness man is with-
> out remorse, in illness woman knows no modesty. (*ibid.*,
> 202)

The second view of nature as morally neutral and blindly
necessary is put by Diderot into the mouth of Bordeu, one of
the characters in his dialogue *D'Alembert's Dream* (1769).
Mlle Lespinasse has expressed the view in conversation with
Bordeu that human behaviour, and more particularly sexual
behaviour, can be judged in terms of how far it conforms to or
deviates from nature. This use of nature as norm Bordeu
briskly rebuts in favour of a revolutionary view of nature which
was to become more powerful in the latter part of the century:

> Everything which is cannot be either contrary to nature or
> outside of nature; this is true of voluntary chastity and con-
> tinence which would be the first of crimes against nature, if
> it were possible to sin against nature. (*ibid.*, 155)

The qualification at the end of this sentence marks the radical
extent of the challenge to the whole notion of seeking in nature
any source of value or any kind of norm. The fact is that
throughout the period it is impossible to separate the shifts in
the use of nature as ethical norm from shifts in cosmology. In
the early eighteenth century the use of nature as ethical value
was closely connected to a cosmology which saw man as an
integral part of a natural order or what Pope called the
'World's great harmony'; this view implied an essentially static nature, which it was assumed had been framed along harmonious and providential lines and had consequently never

evolved. About the middle of the century, however, the tendency to conceive of nature along static and somewhat mathematical lines came to be challenged by a new tendency to conceive of nature along dynamic and somewhat organic lines. *Man a Machine* (1748) by La Mettrie (1709–51) was one of the first provocative statements of this new view and is of lasting importance for the historian of ideas by virtue of its suggestion that the sterile confrontation of two typically eighteenth-century positions – on the one hand the belief that the observable order of nature must imply a wise and benevolent creator, and on the other hand the claim that the observable order of nature could be the result of the operation of pure chance – might be bypassed since, as La Mettrie suggests, 'there might be something else which would be neither chance nor God, I mean Nature'. In other words a typically optimistic expression of the providential view of nature, such as Addison pointing out that the fact that the earth is covered with green, rather than with some other colour less naturally pleasing to the human eye, might afford proof of the foresight and benevolence of Providence, need no longer simply lead to the counter-claim that this is simply the result of chance. While both of these opposed views would see nature as static and unchanging, La Mettrie's view of nature as an organic whole in a constant state of flux pointed the way out of this dilemma. It should be added, however, that the two most famous figures of the French Enlightenment, Voltaire and Rousseau, were never to abandon their belief in an essentially unchanging natural order: Voltaire in his *History of Jenni* of 1775 and Rousseau in his *Profession of Faith of the Savoyard Priest* of 1762 were still to confront the sceptic with a choice between acceptance of the creator implied by the presence of order and 'design' in nature and acceptance of mere chance and randomness in nature. These alternatives are opposed to each other but found a common basis in the assumption of fixity in nature.

The *System of Nature* (1770) by d'Holbach (1723–89) is

one of the most notable restatements and elaborations of the
position explored by La Mettrie; but we may turn back to his
friend Diderot and *D'Alembert's Dream* to see an intuitive
sense of the new idea of nature expressed in terms which are
not so much argued as visionary:

> I am what I am, because it was impossible that I could be
> otherwise. Modify the whole and of necessity you modify
> me; but the whole is in a constant state of change . . . Man
> is no more than a common product, the monster an uncom-
> mon product; both are equally natural, equally necessary,
> equally part of the universal and general order of things.
> (*ibid.*, 113)

In this light, the only answer that can be given to the question
'Why are things as they are?' is 'They are as they are because
they could not be otherwise.' The 'monster' is no longer an
accidental deviation from the otherwise grand and harmonious
design of nature, but, along with 'normal' creatures, the necessary effect of the operation of necessary natural laws. The
'general order of things' is no longer associated with values
such as uniformity, simplicity, economy and constancy, but
with an all-embracing acceptance of nature as a richly varied,
complex, proliferating and changing whole, whose necessity is
ethically neutral.

III

From this new philosophy of nature, d'Holbach sought to
derive an ethic of benevolence towards one's fellow men;
Diderot also explored this line of thought in the *Supplement to
Bougainville's Voyage* and elsewhere, but was equally ready
to explore in *Rameau's Nephew* the possibility that the selfish-
ness and vice in Rameau might be no less 'natural' and no less
justifiable by appeal to nature than the altruism and benevolence of *Moi*. It is this possibility, adumbrated by Diderot in
the suggestive terms of an inconclusive dialogue, which was to

gain currency in the last decades of the century; what for Diderot had been a fascinating but disturbing possibility was to become a fundamental assumption for Laclos (1741–1803) and de Sade (1740–1814), when it was to be subtly and obliquely dramatized by the former and somewhat tediously and over-emphatically reiterated by the latter.

Laclos's *Les Liaisons Dangereuses* enjoyed a considerable *succès de scandale* on its appearance in 1782. It is not difficult in retrospect to understand why, since its implicit ironies undermine, in ways which can still disturb, optimistic assumptions about natural morality, and its challenge to these values is a more direct and far-reaching one than those offered by the interrogations of Rousseau and Diderot. There is, for example, an irresistible deflation of the cult of euphoria associated with natural morality. The rake Valmont, aware that Mme de Tourvel, whom he is intriguing to seduce, is having him followed and watched, resolves to create a favourable impression by going out of his way to help a family of impoverished peasants, knowing that this action will be reported back to her and will thereby help his strategy of seduction. His motives are therefore entirely selfish and hypocritical, yet he relates as follows his feelings when the family gather around him, on their knees, to thank him:

> I will confess my weakness; my eyes filled with tears and I felt an involuntary but delightful impulse. I was surprised by the pleasure which one derives from doing good; and am tempted to believe that those whom we call virtuous are not so meritorious as people like to tell us.
> (Laclos, 1979a, 46–7)

The spuriously 'moral' pleasure in natural benevolence could not be more neatly and ironically suggested.

But it is not through isolated incidents of this kind that the book makes its deepest impact. The novel is a study in seduction and the pursuit of power, but the strategies of seduction serve ultimately to reveal a disquieting view of human nature; the two female victims of Valmont, Cécile de Volanges and Mme de Tourvel, are not really *victims* at all; or, to be exact, they are less victims of Valmont's skills and deceptions than they are victims of their own nature. Neither woman is so much forced or overcome by Valmont as freely giving in to him under the impetus of the sensuality of her nature. Virtue, whether the product of religious education in Cécile or the product of reason and religious faith in Mme de Tourvel, is shown to be ineffectively fragile as a barrier against the corrosively catalytic revelation of their deeper natures which comes from contact with Valmont. There is no room here for the reassuring convention of woman falling an innocent victim.

Alongside this we must set Laclos's presentation of the two main characters of the novel, Valmont and Mme de Merteuil. One of the most striking features of these characters is the extraordinary disproportion between the sustained and elaborate cruelty of strategies of seduction and power which appear to engage all their time and energy, and the brief explanation provided for them. Revenge is mentioned briefly in the second letter but it is very rarely mentioned afterwards, while the lengthy intrigue between Valmont and Mme de Tourvel, which occupies much of the novel, is anyway quite unconnected with this particular motive. In conventional terms of explanation of motive, which we look for in the psychological novel, this imbalance might seem a weakness; in fact, it points to a crucial aspect of the book's originality, since in the absence of any adequate explanation of the behaviour of Valmont and Merteuil — revenge is insufficient; they have no feelings of hate for their victims; it is inappropriate to talk of sadism — Laclos is making the point in a powerfully understated way that their behaviour in its violence and egotism is quite simply 'natural' and does not *need* to be accounted for; it emerges, in the words of Jean-Luc Seylaz, as behaviour whose 'evil' is a 'kind of sustained plenitude' like 'a natural state'

(Seylaz, 1968, 102). This dimension is reinforced by the fact that the dominant perspective in the book is that of Valmont and Merteuil. Innocence under attack was not a new theme in the novel; it had previously been portrayed by, for example, Marivaux in *The Life of Marianne* as well as by Richardson in *Pamela* (1740) and *Clarissa Harlowe* (1749), but both Marivaux and Richardson had organized their works around the moral perspective of the innocent heroine and not around that of the libertine. Laclos departs from this mode: the women tend to be subordinated to Valmont's point of view, and the change of perspective implies a change of moral perspective. Valmont comes to embody the 'norm' from which events are viewed, although Laclos never makes this explicit by statement; the reader is led into an imaginative acceptance of this status accorded to Valmont by the dominant role played by Valmont's correspondence in the epistolary structure of the novel.

With Laclos it is natural to associate de Sade. Unlike Laclos, however, he opts for a mode which is repetitive and over-emphatic in its redefinitions of nature as ethical norm, and he has nothing of Laclos's obliqueness, understatement and irony. His philosophy of nature is essentially that of La Mettrie, d'Holbach and the Diderot of *D'Alembert's Dream*: nature is an impersonal and ethically neutral force, characterized by unending and directionless creation of forms and destruction of forms; it comprehends all, including human existence, which is no more than one of the ephemeral 'combinations and movements' of which the 'unending chain' of nature is composed. We note here a striking example of what Arthur Lovejoy (1961) called the 'temporalising' of the idea of nature as a chain of being: the 'chain of nature' for de Sade is not a structure 'realised all at once and immutably' as it had been in the first half of the century, and was indeed to continue to be in the second half on the century in the eyes of Voltaire and Rousseau; it has been converted into a dynamic sequence but retains the notion, albeit in a temporalized form, that every element in the chain is necessary and could not be other than it is. The difference is that the necessity here is that of blind and directionless determinism and not, as it had been in the earlier static conception of the chain of nature, the necessity for all things to occupy the place they did in the scheme of things as a whole because that scheme was the only rational and right scheme of things.

This radical redefinition of the 'chain of nature' and the consequent redefinition of the idea of 'necessity' in nature had radical consequences for ethics. De Sade's particular contribution was to draw these consequences in the most intransigent terms: no human action can be blamed, since all human impulses and instincts are contained in nature; it follows that the idea of nature can no longer be put to work normatively, as Shaftesbury had done in maintaining that the benevolent social instincts were in accordance with nature's law whereas the selfish aggressive impulses were not, since nature is now seen simply as the sum of what is and which, being as it is, could not be otherwise:

> Nothing is dreadful in libertinism because everything which is inspired by libertinism is inspired equally by nature; the most extraordinary and bizarre actions, those which appear to contravene most plainly all human laws and institutions . . . even those are not dreadful and there is not a single one of them which cannot be evidenced in nature. (de Sade, 1972, 156)

Destruction of life is therefore on this view no more than a 'modification' of the material elements of nature; murder is not a crime according to nature's laws, since it actively furthers the unending processes of transformation and reorganization of matter, which are the supreme law of nature's activity:

Led further on from one conclusion to another and which
follow from each other, one must agree that, far from harm-
ing nature, the action which you commit, by varying the
forms of her different works, is actually advantageous to
her, since you provide in this way the raw material of her
reconstructions which it would be impossible for her to
carry out if you did not further the process of destruction.
(de Sade, 1972, 254)

If we enlighten our minds with what de Sade calls the 'sacred
torch of philosophy' we will recognize that it is the 'voice of
nature' which inspired hate, vengeance and war, 'in a word all
those incentives to ceaseless murder'; and if nature inspires
these impulses, it is because they are indispensable to her;
'how then', asks de Sade, 'can we suppose that we are behav-
ing guiltily towards her, when we are doing no more than follow her aims?' (de Sade, 1972, 255)

It might appear tempting to dismiss de Sade's extreme and
twisted redefinitions of the idea of nature as no more than an
eccentric, if not insane, byway on the intellectual map of the
Enlightenment; but he represents more than that. In the context of the period as a whole, I would see him as making the
same essential point which Laclos had made in the elegantly
understated terms of *Les Liaisons Dangereuses*, for like Laclos, he calls attention to the fragility of the great value upon
which so many different kinds of moral weight had been placed
throughout the eighteenth century – the idea of nature. We
may note that de Sade's almost exact contemporary Bernardin
de Saint-Pierre (1737–1814) was at about the same time still
repeating in the anodyne terms of his *Paul et Virginie* (1788)
the optimistic three-part equation first framed in the early
eighteenth century, when he claimed that the tale illustrates the
'happiness founded on nature and virtue'; and this conjunction
of simultaneous but radically opposed uses of the idea of
nature by de Sade and Bernardin might point a conclusion to

this paper: the idea of nature served unfailingly throughout the period as a point of ethical reference precisely because it could be all things to all men. The shifts of thought which we have traced within the period did not entail shifts in vocabulary, since the idea of nature emerges as infinitely capable of rede-finition. The ready appeal to this 'verbal jack-of-all-trades', as Arthur Lovejoy (1927) described the 'most sacred and most protean' term in the vocabulary of the period, is a con-stant of the literature and philosophy of the Enlightenment; but this by no means signifies a genuine continuity of thought throughout the period. On the contrary, it was continually invested and reinvested with an exceptionally rich variety of meanings on the ethical, as indeed on other, planes. This should make us wary of confident generalizations about the 'thought' of the Enlightenment, but invite us to see in the shifts and ambiguities of the idea of nature in its ethical aspect as variously enrolled by thinkers of the period, what is not one of the least fascinating dimensions of the Enlightenment.

FURTHER READING

Brumfitt, 1972

Cassirer, 1951

Charlton, 1984

Crocker, 1959 and 1963

Ehrard, 1963

Grimsley, 1979

Hampson, 1968

Harris, 1968

Hazard, 1946

Lovejoy, 1948

Mauzi, 1960

Mercier, 1960

Mornet, 1932

Willey, 1948

Naturalizing the Family: Literature and the Bio-Medical Sciences in the Late Eighteenth Century

L.J. JORDANOVA

EDITOR'S INTRODUCTION

Different, even conflicting meanings of nature abounded in the eighteenth century, as we saw in the previous chapter. Often these were presented in terms of oppositions, such as natural versus artificial, nature versus reason, nature versus culture. Such dichotomies are important for two reasons. First, they drew on old, often classical notions and were thus deeply embedded in ways of thinking, so much so that they could be used without self-consciousness as habitual, customary ideas which structured patterns of thought. Second, they had a marvellous capacity for containing contradictions. Raymond Williams (1975) has shown how this worked for the pair country versus city, where the former can be the valued element because deemed pure, natural and innocent. The country can equally be seen negatively as wild, uncouth, and barbaric, yet also as 'natural'.

Such contradictions were not, of course, new in the eighteenth century. Gender and sexuality were intrinsic to many pairs of terms, and they were often given contradictory meanings. Women, and by extension femininity, were commonly identified with nature; men, with culture. Sometimes it could be the other way around, while the feminine and natural realms had both positive and negative connotations. Jordanova's paper discusses such dichotomies and examines some of the ways in which gender and sexuality were written about in eighteenth-century science and literature.

The blending of biology and eroticism is characteristic of the eighteenth century. Natural history, the most descriptive part of the natural sciences, cast its net extremely wide. Everything which could be observed was a proper subject for the natural historian. For example, it is the sheer inclusiveness of Buffon's *Natural History* (1749–1804) which strikes us. While this inclusiveness certainly reinforced an attention to human sexuality as a legitimate object of scientific study, the quite specific interest in reproduction further fuelled it. Buffon's assertion that reproduction was intrinsic to living things, like Linnaeus's discovery of plant sexuality, encouraged the idea that generation, and the feelings that went along with it, were constitutive of living nature.

The licence to speak about procreation which several writers, like Diderot, simply seized, made the biology of reproduction an erotic, partially forbidden field. A closely related eroticism was developing simultaneously in the visual arts where mother–child relations, the female body, and amorous encounters were depicted with frank sensuality by artists such as Greuze (Brookner, 1972), significantly one of Diderot's favourite painters. Doubtless the feeling of defiance in treating sexuality was fuelled by the sense of infringing religious codes. Diderot's *The Nun* (1760) shocks because it goes straight for one of the most controversial issues of the day – the celibacy of priests and nuns. Liberal thinking widely condemned celibacy as 'unnatural' and in doing so raised fears of a declining population as well as provoking hostility to the oppressive alliance between church and state. It is significant that sexuality was the vehicle for such a general critique, as it is in de Sade's writ-

ings, where the worst sexual excesses are invariably committed by aristocrats and priests.

Descriptive natural history, of the kind Buffon and Linnaeus stood for, enjoyed enormous popularity during the eighteenth century. Equally important in terms of writings about sexuality and reproduction was the development of a more theoretically oriented science of life. This science of life, which Lamarck was to name 'biology', focused attention on the whole organism and on its environment. We have already noted how important the environment was in eighteenth-century writings, as in Bernardin de Saint-Pierre's *Paul et Virginie* where the natural world serves as a mirror and guide to the emotions of the main characters. Bernardin also uses the prodigious fecundity of the island as a metaphor of growth. Growth, like 'life', was a key term in the new science of life. Wild and productive as living things were, they also, of course, displayed structure – organization. To stress organic structure directed attention away from the supposedly incommensurable mind/body dichotomy, towards the wholeness and adaptiveness of living beings. A number of concepts were thereby developed, which bridged previously distinct realms and expressed the sense that organisms worked as integrated coordinated units. Jordanova's paper touches on these questions in discussing sympathy, an important bridging concept, which Rodgers treats in more detail in relation to *Tristram Shandy*.

Like Pilkington, Jordanova draws most of her examples from eighteenth-century France. It may therefore be appropriate to ask to what extent the trends she identifies were specific to that country. One characteristic of eighteenth-century France was the importance of state-supported scientific and medical institutions. The Jardin du Roi in Paris, which was devoted to natural history, became the symbolic as well as the practical focus of work on the life sciences in France. With its vast collections and state patronage it was tangible proof of the public commitment to natural history. Whether it would have had quite this significance without Buffon, a figure of considerable literary as well as scientific prominence, as its Director from 1739 until his death nearly fifty years later, is another matter. The fact remains that people could look to the Jardin and to those who worked there as embodiments of the importance of natural history – an activity which both celebrated the variety of nature, and, through taxonomy, imposed order upon nature's chaos. The historian Jules Michelet, who is discussed in a later chapter, idealized the Jardin as an institution which sang hymns to Nature while revealing her mysteries. Also specific to France was the acidity of Laclos and de Sade. The latter in particular can only be comprehended in the context of Revolutionary turmoil, itself a product of the extreme social, economic and political crisis of the end of the *ancien régime*, which made a new moral order, founded on nature, seem a real possibility, especially in relation to sexual and family relations.

In other respects, however, the trends Jordanova mentions can be seen in England too. These include the obsessive investigation of reproduction and sexuality, and the simultaneous attempts to manage it through censuses, philanthropy, family and population policies, and so on. The intimate links between social management and the study of nature were mediated in literary, scientific and medical treatments of such topics as human sexuality. Once again the secular nature of such discussions is striking; they would, after all, have been totally inappropriate in a society which associated sexuality purely with procreation, and procreation solely with marriage sanctioned by an orthodox church. The subversive and erotic elements in eighteenth-century discourse derive from the realization that human sexuality is in fact not at all easy to manage, by church or state, by parents or teachers. The novel, with its permit to describe 'real' life, could hardly ignore a force which seemed to derive its power from nature itself.

F amily and sexuality are themes common to eighteenth-
century science and literature. The bio-medical
sciences were concerned with reproduction and gender as natural phenomena to be explored along with
other facts of nature. At the same time, bio-medical writings
on these themes may be understood as a literary tradition in
that they drew on a specific fund of images and metaphors.
This same language was used in novels, as well as in
philosophical and political writings. In this sense we may
speak of shared cultural resources, a language of nature,
which achieved its force partly because it raised important
social questions about the family as a natural moral unit.
Eighteenth-century literary traditions in general were marked
by a special interest in both the world of nature, often as the
mirror of human feeling or as an escape from society, and the
world of kinship where love and intimacy could be expressed
within the legitimate bounds of the family. This essay
examines the interplay between these two areas, paying particular attention to their implications for the relations between
the domain of nature and that of culture and society.

Referring to a particular literary, medical and scientific
tradition in late eighteenth-century France, I am concerned
with a range of historically specific factors: the definition of
human sexuality in scientific *cum* medical terms, and the
preoccupation with the family as a biological and social unit; a
privileged, private zone of life. When eighteenth-century
commentators discussed such matters as pregnancy, childbirth
and adolescence, they did so with a lively realization of their
dual physiological and social character. Furthermore, physiological processes were tools with which social events
could be explored, and may therefore be said to stand in a
mediating relationship to them. The preoccupation, one might
almost say obsession, with reproduction makes little sense in
isolation from the institution which gives it meaning – the family. There can be no doubt about the widespread interest

among late eighteenth-century writers in the family, both as idea and as lived experience (Flandrin, 1979; Forster and Ranum, 1976; Traer, 1980; Jacobs *et al.*, 1979; Foucault, 1979; McLaren, 1973–4). In relation to languages of nature, the crucial point is that in the family we have an idea which is at once natural and social. It was such an integral element of human existence that its value as a subject of study could scarcely be disputed. Furthermore, it could be treated in a variety of ways: by painters, writers, lawyers, political theorists, economists, administrators, churchmen, medical practitioners and politicians. In the literature and art of the period, both idealized and problematic relationships between family members featured so prominently that their significance cannot be denied (Bryson, 1981; Paulson, 1979; Duncan, 1973, 1981). Historians of science and medicine have been less willing than cultural historians to admit that here, where the social and the biological met, a language of nature, ripe for analysis, existed. To decipher such a language in the context of eighteenth-century images of the family is to do more than illuminate an aspect of culture shared by the humanities and the sciences; it is to perceive the mediation of social relations.

This language of nature was strongly dichotomous in character in that it drew on related pairs of opposite terms as its structuring concepts (Williams, 1975, 1983). Nowhere was this feature more marked than in writings on the family and sexuality, not least because male/female is such a powerfully evocative opposition (MacCormack and Strathern, 1980; Elshtain, 1981; Maclean, 1980). In the course of this chapter a number of such pairs will be discussed:

female	male
nature	culture
private	public
family	society
inside (interior)	outside

body   mind

passion (feeling)   reason

The dichotomous approach can be illustrated by the treatise on *Physiognomy*; first published in 1775–8, by the Swiss pastor Lavater (1741–1801), in which he drew up a series of paired characters designed to evoke metaphorically the differences between the sexes.

> Man is more solid; woman is softer.
> Man is straighter; woman is more supple.
> Man walks with a firm step; woman with a soft and light one.
> Man contemplates and observes; woman looks and feels.
> (Lavater, n.d., 190)

These images of masculinity and femininity pervaded medical and scientific writings, and enabled a holistic view of the human body to be built up. Furthermore, the overlap between these pairs produced a language which incessantly evoked associations, so that to speak of women, for example, was to suggest the realm of private domesticity; one pair stood for and represented the others. But it would be a mistake to construe these pairs as static, with stable meanings; on the contrary, sometimes, as in Lavater, there is a continuum, not a mutually exclusive relationship between the terms. Similarly, whereas female was often related to unmediated nature, as in the power to reproduce, male may also be so related as in the emphasis on brute sexual desire. In these ways a set of complex changing images was built up which both constrained and expressed tension and contradiction.

Scientific and medical writings may be seen as composed of clusters of images and packages of ideas. As a result, detailed textual analysis is imperative if the images are to be unpacked. It further follows that to read with an eye for content but ignoring form and style results in distortions. The approach which involves treating cultural products as integrated wholes may be applied to any kind of writing or art. The example of visual representations is a particularly appropriate one, for it alerts us to the importance of 'ways of seeing', that is, to the power of images to convey complex messages through a vocabulary which accepts ambiguity and contradiction (Berger, 1972, 1980; Bryson, 1981; Paulson, 1979; Williams, 1975, 1983).

The language of late eighteenth-century writings in the bio-medical sciences was significant in three respects: first, it employed words with both common-sense and technical meanings and thereby exploited the imaginative associations they gave rise to; second, there was a deliberate attempt to formulate a common language for mind and body so that different levels of organic complexity could be dealt with in the same explanatory framework; and, finally, there was a growing desire to give notions previously construed as descriptions of stable, physical characters a physiological meaning, reflecting constantly changing internal biological processes. A vocabulary of vital action became necessary which stressed motion, dynamism, process, and change; all these fundamental features of nature demanded expression.

Take the common eighteenth-century notion of 'habit', for example. This concept was of growing importance in the biology and medicine of the period. Standing at the borderline of mind and body, habit expressed common experience, and conveyed the idea of organisms as products of their own life histories. It represented the possibility of behavioural responses to stimuli being incorporated into the physical make-up of living things. For the biologist Lamarck (1744–1829), to take a well-known example, habit expressed the active relationship between plants and animals and their environment. It explained the characteristics both of individuals and of those species developed during the history of the natural world (Lamarck, 1809, vol. 1, ch. vii; Jordanova, 1984, 54–6).

A similar argument applies to terms like 'temperament', 'constitution' and 'sensibility', which were linked in having habit as one of their major sources. The distinctive skeletons and musculature of the two sexes, the physician Cabanis (1757–1808) explained, arise from use and habit and not from rigid, determining structures. Feminine sensibility derived, therefore, from the general habits of women, while it in turn determined the broad parameters of women's lives (Cabanis, 1956, vol. 1, 272–315; Tissot, 1772). The focus was increasingly on the analysis of internal physiological processes. The search for deeper knowledge may be understood both literally and metaphorically, since the most inaccessible areas of the body, and those organic processes that were hardest to observe, claimed greater attention.

The concern with the recesses of the living body carried levels of meaning beyond the explicit claim of physiology to be a new and more sophisticated bio-medical perspective. Those studying the interior of organisms paid particular attention to the female form and its generative powers, thereby raising cultural, social, political and economic questions. But these resonances can only be reconstructed if we accept the full symbolic load carried by the human, and particularly by the female body. The connections between different realms of social life were imaginative, as much as anything. Analysing mediations therefore entails revealing the metaphors on which they were built and their employment in a particular cultural setting. In investigating the reasons for the prominence of reproduction and sexuality in many different forms of eighteenth-century writings, literary and visual materials are particularly valuable. They may, for example, contain elements censored from scientific and medical writings, either consciously or unconsciously, and for a variety of reasons. While we acknowledge the fundamental structural affinities between science and literature, it is nonetheless also the case that the rationalistic conventions of Enlightenment thought adhered to by many natural philosophers allowed fewer open spaces for tensions and unresolved problems than did fiction and poetry of the same period. This does not mean that late eighteenth-century science and medicine evaded the ambiguous and intractable aspects of the world, but rather that in expressing their ideas in written form, natural philosophers strove extremely hard to manage and dominate their materials – a project in which they were, inevitably, only partially successful.

I shall discuss the use of natural imagery in eighteenth-century writings on the family and reproduction by analysing works of fiction such as *Paul et Virginie* (1788) by Bernardin de Saint-Pierre (1737–1814), and *Les Liaisons Dangereuses* (1782) by Choderlos de Laclos (1741–1803), and medical writings such as *On the Relationships Between the Physical and the Moral in Man* (*Rapports du Physique et du Moral de l'Homme*, 1795–6) by the medical philosopher Cabanis, with its lengthy analysis of female physiology.

FROM THE SCIENCE OF MAN
TO THE NATURAL HISTORY OF SEXUALITY

A major impulse towards a naturalistic study of sexuality and the family came from that characteristic eighteenth-century project, the application of scientific techniques to all aspects of human existence to create a 'science of man' (Bryson, 1968; Phillipson, 1981; Staum, 1974, 1980). The science of man took many forms, but two questions with which this chapter is concerned were invariably present. First, there was the issue of the male and female forms of 'man' – a curiously abstract notion which belies the insistent exploration of sex differences. Second, there was the question of the relationship between individuals and groups. The passage from the state of nature to society, whether historical or metaphorical, was undoubtedly problematic. Making the simple assumption that people were, by definition, social beings was not totally satisfying, especially in a context in which the virtues of individuals were idealized and arbitrary patriarchal authority in both the family and society as a whole was severely criticized. There was too much wrong with society for it to be simply 'natural', while the natural virtues of individuals were rarely rewarded in so-called civilized environments. In discussions about the history of human development, about social organization, and about the relationships between individuals and groups, the family therefore occupied a pivotal position. The idea that the family could be taken as a prototype and microcosm of society as a whole was extremely attractive. The family was rooted in nature, and so provided a legitimate foundation for the sexual division of labour and the separation between public and private life (Okin, 1980; Elshtain, 1981, 1982).

Commentators used the family as a natural *cum* social object to explore a wide range of issues. The very inseparability of its natural and social aspects is significant. Furthermore, in speaking about the family, the issues of power, hierarchy and authority were integral questions. The wielding of power within the family, the nature of parental authority, the obligations and duties between spouses, were all debated. An examination of late eighteenth-century writings on family and sexuality, be they political, fictional, medical or scientific, reveals in the language of nature a discourse about power.

The naturalness of the family revolved around two sets of relationships: those between man and woman, and those between parent and child. While some writers discussed relations between siblings, this was usually to make a specific point, to which I shall return shortly. Of all possible combinations, the bond between mother and child held a special place as both the most basic biological and the most significant social relationship. This took the form of a vast literature on pregnancy, childbirth, infanticide, breast-feeding, wet-nursing, swaddling and illegitimacy (Knibiehler, 1976; Forster and Ranum, 1980). Such writings did not necessarily take the precise nature of maternity for granted, however. The medical practitioner William Cadogan (1711–1797) was not alone in aiming in his *Essay on Nursing* (1748) to delineate a more active and significant role for the father in the process of childrearing. The respective contributions and responsibilities of mothers and fathers to their children were not rigid and fixed but were subject to continual re-evaluation.

The fact remains that the mother's relationship to her child, a symbol of the synthesis of nature and society, dominated much writing in late eighteenth-century France. The intensity of the relationship began during pregnancy, and was expressed in terms of 'sympathy', an idea of exceptional richness, which in this period was employed in a number of new ways adding significant levels of meaning to its originally medical connotation of two parts of the body affecting each other (French, 1969, chs 4 and 7; Lawrence, 1979).

> The Mother gives the first Impression or Impulse to the Child, from Whence it is returned with greater Force, by the natural mutual Sympathy and Communication between two equal Sufferers. (Morgan, 1735, 220–1)

The special sympathy between mother and child could not be explained in mechanical terms. It was, on the contrary, a physiological and hence an organic relationship. The physiological language which alone was appropriate for its discussion expressed psychological and social dimensions through a language of life, a vocabulary which conveyed the qualities only the living possessed. Extending the argument about maternal sympathy, Cabanis argued that only women possess the refined and delicate responses necessary for the care of vulnerable infants. For him, maternal love was based in the sensibility which is specific to the female sex. There were degrees of sympathy – that between mother and foetus was more intense than that between mother and baby. There were several levels and types of sympathy – between different parts of the same physiological system, between different areas of the body – and it was manifested in different degrees according to age, sex and the part in question (Cabanis, 1956, vol. 1, 275, 280, 295, 305).

Sympathy and sensibility were closely linked. For Cabanis, sensibility lay at the heart of life itself. It was the closest it was possible to get to a vital principle, but it could only be studied through its effects since its ultimate cause was unknowable (vol. 1, 195–6, 198, 539–40; vol. 2, 266–7, 291–2, 496–7, 498–9). Sensibility explained all aspects of life including human intelligence. Its seat was the brain and nervous system through which all the organs and muscles were connected, providing a physical basis for sympathy. But sensibility was not a passive organic property, it was an active faculty which, for example, acted through the brain on sensations and impressions received by the senses. Sensibility was thus central to the late eighteenth-century project of developing a science of life (Figlio, 1975, 1976).

Sensibility varied with age, sex and behaviour. Woman's distinctive sensibility was lively but unstable. Together with female weakness by comparison with men, the sensibility of women served to captivate the male sex. Man had a different but complementary sensibility which, moreover, served a larger goal: the maintenance of morality. Furthermore, Cabanis explained:

> All civil societies invariably have as their foundation, and, equally necessary for their regulation, the primitive society which is the family. (vol. 1, 293)

Society, morality and civilization all rested upon the union of two opposite elements, male and female, both part of nature, yet finely adapted to their moral functions and social goals.

In sexual reproduction, eighteenth-century writers found a convenient combination of biological, moral and social elements. Cabanis summarized the distinctive features of human gestation to which the key was the special nature of the uterus with its highly developed sensibility. The peak of sensibility reached by the womb during pregnancy served to stimulate the growth of the embryo, and constituted the ability to pass on life. Unlike other species, human babies were not capable of surviving unaided, hence the need for the parental care which women alone could provide by virtue of their physiological delicacy and associated psychological traits (vol. 1, 272, 291–2, 295, 305). These characteristics determined the sorts of work to which the female sex was generally best suited: sedentary, requiring no muscular force, but demanding fine skills and preferably working on small objects (vol. 1, 278–9). In Cabanis's view they were emphatically not to do brain work (vol. 1, 298).

In his *Rapports du Physique et du Moral de l'Homme*, Cabanis moved easily from anatomical through physiological and psychological considerations and on to moral and social ones, aided by concepts like sensibility on the one hand, and by his broad conception of sexuality on the other. From the science of man, he was led on to the dual study of sex differences and social institutions, employing in the process powerful images of femininity and masculinity. But in the fifth section, which dealt with 'the influence of sex [i.e. gender] on the nature of ideas and on moral feelings', the two sexes were not treated with equal attention or in similar detail (vol. 1, 272–315). This part was, in fact, almost exclusively devoted to women, as if sex were more fundamental to female physiology than to male, and the feminine were a deviation from a male norm. The use of dichotomies and metaphor was central to the arguments he developed about the importance of sexuality. He associated women with the inside of the home, the care of children and distance from danger, with modesty, and with weakness, timidity and secretiveness. Masculinity, by contrast, was associated with public debate, politics, reason, forceful energetic personalities, and with strength, daring, enterprise, hard work, and the desire to dominate nature.

The specialness of the mother as the embodiment of feminity is vividly illustrated in Bernardin de Saint-Pierre's *Paul et Virginie*, an extraordinarily popular sentimental novel which idealized the moral goodness of nature. Paul and Virginie were brought up by their mothers, both of whom were without a husband, to become admirable human beings. Their mothers were presented as founts of natural, innate wisdom. It was their destiny to convey simple virtues to their children. Fathers, by implication, are entirely dispensable: the principal role men play in the book is that of mediator between the new moral micro-society in which Paul and Virginie live with their mothers and servants, and the old world, the *ancien régime* of deceit, luxury, artificiality and sorrow. The arbitrary use of power in corrupt Europe had destroyed the simple happiness of human beings, particularly of women.

Bernardin de Saint-Pierre placed the mother/child dyad at centre stage. Both children enjoyed exceptionally intense closeness with their mothers. Great importance was also attached to the relationship between the two children, described as that between brother and sister (they shared the breast milk of both women), although they were not, of course, biologically related. This natural bonding between children was given a political inflection by Mary Wollstonecraft (1759–97) in her *Vindication of the Rights of Woman* (1792) when she suggested that true equality had its origins and its prototype in the mutual respect and love of siblings (1975). Comradeship began with real 'brothers' and 'sisters'; the family was the school for equality and political responsibility.

Bernardin de Saint-Pierre's micro-society had an interesting family structure:

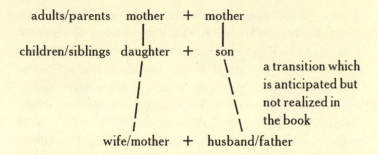

adults/parents   mother   +   mother

children/siblings daughter +   son

                                    a transition which
                                    is anticipated but
                                    not realized in
                                    the book

          wife/mother + husband/father

There was clearly sufficient ambiguity in the relationship between Paul and Virginie to raise the question of incest. In Bernardin's ideal society, mother/child relationships were characterized by maternal sacrifice and transmission of the gift of natural virtue. Those between 'siblings' displayed sharing, identification and sympathy. We never see a full sexual relationship between a man and a woman, for the story does not permit the love between Paul and Virginie to be consummated. However, despite the tragedy of thwarted love, Virginie's death is in its own way an erotic climax.

Bernardin presented the story as a true one, and so, by implication, an account of a way of life which was in principle attainable. His treatment of the physical environment was integral to the plan. The goodness of the micro-society derived partly from its environment: a natural world which was exceptionally fecund, beautiful, and relatively free from human intrusion. Although guided by natural theology, and containing an unconcealed idealization of a 'natural' society, *Paul et Virginie* inevitably contained a dramatic disruption. That the perfect equilibrium should be shattered was unavoidable, even *natural*, not just for the sake of an exciting plot, but for the simple reason that children grow up. And growing up meant awakening sexuality.

In *Paul et Virginie*, Virginie's sexuality was the decisive disruption, both because she reached sexual maturity first, and because the potential consequences of her sexuality – pregnancy – made her more vulnerable than a boy. Prompted by such fears, her mother sent her back to France. Her visit proving a failure, Virginie returned to her tropical paradise only to be drowned in a storm on the way back. She refused to remove her clothes and swim to safety with a naked sailor. Her death was caused by her *modesty*, the quintessentially 'natural' female virtue (Robinson, 1982). The changes of puberty took place in her before she left the island, but she was unable to understand what was happening to her. Her transformation from child to woman was expressed through images of variation, crisis, instability and unpredictability, manifest in mind, body and the physical environment. The picture of awakening sexuality is identical to that found in any number of contemporary scientific and medical treatises. For example, Cabanis characterized puberty as a 'general commotion', 'a general change of all human existence' which demonstrated the effect of the reproductive organs whose highly developed sensibility set up sympathetic responses in other parts of the body through the fluids they secreted and through the nervous system (Cabanis, 1956, vol. 1, 285). The important point is that the natural passage from childhood to adulthood, which physiological changes inevitably produced, was a cause of disruption and conflict as well as a crucial part of human and social continuity.

Bernardin's treatment of adolescence, and his refusal to allow the story to narrate Virginie's attainment of full womanhood, raises the question of how growing up was conceptualized and socially marked. Was it by autonomy from parental control, by entry into the market-place if socially appropriate, by marriage, by becoming sexually active, or by the birth of children? Something of all these was involved, linked as they were by prevailing ideas about sexuality and family. Indeed, by stressing the sexual dimension of adolescence, Bernardin implied the related changes in marital status and fertility, with their economic implications. Adolescence, the in-between state, was deeply threatening. For example, concern about illegitimacy frequently focused on young girls living away from home, working as servants and craving the comfort of a stable relationship, yet lacking the guiding discipline of parents to steer them into a correct marriage (Spacks, 1978; Shorter, 1976; Fairchilds, 1978). Similarly, the premature apprenticeship of young children was offensive to many people who feared that seduction and exploitation were the inevitable consequences; sexual and economic vulnerability went hand in hand, the twin sequelae of lack of parental control (Ariès, 1973; Gillis, 1974; Sommerville, 1982). No matter how attaining adulthood was envisaged, a link was made between sexuality and growth — sex develops, and thus was not seen as an essence but as a dynamic biological process whose natural history could be described.

Sexuality had two meanings which were in tension. It had a positive sense if construed as the impulse to procreate responsibly, portrayed in the almost erotic intimacy of mothers and children in late eighteenth-century painting (Duncan, 1973; Jordanova, 1985). It was seen rather more negatively if sexual expression was premature, illicit, excessive, or simply for carnal gratification. Although in theory this applied equally to men and women, surfeit of passion or voluptuousness was stereotypically associated with feminine weakness. The sense that sexuality disrupts, exploits, is open to both sexes and highly dangerous unless disciplined was explored by Laclos in *Les Liaisons Dangereuses* (Laclos, 1979b, Thody, 1975). He portrayed there a woman, unhampered by husband, children or fear of pregnancy, who was capable of playing the power games of the bedroom — a monstrous creature.

Laclos constructed the book as a series of letters, and like Bernardin de Saint-Pierre, he strove to create the illusion of veracity. The epistolary form gave the impression that convention and custom were exceedingly artificial, for the letters showed how, beneath the surface, people sought power over others. Life was depicted as a manipulative game; people are rarely what they appear to be, since in order to play the game, appearance must mask reality. Human beings are not motivated by passion or true feeling, but by the idea of victory; hence, they do not experience loving and living directly, but instead they take pleasure in a mediated way from the power they hold over others. Individuals are caught in webs of intrigue. Women are just as good at the games as men, maybe even better. Laclos certainly did not depict all human beings as equally corrupt, only potentially so. This is because of the sheer strength of human sexuality. Laclos claimed his book was a moral tale, designed to instruct mothers in particular of the consequences of excessively liberal attitudes towards children. But its subtlety lies in its capacity to explore the nature of human sexuality, as game and intrigue, as duty, and as natural passion.

The success of *Les Liaisons Dangereuses* derives from the perfect matching of the two main protagonists, a man and a woman who plot the downfall of others by sexual means and who are equally capable of playing the game of life – a game which ends with disaster for them both. They also both stand outside the normal family structures which serve as a disciplinary framework. Laclos showed what happened when the two interacting elements of authority and obedience were lacking. The young girl whose virtue was at stake had no father, only a naïve mother. Nor, recasting the argument at another level, did reason prevail over the passions, for people did succumb to their sexual desires – the forces which, although natural, sowed the seeds of disorder. Laclos implied that (male) authority was required to check (feminine/sexual) disorder. Absolute rule and passive obedience was a model of social relationships which no longer appealed to those in the 1790s who preferred to imagine order emerging from the coordinated harmony of body and mind (e.g. Volney, 1934; Jordanova, 1982; Picavet, 1891; van Duzer, 1935). Order was not to be imposed from outside by a separate agent such as the soul, the father or the absolute monarch; rather it would emerge from the inner coherence, harmony and organization of living beings. In physiological terms, this coherence stemmed from the sensibility of the organism and its substratum, the nervous system.

Laclos portrayed a society without arbitrary control, but he could hardly be said to approve of such a situation. In fact, he showed an intuitive reluctance to believe in the possibility of a truly moral society emerging from human nature. Sexuality appeared to him so potentially dangerous and subversive that there had to be rules to constrain its (ab)use which would restore the proper social distinctions between husbands and wives, parents and children, men and women. Families, like society, required a framework of discipline, something which *Les Liaisons Dangereuses* showed mothers alone to be unable to provide. The very absence of male authority figures in the novel was the most powerful argument for their social importance. The lack of strong men indicated not Laclos's idealization of motherhood, but his conviction that fathers are vital.

Like the remarkable works of the Marquis de Sade (1740–1814), we must understand Laclos's book as an inversion of dominant ideology. When he showed men and women equally playing the power games of sex, he was in fact supporting a radical demarcation between the sexes of the kind found in Cabanis. Exaggerating the luxury of the rich and idle which Laclos, like many of his contemporaries, associated with the Parisian court aristocracy, he portrayed a society which was the precise opposite of the one he himself wished to see. While de Sade used some of the same techniques, this was clearly to argue a different case. What these writers had in common, however, must not be lost sight of: namely, that sexuality, natural thought it was, was a powerfully disruptive force at the heart of social relations.

FEMININITY AND LIFE

While sexuality and adolescence, natural phenomena though
they were, seemed threatening forces in late eighteenth-
century culture, the responses to their presence in men and
women were radically different. In placing Virginie, her rise
to sexual maturity, and her virginal death at the centre of his
book, Bernardin de Saint-Pierre evoked a special association
between the female body and the living organism capable of
reproducing itself. At one level this was simply the recognition
of the distinctively female contribution to procreation: pregnancy and suckling. The theme of generation was at the core
of the life sciences during the eighteenth century (Roger,
1963; Delaporte, 1982). Just as the sexuality and reproductive organs of plants elicited enormous interest, so did hermaphrodites and monsters as well as healthy human reproductive
systems, all of which were to be catalogued, described, classified and depicted. Women were the carriers and givers of
life, and as a result, a pregnant woman was both the quintes-
sence of life and an erotic object (Jordanova, 1980a, 1985).
This is of course quite consistent with an emphasis on the
heightened sensibility of women and their wombs, for sensibility was a fundamental organic property.

A better understanding of the identification of femininity
with life can be achieved if the significance of the concept of life
itself is considered (Figlio, 1975, 1976; Canguilhem, 1971;
Jordanova, 1984, 44–57). In the late eighteenth century, life
was commonly associated with activity and plasticity, with the
adaptive powers of organisms to respond to the environment,
and with organization, that is, the structural complexity of a
living being, a concept used to explain the special properties of
animals and plants. Life was a notion of synthesis, system and
fusion. Appropriately enough, it sustained an approach to
sexuality which stressed not the reproductive organs or genitals, but the sex of the whole organism. Every fibre of a female
body carried femininity within it – a femininity which was
acquired by custom and habit. Furthermore, this total female-

ness was adapted to specific biological and social purposes; it
fulfilled a social role. This perspective can be termed organicist in that it stressed the whole coordinated organism, which
then became a model for other entities, such as human
societies. A rigid demarcation between mind and body thus
made no sense, since the organism was one integrated whole.
Hence, clearly, the moral and the social emerged out of the
natural organization of living matter.

Life was, then, a fertile concept. If we think for a moment of
some of its associations, its cultural significance can be brought
into sharper focus: life science, life style, life history, life and
death. Living phenomena were systematically explored, for
example, by correlating behaviour with health, by tracing life
events as they affected the body, by comparing similar
organisms in different environments. All manner of social
relationships were integral to an understanding of living
phenomena because of the dialectical relationship between the
living being and its conditions of existence (Glacken, 1967;
Jordanova and Porter, 1979).

Since it was not the reproductive organs alone which made
men and women different, natural philosophers looked
elsewhere for the distinction. Organisms interacted with their
surroundings, giving sexuality a behavioural dimension, in
that females became full women by doing womanly things, like
breast-feeding their children; to refuse the task was to dena-
ture or unsex oneself, as also happened when women took on
male occupations such as scholarship. Cabanis asserted that
male and female children were strikingly similar and concluded
that sex differences emerge only in the course of development
(1956, vol. 1, 276). As a result, the social and psychological
environment in which an individual was nurtured became of
paramount importance. Each life history, seen from this point
of view, was a complex story, and the body bore the signs of
accumulated experience. One could read a body like a book: it
told the story which the medical practitioner recorded in case
notes. Both the inside of the body and its general appearance

(physiognomy) were scrutinized for evidence of how the female and the male diverge. This was accomplished by, for example, analysing the nervous system, fibres and tissues. The language of fibres and tissues is of great interest because it spoke about the unobservable. In descriptions of the smallest constituents of women's bodies, images of softness, rotundity, delicacy, feebleness and childishness were used. Their muscles were weak and the female nervous system was possessed of great sensibility, yet was softer than a man's. But women were also presented as supple, strong, durable and flexible, and of this their greater life expectancy was adduced as evidence (Barthez, 1858, 181, 184).

The inside of an organism was seen in terms of its sensibility, a term which bridged the physical and the moral (mental) and united them in a single organic base. Significantly, the febrile feminine sensibility was seen as particularly akin to that of children. Although sensibility was rooted in the nervous system, the glands were equally important in the physiology of sex. Glands, including the testicles and ovaries, powerfully affected all other parts of the body through substances they released, changes they prompted in the circulatory system beginning in puberty, and their swelling at this time. Glands formed a physiological system with sympathetic links between member organs. An emphasis on the fine structure of the body went hand in hand with an interest in body fluids. The prominent Montpellier physician Barthez (1734–1806) claimed that women lived longer than men partly because of the rejuvenating effects of menstruation (1858, 184). Spermatic fluid was also deemed to have healthful properties for the women who received it, while losing it illegitimately, through sexual excess or masturbation, had dire consequences for men (Tissot, 1772, 9–11). Blood was clearly of great biological and metaphorical significance. Sex organs affected the rest of the body through the circulatory system, inaugurating new directions in blood flow during puberty which were accompanied by increased tone of blood vessels, more heat, and greater frequency of haemorrhages. Most important was the onset of menstruation at the correct time. The blood of women as their life force was bizarrely depicted by de Sade in *Justine* (1791), where an aristocrat bled to death a succession of young wives for his erotic satisfaction (1966, 633 ff).

Most late eighteenth-century anatomical and physiological accounts assumed that reproduction and sexuality were inseparable. The pregnant woman was thus an object of desire, for she had attained the peak of femininity. The fusion of procreation and sexuality was a consequence of taking the whole, integrated organism as the object of study. The particular interest of de Sade's writings is his *separation* of sexuality and reproduction, one of the most immediately shocking of his ideas. Furthermore, he argued that the separation stemmed from nature herself (1966, 489; Carter, 1979). One consequence of his view was that women and men could be treated equally as vehicles for sexual pleasure. He gave no special status to women because of their capacity to bear children — a striking contrast to the idealization and mystification of female biology found in scientific and medical writings. De Sade raised quite openly the question of infanticide, one of the most highly charged subjects of the period. Infanticide could, he implied, be seen as a rational rather than a criminal act. The world, he allowed one of his protagonists to assert, is overpopulated anyway, and why, he went on to ask, should we bring forth more children to be neglected and rejected by parents who lack the economic resources to care for them (de Sade 1966, 470–1, 650)? This argument called into question common assumptions about the value of human life.

As a perceptive critic of his own society, de Sade must be listened to attentively. Whatever he did or did not advocate in terms of personal conduct, he threw into sharp focus a number of important zones of tension. The most noteworthy of these are the questions of power and money. De Sade showed, in relentless detail, how vulnerability to sexual exploitation was connected with poverty and the lack of social status. By

separating sexuality and reproduction, he allowed the possibility that the human body, male or female, could be an instrument of pleasure; any part of the body could be an erotic zone.
It was not the purpose of anatomical parts that interested him,
but their capacity for sensuality. In abolishing the sanctity
with which human reproduction had been invested, especially
in relation to motherhood, he refused to accord any special
value to female life-giving powers. Women, like men, take
and give pleasure. Or rather, women, like men, buy, sell,
trade and steal for the sake of sexual gratification and power.
If sex is the ultimate form of power, it is important to recognize
that money is the principal means by which it is achieved.
Those who are economically and sexually weak will be rob-
bed; the rich can buy, or just take, what satisfaction they
want. Sex, in other words, is a commodity. In fact, de Sade
argued, it was already treated that way if only the surface ven-
eer were skimmed off. The body, for him, was already in the
market-place. It was an object bought and sold daily, frequently under the guise of institutions like marriage, which
supposedly protected and cherished human beings while in
fact treating them as cattle.

De Sade's view was the reverse of the medical organicism
discussed earlier. Where the medical writers saw life, resisting
the reduction to the status of an object, he saw the reduction
already accomplished. Where they revered the feminine, he
demystified it. Where they treated the human race as a natural
unit, a biological entity, he perceived its fragmentation into the
rich and powerful, the poor and weak.

The insight that sex was treated as a commodity was hardly
new with de Sade. Writers on prostitution had noted that sexual and economic exploitation went hand in hand (Jones,
1978). They generally assumed that treating women as instruments of sexual pleasure was wrong because it prevented them
from fulfilling their proper destiny as wives and mothers.
Furthermore, they implied that whereas there was little inherently wrong with men treating sex as a commodity, there was

when women did so. This asymmetry in the argument prompts us to ask why it was so important for women to be placed in the mysterious, sacred role of life-giver.

Concern with the value of life and of individual lives as abstractions dominated many areas of scientific, medical and philosophical inquiry. Some examples were the attempts to produce adequate mortality and morbidity statistics, reliable life tables and analyses of infant mortality (Rosen, 1976; Glass, 1978; Cullen, 1975, 1–16; Gonnard, 1923; Coleman, 1977, 1982; Buck, 1982; McManners, 1981, ch. 4). Here the bare facts of life and death were quantified, and ways suggested of improving the quality as well as the quantity of life. Early demographic work was an attempt to bridge the public and private domains because aggregate population, and its profile, was the concern of the state, even if produced by the actions of individuals in their most intimate relationships. An individual's capacity to give life depended on many physiological and anatomical variables as well as psychological and social ones. Private, individual acts of sex and reproduction had public consequences in the size and health of the population and its labouring potential. Quantification was one way of dealing with the problem of how to manage human resources. Improving the quality of mothering was seen as an important step towards the goal of bettering the population. The private behaviour of women as reproductive beings and their physiological competence were of great interest to those attempting to develop a scientific, quantitative analysis of human life. Each life was assigned a value based on what it could produce: work in the case of men, healthy children in the case of women. This value was expressed in numerical terms if life insurance or membership of friendly societies was involved. In this sense human life was already treated as a commodity; the mentality of mercantilism was well established (Rosen, 1974; Wilson, 1958).

By contrast, the mentality of the organicist approach was based on the assumption that living things were integrated

wholes, ensembles of functions. Such views tended to lead to
assertions about the inviolability of life. Since the distinctive
features of living things did not adhere in any one part of them,
as they would according to mechanist or dualist presuppositions, but were diffused through every fibre of the body, viv-
isection or any sort of ruthless experimentation was frowned
upon. The sacred value of life had to be respected. Furthermore, there were degrees of living complexity or organization,
with those beings which were most structurally elaborate,
closest to the peak of life, being given special status.

This special status was also assigned to women and young
children: women because they gave life, children because they
had recently received it. In them the full mystery of life was
manifest. One can state this another way by saying that
women and children were those people who should not be
treated as objects or commodities. Life was placed in opposition to commodity. To the sets of pairs mentioned at the beginning of the chapter, some more may now be added:

nature	culture
women and children	men
life	commodity
privacy of the home	public market-place

We can now go a stage further and ask about the implicit
meanings of such dichotomies. Clearly the central issue is the
treatment of human life as if it were a thing. If we want to
understand the special significance of the feminine and the
infantile as natural categories, we should look at what their
mystification concealed. A form of social relations which
treated persons as objects was thereby veiled by a language of
nature in which reproduction and sexuality were made both
natural and sacred via the anatomy and physiology of women.
Since the language was a predominantly masculine one, it may
be understood as a projection onto the feminine of something
men were actually, or in danger of, losing. This 'something'

was captured and retained by being associated with the 'other' – woman and child. The family then became the principal occasion for the mingling of these two elements, hence the need to stabilize the family through the physical presence of women and children within the home as symbols of life and personhood. For this reason the apparent violation of children through labour carried a very strong symbolic load.

One of the most potent expressions of these ideas in the eighteenth century may be found in the writings of Rousseau, and especially in his *Emile* (1762). He was in fact virtually the only author Cabanis referred to when writing about sexuality. Other medical writers concerned with femininity and sexuality like the French physician Pierre Roussel (1742–1802), as well as authors of more conventionally literary works like Bernardin de Saint-Pierre, were similarly indebted to Rousseau (Roussel, 1777; MacCormack and Strathern, 1980, chs 2 and 3; Le Doeuff, 1981–2; Knibiehler, 1976). Rousseau spawned a literary and ideological tradition, seductive for its capacity to draw together political, personal and scientific elements, and with a strong aesthetic dimension. This tradition was highly compatible with the approaches to natural history at the Muséum National d'Histoire Naturelle (formerly the Jardin du Roi) in Paris which nourished the imagination of several generations of Frenchmen in the eighteenth and nineteenth centuries (Huss, this volume; Kaplan, 1977; *Centenaire*, 1893; Jordanova, 1980b).

CONCLUSION

The idea of privacy was evoked in a number of ways as a result of giving women and children the status of not-commodity, carriers of life. Privacy was identified with domesticity, with surveillance of intimate acts, with voyeurism and the erotic, and with the interior of the body, what was not normally seen, the 'private parts'. In the very process of separating off the female and private from the male and public, the impulse to

examine, probe, violate and penetrate the former was generated. At the same time as Cabanis waxed lyrical about the
suppleness of the fibres of the female body, sex organs were
increasingly explicitly depicted in medical treatises, and erotic
elements were present in conventional anatomical drawings
and models. Medical practitioners probed, and then wrote
about, the most private aspects of people's lives. They made
moral tales out of case histories; but the drive to know about
the private aspects of people's lives went far deeper than that.
In his famous treatise on masturbation, first published in
French in 1760, the Swiss physician Tissot (1728–97) took
the notion that it is important to penetrate into the most private
aspects of people's lives a stage further (Tissot, 1772; Donzelot, 1980). He did not advocate *medical* intrusion, but
rather that the parents should oversee children at every possible moment in order to guard against their masturbating tendencies. His advice contained strikingly violent undertones:

> Be particularly careful in the choice of a preceptor, watch
> over him and his pupil with that vigilance, which an atten-
> tive and enlightened father of a family exerts to know what
> is done in the darkest recesses of his house; use that vigi-
> lance which discovers the coppice where the deer has taken
> shelter, when it escaped all other eyes: this is always possi-
> ble when it is earnestly pursued. (1772, 43)

Tissot presupposes an intimacy between parents and children
which gives the former the right to see and know all in relation
to their offspring.

Children were placed in an ambiguous situation when
associated with the female domain of domestic privacy.
Women could be conceptualized in this way by presenting
their sexuality and their reproduction capacities as one and the
same thing. For children the situation was more equivocal
when they reached adolescence, as we saw in the case of Virginie. In *Paul et Virginie* children were shown as non-sexual

beings, and Bernardin de Saint-Pierre did not describe the whole transformation from childhood to full sexual maturity. It was too explosive, too threatening, for him to be able to do so. Yet children had to make the transition from childhood to adulthood, from being subject to their parents to being parents themselves.

Tissot's concern about masturbation implied that, in some sense, children *were* sexual beings; why else would their secret activities need to be controlled? The awkwardness of growing up, both in reality and in imagination, could not be solved easily. One approach was to select an age at which the passage from one status to another could be deemed to have taken place. The tensions and difficulties of so doing were nicely portrayed in debates on the age at which children should work or be considered legally competent. At a deeper level, these debates were about when children might pass from the private to the public, when they might enter the world of commodities, and when they might become sexually active. Once working, they lost their special status close to the source of life; they entered the public domain and became economic persons. Hence the concern about child prostitution, which violated the economic, the sexual and the social dimensions of childhood simultaneously.

Forms of shorthand were developed to designate the special way in which women and children were carriers of life. The pictorial treatment of children in the period as innocent, as simple, as close to nature, playful, and, most significantly, as implicitly erotic. is one example. Another is the treatment of the breast, which took on symbolic significance in the ways it was extolled for its beauty and its valuable biological function. It also stood for the attraction between men and women, since it was a *visible* sign of femininity which suggested the importance of reproduction (Roussel, 1777). It did so all the more powerfully in an environment where wet-nursing was commonplace and a known killer of babies (Sussman, 1982). The mother's refusal or willingness to give her breast to the child meant, symbolically, and sometimes literally, death or life. The arrival and departure of the wet-nurse were common themes in painting of the period, which also on occasion depicted the mother giving suck or about to do so (Gélis *et al.*, 1978). This sign-language relied on putatively natural objects and processes to contain and express a wide range of social and cultural meaning.

This essay has explored some of the complexities involved in late eighteenth-century treatments of sexuality, reproduction and the family as phenomena which were at once natural and social. There were important political, economic, social and ideological questions raised by such treatments. The language in which these questions were couched, shared by scientific, medical and literary accounts, is among the most important keys to their historical significance. It was indeed a language of nature, full of tensions, ambiguities, and fruitful associations, and serving to conceal as well as to reveal. It drew upon anatomy and physiology, and was sustained by the growing scientific and medical interest in a science of life. To chart the development of biology without recognizing the larger cultural context which gave meaning to the concept of life, or to read novels depicting sexual experience and kin relations in isolation from the scientific and medical treatments of those subjects, results in a partial and distorted historical perspective. Science and literature, united in eighteenth-century culture, must be reunited by the historian.

ACKNOWLEDGMENTS
I wish to thank Gillian Beer, Roger Cooter, Elaine Jordan and Angela Livingstone for their help in preparing this essay.

FURTHER READING

Boucé, 1982   Goldberg, 1984
Eagleton, 1982   MacCormack and
Elshtain, 1981   Strathern, 1980

Sensibility, Sympathy, Benevolence: Physiology and Moral Philosophy in Tristram Shandy

JAMES RODGERS

EDITOR'S INTRODUCTION

The separation of mind and body articulated so clearly by Descartes posed severe problems to later generations. He had acknowledged that the two elements interacted, but failed to provide a satisfying account of how this actually happened. The postulated role of the pineal gland as the point of contact proved largely unconvincing. The nature of mind/body interaction was one of the most challenging conceptual problems facing those interested in physiological and biological science during the eighteenth century. As Rodgers shows, there were many common human experiences that shed light on the matter, such as crying, blushing, sexual desire, erection, and feelings of sympathy towards fellow human beings. Sterne is particularly interesting in the subtle and complex way he explored these themes in fictional form. He continually called into question simplistic accounts of human nature by showing that the key concepts of eighteenth-century physiological and social thought — sensibility, sentiment, sympathy and benevolence — had many, not always compatible meanings. In doing so, he also subverted comfortable notions about the progress of science coming about by means of a clear, simple, direct vocabulary — a notion to which those concerned with classification were particularly committed. Rodgers shows that Sterne undermined any idea of 'verbal fixity'.

The power of Sterne's writing derives in part from the fact that natural philosophers and natural historians did indeed espouse a theory of language as integral to the growth of knowledge. The debates about language that took place during the eighteenth century were also important because they were the occasion for some hard thinking about the nature of the human mind and of the soul. Through the discussion of what is generally referred to as 'materialism' – the thesis that only matter exists in the universe – fundamental religious issues were canvassed. The fact that physiological ideas mediated other levels of concern allows Rodgers to hint at a point made earlier in the essays by Pilkington and Jordanova. Such matters struck at the heart of social relations. We can see this very clearly in the treatment of sympathy, which, as Rodgers shows, was used to explore relationships between human beings, especially in relation to benevolence and charity. In a century particularly concerned with secular philanthropy, its rationale and functions, and with the role of individual benefactors, the precise interpretation of sympathy was a matter of some importance. Furthermore, Rodgers indicates that even within physiology, sympathy was a highly complex term.

Tristram Shandy is a further testimony to the importance of sexuality for eighteenth-century writers. The book often alludes to the human sexual impulse, which is treated with great candour. Sterne inquires just how far people do consciously control their own erotic behaviour – a point nicely exemplified by the difficulties of explaining erection, particularly in trying to see how a physiological process can be controlled by the imagination but not apparently by the will. The difficulties of explaining the will, soul, mind and imagination in naturalistic terms were general in the life sciences of the period, which registered the widespread disenchantment with purely mechanistic accounts, a point exemplified by Diderot's writings.

Yet some mechanistic accounts were highly influential, such as that by the philosopher and physician David Hartley (1705–57). He strove to show how all mental processes could be understood in terms of the association of ideas (in the tradition inaugurated by John Locke) and by the vibrations of organic fibres. The resistance to what was often construed as a crude, simplifying, reductionistic Cartesianism is of great historical significance because it focused attention on the language of science. A fresh vocabulary for the new science of life was needed, the terms borrowed from natural philosophy (i.e. the physical sciences) having proved unequal to the task. Most commentators were happy to use distinctively organic terms like sensibility and irritability, following the influential physiologist Haller (1708–77), but they meant entirely different things by them. The resulting debates revealed that conceptualizing natural processes and deploying a complex language were two facets of the same intellectual challenge.

One consequence of these wide-ranging discussions on the nature of 'life' and on 'mind/body' was a flowering of interest in the nervous system. This was a logical development from the Cartesian and Lockean positions, for the nervous system provided the place where mind and body interacted and sensations became ideas. It was not an easy natural object to study, however, since discriminating different parts of the brain on observable grounds proved difficult, although theorists maintained that the brain and the nervous system were composed of distinct faculties. It was especially hard to perform experiments, or even to dissect these parts in a human body. Bodies for anatomizing were not freely available and experiments on living creatures had to be confined to animals. As a result there was great interest in the 'natural experiments' provided by unusual medical conditions that threw light on nervous function. At the same time, the brain stood for something special, even uniquely human, for it was, according to traditionalists like Haller, the seat of the soul.

Perhaps the most important consequence of the interest in nervous action was the use of the nervous system as a metaphor for human society. The link with sympathy as a term in moral and social thought was particularly important once investigators had identified the nervous system as the major physiological system underpinning sympathetic relations between organs. The coordination between different social and political structures could be neatly analogized with the function of the nervous system in the body. Through discourse on the nervous system, writers could pose political and social questions. How did the different parts of human society hang together? What were the relationships between the parts? Were some superior to others, and hence legitimately dominant over them? The term 'parts', appropriate in physiological debate, has a conveniently neutral ring to it. For 'parts' one can substitute 'classes', 'orders', occupations' or 'social interest groups' as the social equivalents.

Through the study of a work like *Tristram Shandy*, we can reconstruct some of the resonances of key terms in scientific and medical thought, precisely because such terms were common to science and literature. Furthermore, for Rodgers, Sterne's impact is essentially subversive in that he never used a concept without pointing out its myriad meanings and multiple associations, thereby undermining a single authoritative interpretation. Hence, the vocabulary common to science and literature was in fact deployed somewhat differently in the two fields. In science, writers strove to control ambiguity and free associations partly because a quite clear set of intellectual, religious, moral and social consequences followed from the precise manner in which they used their key concepts. Sterne, by contrast, knew no such constraint, but played with words, with ideas about words like 'sensibility' and 'irritability', and with concepts of life and human nature.

Words and their meanings perplex the male Shandys, Walter, Toby and Tristram himself, the narrator of Laurence Sterne's mock-autobiography, *The Life and Opinions of Tristram Shandy, Gentleman* (1759–67). As the novel progresses, Tristram learns that his father's logorrhoea springs from numerous sources and that his uncle's taciturn simplicity is very complex indeed. He also discovers that words themselves are many-layered, loaded with associations reverberating beyond their literal meanings. Throughout the novel's nine volumes, the intricate relations between words, their meanings, and the events they describe continually confound the Shandy family. In scrutinizing his narrator and revealing his characters' shortcomings as they struggle with language, Sterne satirizes overly systematic, rational thought. He also plays a major part in the establishment of sentimentality as a dominant literary attitude in late eighteenth-century Europe. As part of this productive play with language and ideas, Sterne's fiction exploits and criticizes contemporary science, particularly the emerging field of physiology.

During the eighteenth century, study of the workings of the human body (and its corresponding mental dispositions) emerged from its grounding in the ancient doctrine of the four humours – phlegm (phlegmatic), blood (sanguine), black bile (melancholic), and yellow bile (choleric) – derived from Galen, the second-century AD Greek physician and anatomist. For 1,500 years, both physicians and their patients accepted the idea that the balance of these four bodily fluids determined both physical and psychological health. Beginning in the seventeenth century, this holistic account of mind/body interaction was supplanted by a view of the human body as a machine. The rationalist philosophy of René Descartes (1596–1650) produced the influential dualism of two substances, the immaterial thinking and the materially extended, and William Harvey (1578–1657) explained the

blood's circulation as a result of empirical, experimental investigation. Their successes generated ever more radical attempts
to separate apparently mechanical bodily functions from the
mind's spiritual domain. In reaction, the natural philosopher
Georg Ernst Stahl (1660–1734) and his followers, called
'vitalists', asserted that the rational soul controls man's physical functions. Despite this vigorous opposition, mechanistic
explanation found its clearest and most provocative statement
in Julien Offray de La Mettrie's *L'Homme Machine* (1747)
and David Hartley's *Observations on Man* (1749).

Although La Mettrie's materialism denies the necessity for
an immaterial soul while Hartley's maintains a place for it,
both explain muscular motion and even human thought solely
on mechanical and materialistic principles. Holism is thus
restored, but a more precisely explanatory machine replaces
the vague humouralism of the ancients. The vitalism of the
Stahlians is moribund, and the Christian 'soul' virtually
abandoned. Such a state delighted the subversive French
philosophes and dismayed their more pious British contemporaries. At this stage, in the 1750s and 1760s, two developments of lasting significance occur: (1) Albrecht von Haller
(1708–77) establishes experimentally the distinction between
irritability (unfelt automatic response to stimuli) and sensibility (response based on or accompanied by feeling) as sources
of muscular motion. Haller's work has been seen as a 'turning
point' in the development of the life sciences (Roger, 1980,
274) and as the foundation of the science of physiology. (2)
Robert Whytt (1714–66), Professor of Medicine at Edinburgh, and the *philosophes*, most notably La Mettrie and
Denis Diderot, assert the importance of sensibility or 'feeling'
as the single distinguishing characteristic of life (Moravia,
1978, 45–60).

In addition to its importance for science, the term 'sensibility' has great significance for later eighteenth-century literature. Exploring sensibility's developing meaning in physiolog-

ical, psychological, philosophical, and literary contexts is necessary in order to understand more fully both the word itself and the interrelations of those contexts. Furthermore, other terms closely related to sensibility – sympathy and senti- ment – stand in need of explanation as they take on varying meanings in the discourses of natural science, social thought, and imaginative literature. Out of such discussion, firmly grounded in physiology, can grow a more complete apprehen- sion of the place occupied by benevolence, the fundamental moral virtue of good will, in eighteenth-century writing.

Sterne recognizes that sentiment and benevolence are based on neither reason nor passion nor mechanical reaction, but on a conflation of reason and emotion allied with imagination. In this, Sterne's view of the basis for moral action and generous sentiments is similar to notions argued in the philosophical works of his two contemporaries David Hume (1711–76) and Adam Smith (1723–90). Sterne's fiction, however, develops the ramifications of such a view more vividly than the work of either philosopher. While demonstrating the complexity of apparently simple 'feeling', Sterne also exposes the self-indul- gent and self-protecting aspects of the innocent-seeming avocation, the tenaciously pursued hobby-horse. In addition, he recognizes the sexual basis of much human thought and altruistic feeling (Brady, 1970, 41–56). Sterne's literary use of physiological terms provides a strong critique of both natural philosophy and moral philosophy. Their solemn rationalizing and unselfcritical empiricism fail to explain the living creature, the social interactions of a few 'humourous' characters, or the introspective mind of Tristram Shandy.

Studying the works of Sterne and certain physiologists reveals parallel lines of development in common categories of thought about similar problems. Sterne, however, surpasses his scientific and philosophical contemporaries by continually undercutting their empiricist use of language, the pervasive and all-important assumption that words can be made to rep-

resent ideas of things without ambiguity. For Sterne, words
do not simply represent ideas or things, nor can they be made
to do so except in the most artificial of languages – that is, in a
language incapable of describing and expressing life. More
specifically, through his intentional ambiguity in employing
sensibility, sympathy, and sentiment, he criticizes their use in
physiological and philosophical works and is led to fresh views
of that key concept of moral philosophy – benevolence.

I

Sterne's critical view of the relations of sensibility and benevolence appears at its most sensitive in those parts of *Tristram
Shandy* where he displays the complex interplay between sentiment and power. In depicting Tristram's apparently
exemplary Uncle Toby, the novel shows that the capacity for
sympathy and benevolence need not preclude a massive and
wounding insensitivity. Sensibility and power also provided
the central issues for a physiological controversy raging at the
time of *Tristram Shandy*'s composition. In a series of publications in the 1750s and 1760s, Whytt and Haller – one of the
most eminent scientists and prolific writers in Europe –
debated the nature of animal motion. Central to the controversy were the definitions and relative importance of irritability and sensibility, and the place of the 'soul' in human life
(French, 1969, 63–76). One focus of this debate – the nature
of erection and causes of sexual impotence – pervades *Tristram
Shandy*. Whether Tristram's Uncle Toby, severely wounded
in the groin at the siege of Namur, is able to father children not
only engages the curiosity of his pursuer, the Widow Wadman, but also becomes the central theme of the novel's concluding volumes. On this physiological phenomenon, with its
mysterious causes, significant scientific and literary discourses
converge.

    In the light of contemporary physiology, the state of Toby's
procreative powers is intimately bound to his sentimentality

and benevolence. For the eighteenth-century moralists, the motivation for an act of good will is at least as important as the act itself (Randall, 1962, I, 741). Hume, in *An Enquiry concerning Human Understanding* (1748), refers approvingly to Francis Hutcheson (1694–1746), the Scottish philosopher of 'moral sentiment': 'But a late Philosopher has taught us, by the most convincing Arguments, that Morality is nothing in the abstract Nature of Things, but is entirely relative to the Sentiment or mental Taste of each particular Being; . . . Moral perceptions therefore, ought not to be classified with the Operations of the Understanding, but with the Tastes or Sentiments' (in Randall, I, 803). This moral sentiment is closely connected to sexual impotence in *Tristram Shandy*. Indeed, one critic, R. F. Brissenden, holds a view similar to the Devil's and Mrs Wadman's that turns 'uncle *Toby*'s virtue thereupon into nothing but *empty bottles*, *tripes*, *trunk-hose*, and *pantofles*' (Sterne, 1940, IX, xxii, 626). Brissenden writes. 'The significance of Uncle Toby as a symbol not only of goodness, but also of impotence, is not always recognized. . . . Nor is it usually recognized just how much Toby's goodness depends on his impotence — although Sterne tries to make it clear that there are very good physical reasons for Uncle Toby's modesty' (1974, 211). Sterne, however, makes nothing very clear, least of all the question of Toby's impotence and its influence on his modesty and benevolence. Although the novel's testimony concerning Toby's manhood is finally inconclusive, throughout the book Tristram insinuates that his uncle is unable to carry out the conjugal duties the Widow Wadman so eagerly anticipates. Whether Toby is really impotent or whether Tristram as narrator merely treats him as such, the nature of impotence, the causes of erection, and their influence on the moral sentiments remain significant.

As early as the sixteenth century, Montaigne, the French sceptic whose *Essais* Sterne read avidly, saw clearly the mental origin of some impotence (Johnson, 1968, 5). Only in the eighteenth century, however, did medical writing display a growing awareness of the role played by the imagination and emotions in the seemingly wholly physical phenomenon of erection. For instance, the anonymous *Tabes Dorsalis* (1758) quotes the influential Dutch physician and chemist Hermann Boerhaave (1668–1738): 'The Muscles concerned in this Action, are not to be reckoned among the Class of vital or spontaneous Muscles, since of themselves they do not act in the most healthy Man; but they are rather in a Class *sui generis*, being under the influence of the Imagination. The Will has no influence either to suppress, excite, or diminish their Action, Etc' (14). Here a fascinating special case arises to challenge both mechanists and vitalists, both believers in predestination and upholders of free will. This peculiar set of muscles responds neither to the uncontrollable spontaneous impulse nor to the conscious will. The mysteries of erection and impotence thus provide a focal point for the controversy between Haller and Whytt on the source of movement in the animal body. In 1751 Whytt's *Essay on Vital and Other Involuntary Motions of Animals*, began the argument, and the debate continued in books and pamphlets ending with Haller's *Ad Robert Whyttii nuperum Scriptum Apologia* in 1764 (French 1969, 63–4). Both Haller and Whytt, while disagreeing with one another, objected to the current, simplistic view that the cause of erection is the nerves' mechanically constricting the veins leading from the penis (French 1969, 61).

Whytt's *Essay* first mentions Haller to attack his view, put forth in *First Lines of Physiology* (1747), that compression of the veins causes erection of the penis. Whytt posits that 'the seed in the *vesiculae seminales*' or lascivious sights and ideas stimulate the arteries, not the veins, to more rapidly 'vibrating contractions', and that these contractions cause arterial blood to enter the penis faster than the veins can carry it off (Whytt, 1751, 98–100). Haller's explanation, published in English in 1754, responds to Whytt. Compression of the veins in the penis causes erection, but Haller rejects a simple mechanism independent of mind and admits that what causes this compression 'remains to be explained' (Haller, 1754, II, 278). For Haller, the physiology of erection ultimately depends on irritating the nerves of the penis and the urethra by 'external friction, or from venereal thoughts or dreams, a redundancy of good semen', and other physical causes (Haller, 1754, II, 281).

Both Haller and Whytt see the great influence of the mind over the body in causing erection. Haller finds this mental influence a special case of irritability applicable only to erection, while Whytt places erection among a set of analogous mind/body interactions. While explicitly attacking Whytt's view, Haller explains: 'The Irritability of the genitals seems to be of a particular nature, in so far as voluptuous ideas are the most proper *stimulus* to put them in motion. . . But in whatever manner these irritations are produced, the effect of them is always to constrict the veins, and to retard the motion of the blood through them' (Haller, 1755, 682–3). This 'particular nature' is denied by Whytt: 'As the erection of the *penis* often proceeds from lascivious thoughts, it must be ascribed, in these cases at least, to the mind, notwithstanding our being equally unconscious of her influence exerted here, as in producing the contraction of the heart' (Whytt, 1751, 301). Thus, Whytt places erection among other examples of the will's unconscious working. In a later work he reiterates his position by comparing the 'increased motion of blood in the arteries' to the motion in the salivary vessels of a hungry man presented with food (Whytt, 1755, II, 70).

Whytt explains in terms especially pertinent to Tristram's retiring Uncle Toby this unconscious, involuntary, yet not spontaneous physical phenomenon:

> We cannot, by an effort of the will, either command or restrain the erection of the *penis*; and yet it is evidently owing

> to the mind; for sudden fear, or any thing which fixes our
> attention strongly and all at once, makes this member
> quickly subside, though it were ever so fully erected. The
> titillation, therefore, of the *vesiculae seminales* by the
> semen, lascivious thoughts, and other causes, only produce
> the erection of the *penis*, as they necessarily excite the mind
> to determine the blood in greater quantity into the cells.
> (Whytt, 1751, 314)

The mind definitely mediates between cause and effect here
and is necessary to control erection, yet the mind itself is in this
case beyond conscious control. There is no question of a mindless, mechanical irritability at work, and yet Whytt insists that
the mind is insensible of its own working. (Such discussion of
the unconscious appeared in a surprisingly large amount of
eighteenth-century medical writing (Rousseau, 1980, 155–
6)). The imagination, although Whytt does not name it, seems
through the unconscious mind to control erection and to supply
the middle ground between involuntary response and willed
action. Attesting to the power of memory and imagination,
Whytt states that 'the remembrance or *idea* of things, formerly
applied to different parts of the body, produce almost the
same effect, as if they themselves were really present' (Whytt,
1751, 252). When Whytt offers mental fixation and fear,
both products of the imagination, as causes of detumescence,
his theory applies particularly well to Toby. He dwells defen-
sively in an imaginative reconstruction of his manner of life
before the traumatic injury to his groin. He also shuns adult
encounters with women.

Concerning the first threat to Toby's potency – mental fixation – the eager Mrs Wadman must wait for Toby's hobby-
horse, his bowling-green as mock battlefield, to be put out to
pasture before she can hope to titillate him. Only an exercise of
patience, it seems, can finally overcome his fixation on the
pre-traumatic past. Tristram is not so forthcoming about the

removal of the second threat to Toby's potency, his fear of
sexual injury. Corporal Trim, the faithful Sancho Panza to
Toby's Quixote, can help to mitigate the effects of Toby's
modesty, but it appears that Trim's information about Mrs
Wadman's 'humanity', i.e. her sexuality, only reinforces
Toby's fear of women. Fear for his own safety, particularly in
the tender parts of his anatomy, may be very strong in Toby.
Mrs Wadman would have read about such problems when she
consulted James Drake's *New System of Anatomy* (1707), as
Tristram tells us she did (IX, xxvi, 636). Drake writes:

> An Alternation, as occasion requires, of *Erection* and
> *Flaccidity*, was absolutely necessary, the first, to the Per-
> formance of its Office, the latter, for the Security of the
> Part: Since without an *Erection* it were impossible to emit,
> and lodge the Seed where it ought to be, and with a Con-
> stant one, almost as impossible to secure the Part from
> many of those Injuries to which it would be perpetually
> expos'd; not to mention the loss of Instigation, which must
> be a necessary Consequence of Constant Erection. (Drake,
> 1707, I, 256–7)

Security from injury plays a large part in Toby's mental make-
up, and insinuations about his potency accompany Tristram's
indirect statements about his own capacities. These references
are meant to amuse, but they also suggest that further consideration of erection can yield insights into Sterne's binding of
character to physiology.

Whytt's discussion of erection and its connection to other
mind/body relations is even more pertinent than Drake's:

> By an increased oscillatory motion of the small vessels,
> which we have assigned as the cause of the erection of the
> *penis*, we daily observe a variety of sudden and surprising
> changes produced in the circulation. To this is to be
> ascribed the profuse secretion of the pale limpid urine, to

which hysterical people are so liable; as also the great discharge of tears from the lachrymal vessels, in people
affected with great joy or grief. And the blushing, or red-
ness and glowing warmth of the face, which attends a sense
of shame, is not owing to the constriction of the temporal
veins by means of the nervous filaments from the *portio
dura*, which surround them*, but to an increased oscillatory
motion of the small vessels of the face . . .
*Haller, not in Boerhaave. . . [Whytt's note]
(Whytt, 1751, 101–2)

Whytt attacks Haller while expressing his firm conviction that
the mind wields great influence over the body. More specifically, he emphasizes the oscillation of the blood vessels as the
common cause of erection, blushing, and the production of
tears. With this claim, he provides a link in physiological
speculation between sexuality and sentimentality, a connection Sterne explores in an original way. Sterne implies the connection of erection and blushing when Trim paints a picture for
Toby of the possibilities inherent in the bowling-green fortifications. The imagination triggers Toby's reaction:

> This identical bowling-green instantly presented itself, and
> became curiously painted, all at once, upon the retina of my
> uncle *Toby*'s fancy; – which was the physical cause of mak-
> ing him change colour, or at least, of heightening his blush
> to that immoderate degree I spoke of.
>
>   Never did lover post down to a belov'd mistress with
> more heat and expectation, than my uncle *Toby* did, to
> enjoy this self-same thing in private; . . . so that the idea of
> not being seen, did not a little contribute to the idea of plea-
> sure pre-conceived in my uncle *Toby*'s mind. (II, v, 98–9)

Sterne links his blatantly auto-erotic suggestion with the blush
and imagination. The Tristram of the early volumes can quite
confidently discover causes and find a physical explanation
where a mental one might be expected. Later in the novel,

Tristram describes a similar sequence when Trim remembers the feelings aroused by his nurse's massaging of his wounded leg (VIII, xxii, 574). Here a different Tristram discovers only the mind at work where his mechanistic earlier self would have seen a physical cause. Exploring the concept of sympathy, a term that permeates the writing of the later eighteenth century, should illuminate both the change in Tristram as narrator and the mind/body connections made by Sterne and Whytt. In the eighteenth century, sympathy carried many meanings, physical, psychological, and moral.

II

A brief account of the general controversy over irritability and sensibility will elucidate the physiological aspects of sympathy and also reveal the broader issues at stake in the discussion of impotence and erection. About 1660, Francis Glisson, reacting to the inroads made by the mechanists in natural history, set forth the irritability of the animal fibres as their distinguishing characteristic. Almost a century later, Haller would make this idea more widely accepted by expressing it in more generally understandable terms (Foster, 1924, 287). Haller says quite simply: 'I call that part of the human body irritable, which becomes shorter upon being touched: . . . I call that a sensible part of the human body, which upon being touched transmits the impression of it to the soul' (Haller, 1755, 658–9). Whytt, however, could not accept Haller's claim that some parts of the body could be irritable without being sensible as well. Referring to Haller, he says: 'As for our author's third argument, *viz.* that parts destitute of feeling are irritable; there is not so much as one instance given of a part being irritable that is naturally insensible and destitute of nerves' (Whytt, 1755, II, 158–9). Shunning mechanism, both can agree that some bodily parts are irritable and that sensibility depends on the presence of nerves; Whytt insists, however, that all parts must be sensible, and this position Haller rejects.

One of the most important bodily parts about which they disagree is the heart, so important to sentimentalists for many years to come. Over a century earlier, Harvey had demonstrated to Charles I the insensitivity to touch of the Earl of Montgomery's exposed heart (Keele, 1957, 68). Both Haller and Whytt refer to this event, but for different ends (French, 1969, 73). Haller states: 'The heart, which is very irritable, has but a small share of sensation, and upon touching it in a living person, a fainting is thereby occasioned rather than pain' (Haller, 1755, 676). He argues that the heart from reason 'ought to be' and from observation 'is actually' seen to be 'endowed with the greatest irritability' (687). Whytt, on the other hand, maintains the heart's sensibility, contrary to the experience of Harvey and arguments of Haller. Whytt claims that in their experiments Harvey and Haller had touched only the callous pericardium surrounding the heart while the truly sensible cardial surface is its interior, which reacts to the stimulus of the inrushing blood (Whytt, 1755, II, 156–8). Haller's rather sneering, but ironically self-condemning, rejoinder to Whytt's ideas states that 'Anatomy gives us but little light into this subject' (Haller, 1755, 689). He points out 'that an animal whose *thorax* is opened is in such violent torture, that it is hard to distinguish the effect of an additional slight irritation' (672).

Surely the sentimentalist who loved dogs or asses would feel outrage at such treatment of fellow creatures and also be moved to defend the sensibility of the heart. Parson Yorick's observations in Sterne's *A Sentimental Journey* (1768) express just such an outlook, but as Sterne knew, even more was at stake. In the 1740s, the outspoken La Mettrie was the first to see the broader significance of muscular irritability. In fact, he provocatively dedicated *L'Homme Machine* to Haller – an act that outraged the supporters of the pious physiologist (Vartanian, 1960, 95). In his scandalous book, La Mettrie uses irritability to explain the 'inherent powers of purposive motion' in the organism and hence to eliminate the need for a soul (Vartanian, 1960, 18). Aram Vartanian concludes that 'La Mettrie's discussion . . . views the phenomenon of irritability as the key to the mystery of life itself, and proposes to erect the mechanistic theory of mind on this firm biological foundation' (22). In the La Mettrian scheme, the soul as either Whytt's sentient principle or the Christian's immortal reality is left without place or function. As a contemporary physician, William Smith, pointed out, Whytt's defense of sensibility's presence throughout the body entails the divisibility and extension of the soul, and this doctrine makes Whytt an unwitting ally of La Mettrian materialism (French, 1969, 42). Thus, this technical, physiological dispute was seen to touch on the most profound religious questions.

Even though physiology offered little to defenders of the soul, it was not entirely barren for the sentimentalists because it made sympathy a key component of physiological explanation. French explains: 'Thus the whole dispute over irritability centered around the *nature* of irritability — whether it was a characteristic of matter, or of a life-force — and its relationship to sensibility.' Whytt's perception of this relationship allowed for further development in 'the idea of reflex and sympathy', in opposition to mechanism (70). Whytt made sympathy the basis of involuntary muscular movement and non-rational mental phenomena. The physiologists argued the degree to which sympathy is a necessary, mechanical, irritable response and to what extent it is dependent on sensation, perception, and conscious control. In fact, the nature of sympathy was a central issue in the physiological dispute over sensibility and irritability as it was in the religious, philosophical, and political discussions of Sterne's time.

III

In the eighteenth century, the word 'sympathy' carried with it a history of changing meanings. The resulting confusion prompted Whytt to complain: 'The sympathy of the nerves [is] a phrase indeed oftener used than well understood!' (Whytt, 1751, 181–2). We can attempt to understand the word, and the ways Sterne uses it, by tracing its history. The three main usages of sympathy in Sterne's lifetime were as: (1) an occult force, spurned by mechanistic science; (2) a useful physiological concept, revived by the mechanists and taken over by their opponents; and (3) a social mechanism or sentiment important to moral philosophy. *Tristram Shandy* reflects aspects of all three.

The term 'sympathy' (*sympatheia*) meant for the ancient Stoic philosophers the mutual suffering in an organism of all or some of the parts when one is affected. They used this organic conception to explain the relationship of mind to body: the *psyche* like a spider hurries to the site of a wound in the web-like body as if she herself suffers (Rather, 1965, 205, n. 2). This kind of relationship became a significant part of alchemical lore and a *bête noire* of the mechanical scientists. In the *Dialogue Concerning the Two Chief World Systems* (1632), Galileo, famous as an experimental scientist but also a powerful polemicist for Copernican astronomy and mathematically based physics, recognizes and attacks the obscurantist nature of the word as used by astrologers and alchemists. Simplicio represents their beliefs, while Sagredo appears to represent Galileo himself:

> Simplicio: But we who restrict ourselves to philosophical terminology reduce the cause of this and other similar effects to *sympathy*, which is a certain agreement and mutual desire that arise between things which are similar in quality among themselves . . .
> Sagredo: And thus, by means of two words [i.e. sympathy and antipathy], causes are given for a large number of events and effects which we behold with amazement when

they occur in nature. Now this method of philosophizing seems to me to have great sympathy with a certain manner of painting used by a friend of mine. He would write on the canvas with chalk: 'This is where I'll have the fountain, with Diana and her nymphs; here, some greyhounds; there, a hunter with a stag's head. The rest is a field, a forest and hillocks'. He left everything else to be filled in with color by a painter, and with this he was satisfied that he himself had painted the story of Acteon – not having contributed anything of his own except the title. (Galileo, 1967, 271)

At the turn of the eighteenth century, H. M. Herwig, ignoring the scorn of the mechanical philosophers who followed Galileo's lead, defines sympathy as 'a mutual and natural affection and combination between natural things, arising from a peculiar and occult cognation'. (Herwig, 1700, 21) This product of 'occult cognation', or imperceivable affinity, explains for Herwig the dependence of all 'chemical mixtures' on the influence of the sun (9–10). As late as 1744, the anonymous *Hermippus Revivified* could justify its ancient but outrageous doctrine – securing health in an old man by his taking in the breath and perspiration of young virgins – on the grounds of sympathy as described by 'the Learned [Roger] Bacon' (78–9), the thirteenth-century monk and scientist accused of practising black magic. Although out of the mainstream of scientific thought, this occult conception of sympathy remained alive well into Sterne's maturity. Its ability to irritate the mechanists Sterne would have found attractive, but the more common, mechanistic usage of the term draws his most penetrating gaze.

Outlining the ideas of eighteenth-century physicians concerning sympathy will demonstrate just how insightful and original Sterne's view is. Relating the physicians' conceptions to Sterne's accounts of sympathy will also clarify his attitude towards the roles of reason, imagination, and emotion in sympathy and will show his rejection of mechanical accounts of mindless human sympathy.

When Tristram discusses his own writing in *Tristram Shandy*, Sterne seizes the opportunity to ridicule mechanistic conceptions of mind. In one instance, Tristram looks for a 'sixth sense' to help him translate the tales of his father's beloved Slawkenbergius and asks: 'What can he mean by the lambent pupilability of a slow, low, dry chat, five notes below the natural tone?' He then confesses: 'The moment I pronounced the words, I could perceive an attempt towards a vibration in the strings, about the region of the heart. – The brain made no acknowledgement.' Then, Tristram portrays the 'sentimental part' of such wordless and brainless communication between lovers collapsing under the threat of clashing chins and smashed foreheads (IV, i, 273). Such a farcical deflation of an idea generated by the ridiculous Slawkenbergius's absurd locution negates attempts to take seriously this vibrationist sentimentality. In the novel's final volume, Tristram says that "the kindliest harmony vibrating within' him provides a 'secret spring either of sentiment or rapture' in keeping with 'every oscillation of the chaise [in which he is riding] . . . whether the roads were rough or smooth'. Through the course of the novel, Tristram has learned to distrust talk of secret springs, particularly mechanical ones harnessed to horses (Rodgers, 1978, 122–33). Furthermore, this discussion of vibrations introduces the Maria episode where sentimentality is burlesqued by its sexually self-indulgent conclusion. Clearly, Sterne wishes to show that such mechanistic conceptions of harmonious feelings are ludicrous. Sterne's employment of phrases such as 'vibration in the strings, about the region of the heart' and his talk of 'secret springs' and 'oscillations' mocks the language of contemporary scientific accounts of sympathy.

Mid-century physiologists sought precise explanations of the power of sympathy, thought to be wide-ranging within the body. Whytt in his work on nervous disorders lists at length the sympathy between various organs and functions of the body. Such obvious connections as those between the windpipe and coughing or the lungs and chest muscles are noted, but he also includes more surprising ones between the ears and womb or the intestines and nose (Whytt, 1765, 18–24). To account for such a variety of linkages, physiologists began to place sympathetic action in the nervous system itself. Robert Willis's *On the Souls of Animals* (1694) is the first work to connect sympathy with the nervous system. For Willis, sympathetic reactions are controlled by the 'intercostal' and vagus nerves but are linked to the brain as well. From the appearance of Willis's book, sympathy was used to relate sensation and action to the emotions. It was seen to account for involuntary reactions to pleasure or pain and for such phenomena as blushing or palpitation caused involuntarily by emotion (Keele, 1957, 81–2).

The iatromechanists, physicians who hoped to use mechanical principles to explain all bodily actions, accounted for these connections by moving from a concern with animal spirits to an emphasis on the nervous fibres' condition (Furst, 1974, 159–200). George Cheyne (1671–1743), perhaps the most popular medical writer of his day, uses a musical metaphor to suggest the mechanical manner in which soul and body interact:

The Human Body is a Machine of an infinite Number and Variety of different Channels and Pipes, filled with various and different Liquors and Fluids. . . . the Intelligent Principle, or *Soul*, resides somewhere in the Brain, where all the Nerves, or Instruments of Sensation terminate, like a *Musician* in a finely fram'd and well-tun'd Organ-Case; . . . these Nerves are like *Keys*, which, being struck on or touch'd, convey the sound and Harmony to this sentient Principle, or *Musician*. (Cheyne, *The English Malady*

(1735), 4–5; in Furst, 1974, 180–1)

Nerves either too taut or too lax will throw the mind and body
out of harmony and impair sympathetic responses. In 1752
Thomas Simson, another physician–writer, claims that 'every
Philosopher is now satisfied' that bodily connections work
through the 'flexible fibres', which need to be properly tuned
'by the mediation of the Mind' (Simson, 1752, 29, 84–5).
On the other hand, the more traditional Richard Mead, who
is savagely satirized in *Tristram Shandy*, still clings to the doctrine that disease is sparked by consent with the other organs
and that 'the instruments of this sympathy are the animal
spirits . . . being hurried by the passions' (Mead, 1762,
569).

Both Haller and Whytt repudiate such claims to understanding the detailed relations between mind and body or the
fine structure and functions of the nervous fibres. They do,
however, make significant and differing comments on bodily
sympathy. Haller contends that 'the consent of parts' comes
from five causes, four purely mechanical and one dependent on
the mind, i.e. 'some cause [from one nerve] acting on the common sensory, and beginning of the nerves' (1754, II, 102–3).
Haller openly admits his 'ignorance in the mechanism of this
ultimate law' of the junction of mind and body, but he firmly
rejects the need for mind to be present for all movement (105,
108).

Whytt also admits ignorance of how the nerves work and
rejects such discredited explanations as 'the hypothetical
motions and *countermotions* of the animal spirits'. He does,
however, claim that the concepts of the sensibility and sympathy of the nerves explain some things more clearly, such as
the production of tears. He concludes that, just as Newton
triumphed over Descartes without knowing how gravity
works, natural philosophers can triumph over faulty explanations without certain knowledge of first principles (Whytt,

1765, vi–vii). He explicitly rejects mechanism alone and invokes '*consent*, which, as it depends upon feeling, cannot be explained upon mechanical principles' (32). In his earlier *Essay*, while still retaining the word 'spirits' for convenience and calling the body a 'machine', Whytt explains that sympathy, 'or consent observed between the nerves of various parts of the body, is not to be explained mechanically, but ought to be ascribed to the energy of that sentient BEING . . . in the brain' (Whytt, 1751, 183). Thus, the brain and feeling are necessary to every bodily movement. Sympathy, Whytt emphasizes, is not 'owing to the communication between the nerves' as is 'the prevailing opinion' (Whytt, 1765, 37). These physiological ideas of Whytt's were to have effects on conceptions of social or moral sympathy too.

IV

John Hunter's *Treatise on the Blood* (1794), recording ideas the eminent anatomist-surgeon developed just after the mid-century, presents an elaborate scheme of sympathies, including those of the body and of the mind. This second kind, he explains, 'depends upon the state of others' and is 'the first of the social feelings'. It exists 'to excite an active interest in favour of the distressed, the mind of the spectators taking on nearly the same action with that of the sufferers' (Hunter, 1794, 6). In this representative description of social sympathy, Hunter provides just one example of a medical man writing of sympathy and benevolence, something quite common from mid-century on. Whytt himself discusses a connection between bodily and social sympathy. His writing demonstrates how the language of physiology provides, through analogy, a language for morality as well:

> There is a remarkable sympathy, by means of the nerves, between the various parts of the body; and now it appears that there is a still more wonderful sympathy between the

nervous systems of different persons, whence various motions and morbid symptoms are often transferred, from one to another, without any corporeal contact or infection.

In these cases, the impression made upon the mind or *sensorium commune* by seeing others in a disordered state, raises, by means of the nerves, such motions or changes in certain parts of the body as to produce similar affections in them. (Whytt, 1765, 219–20)

Earlier, Whytt had drawn an explicit but unexplained, 'easy and natural' analogy between sympathetic bodily functions and the workings of 'a kind of SENSE respecting *Morals*' (Whytt, 1751, 288–9). Ironically for one who devoted his life's work to combating the mechanists, Whytt's rooting social sympathy in physiological language makes it seem mechanical. Furthermore, he treats sympathy between persons in terms of pathology. Sterne presents both of these aspects of sympathy in *Tristram Shandy*: he wishes to discredit the first and to explore the second.

A passage from Volume VIII shows how subtle and acute Sterne is when dealing with sympathy and sentiment. He implicitly criticizes the simplistically mechanical notions of some of the physiologists and philosophers. He shows that sympathy involves more than harmonious vibrations and that the 'moral sense' is no unmixed perception:

Every body, said my mother, says you are in love, brother *Toby* – and we hope it is true.

I am as much in love, sister, I believe, replied my uncle *Toby*, as any man usually is – Humph! said my father – and when did you know it? quoth my mother –

When the blister broke; replied my uncle *Toby*. (VIII, xxxii, 585)

Toby equates the sensation created by the breaking of the blister on his arse with the raptures of love, and Sterne uses this passage as a warning against a simplistic interpretation of events. While Toby's body tells him he is in love, his means for interpreting what his body is saying derives from a story that Trim, his servant, has just told him. Trim tells how the fair Beguine's therapeutic massage of the area around and above his injured knee caused him to know he was in love (VIII, xxii, 573–5). The story softens Toby up for Mrs Wadman's amorous assaults and, at the same time, demonstrates to him how love is recognized: by reading the signals that come from the body's physical states. As Tristram tells us of the meaning of the blister:

> He had mistook it at first. . . . by trotting on too hastily to save [a beautiful wood] – upon an uneasy saddle – worse horse, &c, &c. . . . it had so happened, that the serous part of the blood had got betwixt the two skins, in the nethermost part of my uncle *Toby* – the first shootings of which (as my uncle *Toby* had no experience of love) he had taken for a part of the passion – till the blister breaking in the one case – and the other remaining – my uncle *Toby* was presently convinced, that his wound was not a skin-deep-wound – but that it had gone to his heart. (VIII, xxvi, 579–80)

The blister, or body, does not automatically, mechanically signal love or any other sentiment. For a sentiment, such as love or benevolence, based on sympathy to come about, feeling from the body must combine with a thought process working in a social context. In this respect, Sterne's view of sentiment bears a close resemblance to David Hume's use of the word in his analysis of human nature.

To understand both Sterne and Hume, one must be aware of a shift in the meaning of the word 'sentiment' in general eighteenth-century usage, a shift reflected in the writing of the philosopher and novelist. The 1783 edition of Chambers's widely-read *Cyclopaedia* clearly spells out the change: 'The word *sentiment*, in its true and old English sense signifies, *a formed opinion, notion*, or *principle*; but of late years, it has been much used by some writers to denote an internal impulse of passion, affection, fancy, or intellect, which is to be considered rather as the cause or occasion of our forming an opinion, than the real opinion itself' (Chambers, 1783, 'Sentiments'). Chambers describes the change brought about by the influence of the 'moral sense' school of philosophers, Shaftesbury, Hutcheson, and Hume. They use 'sentiment' rather loosely to mean a 'mental feeling' or an 'emotional thought'. Hume, for example, sometimes uses 'sentiment' in a confusing, but convenient way. His 'moral sense' is the result of feeling, 'of individual pleasure/pain responses', but this feeling is also the result of judgment, or 'reasoning,' and has its concurrent weight or moral force (Brissenden, 1968, 95, 106–7).

Hume develops this concept perhaps in opposition to overly simplified notions of sentiment as a mere feeling or passion, the sole motivator of human action. Ironically, Hume himself may bear some responsibility for the appearance of such notions with his proclamation that 'reason is, and ought only to be, the slave of the passions' (in Roberts, 1973, 109), and in his projecting 'to prove *first*, that reason alone can never be a motive to any action of the will; and *secondly*, that it can never oppose passion in the direction of the will' (Hume, 1888, 413). An enthusiastic *philosophe*, Helvétius (1715–71), could use this kind of statement to declare that 'from the moment we regard corporeal sensibility as the first principle of morality, its maxims cease to be contradictory . . . [and] its principles being freed from the darkness of speculative philosophy, will become evident, and the more generally adopted' (in Bredvold, 1961, 49). This statement from Helvétius's *Treatise on Man* would not suit the Hume who makes clear what he means by sentiment in the *Enquiry Concerning the Principles of Morals* (1751): 'As justice evidently tends to promote public utility and to support civil society, the sentiment of justice is either derived from our reflecting on that tendency, or . . . arises from a simple original instinct in the human breast . . . and is not ascertained by any argument or reflection.' He concludes that 'The necessity of justice to the support of society is the *sole* foundation of that virtue. . . . Usefulness has, in general, the strongest energy and most entire command over our sentiments' (in Randall, 1962, I, 844). The judgment of usefulness can come only from reasoning, and thus reasoning is the basis of at least some sentiments.

Sterne's writing also recognizes the complexity of sentiment and opposes moral oversimplification. Tristram does, however, present sentiment as simple emotion in the earlier portions of *Tristram Shandy*. He provides both tearful and leering contexts for the word. First, the melodramatically sentimental address to his Uncle Toby: 'Here let me thrust my chair aside, and kneel down upon the ground, whilst I am pouring forth the warmest sentiments of love for thee, and veneration for the excellency of thy character, that ever virtue and nature kindled in a nephew's bosom. − . . . for each one's sorrows, thou hadst a tear, − for each man's need, thou hadst a shilling' (III, xxxiv, 224). Tristram here appears disinterestedly overcome by the contemplation of benevolence, but one senses that he bathes himself in self-indulgent emotion. In the second example, he uses the word 'sentiment' to tease a frequent victim:

− Surely, Madam, a friendship between the two sexes may subsist, and be supported without − Fy! Mr *Shandy*: − Without any thing, Madam, but that tender and delicious sentiment, which ever mixes in friendship, where there is a difference of sex. Let me intreat you to study the pure and sentimental parts of the best *French* Romances; − it will really, Madam, astonish you to see with what a variety of chaste expression this delicious sentiment, which I have the honour to speak of, is dress'd out. (I, xviii, 49)

Never was so 'pure' a feeling so lasciviously expressed. Even in these early presentations of 'simple' sentiment, Tristram's tone, histrionically exaggerated or mockingly coy, reveals a distrust of his own use of 'sentiment'.

Sterne also discusses sentiment outside his novels in the sermons where, like Hume, he presents the role of reason in determining sentiment and benevolent action. In 'Philanthropy Recommended', Sermon III of Volume I of *The Sermons of Mr. Yorick* (1760), Sterne recounts in detail the reasoning behind the Good Samaritan's reaction to the Jew. He stresses that the Samaritan's reaction is not a mechanical reflex, but a sentiment that is the result of a rather complex, although instantaneous, train of reflection. The Samaritan's benevolent action is based on principle, not impulse:

> So that the Samaritan, though the moment he saw him he had compassion on him, yet, sudden as the emotion is represented, you are not to imagine that it was mechanical, but that there was a settled principle of humanity and goodness which operated within him, and influenced not only the first impulse of kindness but the continuation of it throughout the rest of so engaging a behavior. (IX, 45–6)

Sterne then recounts what has happened in the Samaritan's mind: (1) immediate shock and concern; (2) realization that the Jew is the traditional enemy; (3) reconciliation by recognition of their common humanity and the Golden Rule; (4) realization that the Jew is a stranger; (5) reconciliation by recognition of the common conditions of life for all; and (6) decision to help the Jew, '– and if I can do nothing else, – I shall soften his misfortunes by dropping a tear of pity over them' (45–8). Similarly, in 'The Levite and His Concubine', Sterne presents the details of the Levite's thinking that lead to the final determination to forgive and win back his concubine (291–4). The sermons make explicit the meaning of sentiment in the view of Sterne as preacher.

When Sterne turns from sermons to fiction, he employs a

considerably less pious narrative voice. Tristram comments on Mrs Wadman's strategy for inflaming his uncle's heart:

> It is a great pity, – but 'tis certain from every day's observation of man, that he may be set on fire like a candle, at either end – provided there is a sufficient wick standing out; if there is not – there's an end of the affair; and if there is – by lighting it at the bottom, as the flame in that case has the misfortune generally to put out itself – there's an end of the affair again. (VIII, xv, 553)

Presumably, moving the body will generate the momentary passion of lust, but for the sentiment of love to be created, the mind must be involved as well. But, of course, the mind changes. Love, like the other sentiments, can exist only in a dynamic situation subject to the transformations in the relationship of the two people involved. Thus, the comic distrust of sentiment evidenced in *Tristram Shandy*'s first volumes changes to understanding, if only partial understanding, in the latter. Tristram is learning about the nature of sentiments, particularly love.

Even the virtuous sentiments associated with human sympathy are subject to the restraints created by the mind's powers and limitations. John B. Radner demonstrates that eighteenth-century moral philosophy developed 'a growing sense . . . that compassion depends on various deliberate mental efforts, and so differs from emotional contagion or emotional identification' (1979, 192) Hume's presentation of sympathy as a mechanical response in the *Treatise of Human Nature* (1739–40) is replaced by his stressing the role of a more active imagination in generating benevolent sympathy in the *Enquiry* of 1751 (Roberts, 1973, 92–7). Similarly, Tristram learns that his Uncle Toby, the apparent exemplar of benevolence, is limited by his imagination and reason. Toby is far removed from any simple mechanical reaction. In the Story of Le Fever, Toby can temporarily turn 'the siege of *Dender-*

mond into a blockade' in order to consider more fully 'how he himself should relieve the poor lieutenant [Le Fever] and his son' (VI, viii, 423–4). Revealingly, in the earlier, more satirical Volume II, Toby's sympathy, and that of the other men, seems to have disappeared. Walter, Tristram's father, addresses Toby:

> – But so full is your head of these confounded works, that tho' my wife is this moment in the pains of labour, – and you hear her cry out, – yet nothing will serve you but to carry off the man-midwife. – *Accoucheur*, – if you please, quoth Dr. *Slop*. – With all my heart, replied my father, I don't care what they call you, – but I wish the whole science of fortification, with all its inventors, at the devil; – it has been the death of thousands, – and it will be mine, in the end. – I would not, I would not, brother *Toby*, have my brains so full of saps, mines, blinds, gabions, palisadoes, ravelins, half-moons, and such trumpery, to be proprietor of *Namur*, and of all the towns in *Flanders* with it. (II, xii, 112–13)

Of course, Walter's reference to his wife's sufferings, like his outburst condemning war, is the result, not of great sympathy, but of great annoyance with Toby. All Walter says has an element of truth in it, but his motive for saying it is suspect. That 'all my heart' goes with a direct insult suggests that his expressions of sympathy may be employed as weapons. This impression finds reinforcement in the certainty that Walter will never actually do anything but talk either about Mrs Shandy's crying out or about 'the death of thousands'.

Toby, on the other hand, can placidly ignore Walter's tirade for the same reason that he can ignore his sister's cries and the horrors of war. His inner defences – his hobby-horsically compulsive study of fortification and his immense imaginative blind spot in sexual matters, his modesty (II, vii, 102) – have been created to ensure that he remains insensible and, thereby, insensitive to them all. His mind works to blot them out. By contrast, his servant Trim's narration – and Trim is noted for his rhetorical skills – forces the realization of the distressed Le Fever's plight into Toby's imagination; only then can sympathy work to trigger his benevolence. For Walter's words and his sister's cries, Toby has adequate defences, but to Trim's verbal sieges, assaults, and undermining, all working on the imagination, Toby must fall as he does again and again throughout the novel.

V

Another aspect of Walter's outrage, its extreme fury, suggests the power inherent in Toby's self-defensive manner – the power not only to protect himself, but also to inflict wounds of his own, and the power of sympathy and benevolence to wreak their own modest and sentimental destruction. Sterne recognizes that Toby's sympathy does not console his brother, while new theories do. Likewise, Walter's kindness does not cure Toby: his hobby-horse does (De Porte, 1974, 149–51). Tristram himself says: 'Before an affliction is digested, – consolation ever comes too soon; – and after it is digested, – it comes too late' (III, xxix, 216). Sterne not only recognizes limits to benevolent sympathy, however; he also envisions its power to do positive harm. To understand the nature of this power and the extent of Sterne's departure from the views of philosophers and physicians, we need to look further at eighteenth-century views of benevolence and its agent, sympathy.

Chambers's *Cyclopaedia* of 1783 provides a clear definition of benevolence and equally clearly outlines the conflicting theories about its source:

Benevolence, *Universal*, in *Ethics*, denotes a hearty desire of the good of mankind, evidencing itself, as ability and opportunity offer, in the chearful and diligent practice of whatever may promote the well-being of all. Some have traced the origin of this affection in self-love; others again in some INSTINCT or determination of our nature, antecedent to all reason from interest, which influences us to the love of others, and they have accordingly made it the foundation of universal VIRTUE: others more properly ascribe it to the *intelligent* constitution of human nature, and observe, that it arises not from instinct, but from the natures and necessities of things. (Chambers, 1783, 'Benevolence')

Benevolence was seen as dependent on the working of sympathy, but benevolence might be merely 'instinct'. Likewise, social sympathy could be merely mechanical, an extension of physiology into morality. A century earlier, the Latitudinarians, Anglican ecclesiastics who embraced scientific reasoning, had 'recognized the mechanical character of sympathy' (MacLean, 1949, 403). Nevertheless, one of their most distinguished representatives, Isaac Barrow (1630–77) could find in 'charity' and 'the impulse to sympathize with other human beings' evidence of man's descent from the divine, not merely of mechanism. The proof of this for Barrow resembles Hume's thinking on sentiment, for Barrow notes the ability of 'wit', human intelligence, to block the soul's immediate response to others (Tuveson, 1967, 77). Thus, two traditional views of sympathy outlined by Chambers have roots in the seventeenth century.

But what of Chambers's 'intelligent constitution of human nature', his third posited source of benevolence? Chambers probably refers to the kind of arguments occurring in Adam Smith's *Theory of Moral Sentiments*, which appeared in 1759 – the year of the first instalment of *Tristram Shandy*. Kenneth MacLean demonstrates that Smith and Sterne were original in stressing, not the egotistical or mechanical nature of sympathy and benevolence, but their solid grounding in a pictorial imagination. For Smith, 'the image [of suffering] in itself wounds the mind somewhat in the way a blow hurts the physical body' (MacLean, 1949, 401). The imagination and physiological analogy underlie a concept of sympathy where reason cannot control the passions, but mind nevertheless is essential to the working of sympathy. The imagination empowers sympathy's good work, but the philosophers and physicians also developed theories about the final purpose of sympathy as well as about its functioning. They began to ask what sympathy does for the organism and its survival, not only what moral or religious end it serves.

One of Whytt's notions about sympathy reveals a 'biological' aspect of Sterne's portrayal of sympathy and benevolence in *Tristram Shandy*. Early in the century, the third Earl of Shaftesbury (1671–1713) argued in his influential *Characteristics of Men, Manners, Opinions, Times* (1711) that moral principles spring from a natural source. For Shaftesbury, man's social passions come from a biological impulse for survival, not from some hope of redemption nor a sense of spiritual elevation (Tuveson, 1967, 83). Whytt develops Shaftesbury's insight by arguing that 'All these [sympathetic motions] are the efforts of nature to free the body of something hurtful; and are so many instances of that principle of self-preservation so conspicuous in all animals. These motions, therefore, cannot, in my opinion, be referred to any connexion or communication among the nerves, but to the brain itself, and to that sentient *being* which animates our whole frame' (Whytt, 1765, 72–3). Thus, the soul, the 'sentient being', acts in sympathy. While driving off the materialists and mechanists, Whytt gives the soul power in a process like homeostasis, the maintenance of a life-preserving equilibrium within the body.

Sterne also juxtaposes the sympathetic reactions of mind and body. The lachrymal glands in producing tears act quite like a safety valve, protecting the body and soul from the pathological consequences of grief. While reading Yorick's 'Sermon on Conscience', Trim pictures his brother Tom suffering the tortures of the Inquisition described in the sermon's

text. As a result, 'The tears trickled down *Trim*'s cheeks faster than he could well wipe them away. . . . Come, *Trim*,
quoth my father, after he saw the poor fellow's grief had got a
little vent, – read on, – and put this melancholy story out of thy
head' (II, xvii, 125). Clearly the imagination supplies Trim
with a representation of his brother's suffering. His tears
would hardly have flowed so copiously for the sufferings of a
stranger or without Yorick's vividly written descriptions.
More than mechanism is at work. Furthermore, Sterne's use of
the word 'vent' suggests that the excretion of tears provides a
necessary physical outlet for fluids and emotions that would be
harmful if kept within.

For Sterne and Whytt, then, the action of mind precludes a
merely mechanical account of sympathy and benevolence, but
neither is the mind's role simply rational. As Trim reads on,
Sterne shows that sympathy depends on imagination and can
override the hobby-horse, a creature of the rigidly closed
mind. Trim reads the Sermon:

> 'his body so wasted with sorrow and confinement'. – [Oh!
> 'tis my brother, cried poor *Trim* in a most passionate excla-
> mation, dropping the sermon upon the ground, and clap-
> ping his hands together – I fear 'tis poor *Tom*. My father's
> and my uncle *Toby*'s hearts yearn'd with sympathy for the
> poor fellow's distress, – even *Slop* himself acknowledged
> pity for him.] (II, xvii, 138)

A moment later Walter protests Trim's reaction: "'Tis not an
historical account – 'tis a description.' Yet Walter acknowledges the power of the imaginative description by releasing
Trim from the further 'cruelty' of having to read on (II, xvii,
139). All are moved. In this instance, the ruling passion
becomes benevolence. It temporarily displaces everyone's
hobby-horses, and sympathy therapeutically conquers all.

Sympathy alone, however, proves impotent. As Brissenden points out, 'When the theoretical point of the sermon is

being made . . . , Dr. Slop falls asleep; his heart can be moved, but his reason remains deaf to all attempts to convince it' (Brissenden, 1974, 215). The physician Charles Collignon in 1764 makes a similar point about the role of reason in making an emotion such as benevolence work to the best advantage:

> But [my argument] is not designed to deny, that we are liable, without great care, to be byassed by some internal feelings. The Sects of Philosophers probably first arose, from the constitutional dispositions of their respective founders. It would not, perhaps, have been an easy attempt to have made *Cato* an *Epicurean*, or *Mark Anthony* a *Stoick*. . . . But yet may we bend, what we cannot break; and prune the luxuriancies, of what we cannot eradicate; and so blend the jarring ingredients of a faulty frame, as to become happy to ourselves, and profitable to others.
> (Collignon, 1764, 12–13)

For Collignon, the emotions, when properly channelled, may lead the individual and those he touches to greater happiness. Such is the reasonable ideal of the benevolent doctor. Although Sterne, as preacher, shared Collignon's hopes for virtue to work through a balanced effort of the passions and reason, *Tristram Shandy* contains a much more sceptical outlook on sympathy and benevolence. Sterne shows how self-serving and self-preserving these 'virtues' can be.

In *Tristram Shandy*, Sterne offers an object lesson in the power, for good or ill, of sentimental benevolence. Furthermore, in contrasting Toby's phlegm, his calm self-possession, to Walter's choler, his angry outbursts, Tristram suggests the source of Toby's extraordinary good nature:

> My uncle *Toby* was a man patient of injuries; – not from want of courage, . . . nor did this arise from any insensibility or obtuseness of his intellectual parts; – for he felt this

insult of my father's as feelingly as a man could do; – but he
was of a peaceful, placid nature, – no jarring element in it,
– all was mix'd up so kindly within him; my uncle *Toby* had
scarce a heart to retaliate upon a fly. (II, xii, 113)

Tristram seems to be saying that Toby's nature is a mixture of
elements – courage, sensitivity, intelligence, serenity – and
that his goodness of heart dominates all. To demonstrate his
point, Tristram tells the notorious story of Toby's kindness to
an 'overgrown' fly that 'tormented him cruelly'. Tristram
claims that, by a 'secret magic' perhaps analogous to music,
Toby's 'universal good-will' became the source of at least 'one
half of my philanthropy'. Still an experimental, theorizing
mechanist at this early stage of the novel, Tristram follows a
contemporary line of thought about the transfer of emotion
through harmony, through resonating nervous fibres.

Sterne, however, muddies the illusory clarity of any 'scientific' understanding of feeling. In the next paragraph, Tristram first renounces his earlier belief in 'mere HOBBY-HORSI-
CAL likeness' (a man and his hobbies are one) as the one way to
understand human character. He now intends to disclose
Toby's 'moral character'. What then follows is a description
of Walter's, not Toby's, character that nevertheless reveals
something important about the benevolent captain. Walter,
we find, 'was, however, frank and generous in his nature; – at
all times open to conviction; and in the little ebullitions of this
subacid humour towards others, but particularly towards my
uncle *Toby*, whom he truly loved; – he would feel more pain,
ten times told (except in the affair of my aunt *Dinah*, or where
an hypothesis was concerned) than what he ever gave' (II, xii,
114). Walter uncontrollably spews forth cutting remarks but
suffers ten times more pain from their backlash of remorse than
Toby feels in receiving them. Toby's system of psychic fortifications proves to be strong indeed and wounding as well.

Toby's hobby-horse as whipping boy accounts for this state

of affairs. Tristram explains that, 'A man's HOBBY-HORSE is as tender a part as he has about him', so the hobby-horse feels the sting, 'and very sensibly too'. Nevertheless, because it is 'about him', not within him, it actually acts like a suit of armour by taking the brunt of the blows while allowing the man inside to carry on uninjured. Walter has no such defences:

> For as soon as my father had done insulting [Toby's] HOBBY-HORSE, – he turned his head, without the least emotion, . . . and look'd up into my father's face, with a countenance spread over with so much good nature; – so placid; – so fraternal; – so inexpressibly tender towards him; – it penetrated my father to his heart: He rose up hastily from his chair, and seizing hold of both my uncle *Toby*'s hands as he spoke: . . . – forgive, I pray thee, this rash humour which my mother gave me. (II, xii, 115)

In contrast to Toby's serene absorption of his brother's jibes, Walter's outflow of words responds to painful injuries. Here, as elsewhere, Toby's goodness does the damage. The more benignly forgiving Toby is, the more Walter accuses himself, feels agonies of remorse, and himself grows sentimental.

Other instances in the novel show Toby's defensive kindness and modesty and their ability to infuriate Walter. A characteristic exchange between the brothers results in the uninjured Toby's whistling of 'Lillabullero' after Walter again has felt all the pain:

> 'Tis a pity, said my father, that truth can only be on one side, brother *Toby*, – considering what ingenuity these learned men have all shewn in their solutions of noses. – Can noses be dissolved? replied my uncle *Toby*. –
> – My father thrust back his chair, – rose up, – put on his hat, – took four long strides to the door, – jerked it open . . . (III, xli, 239)

Walter goes through further gesticulations fuelled by his pent-

up rage at this characteristic misunderstanding of words, but
when he explodes, it is with the impotence of a toy cannon: 'the
curse came charged only with the bran, – the bran, may it
please your honours, – was no more than powder to the ball'.
Tristram then explains that Walter's explosions are touched
off by painful internal combustions and that Toby's kind-
hearted fortifications prove almost impregnable:

> . . . it is one of the most unaccountable problems that ever
> I met with in my observations of human nature, that nothing
> should prove my father's mettle so much, or make his pas-
> sions go off so like gun-powder, as the unexpected strokes
> his science met with from the quaint simplicity of my uncle
> *Toby*'s questions. – Had ten dozen of hornets stung him
> behind in so many different places all at one time, – he could
> not have exerted more mechanical functions in fewer sec-
> onds, – or started half so much, as with one single *quaere* of
> three words unseasonably popping in full upon him in his
> hobbyhorsical career.
>   'Twas all one to my uncle *Toby*, – he smoked his pipe on,
> with unvaried composure, – his heart never intended
> offence to his brother, – and as his head could seldom find
> out where the sting of it lay, – he always gave my father the
> credit of cooling by himself. (III, xli, 239–40)

Walter suffers from Toby's simplicity while Toby remains
innocent and insensible. Tristram himself notes Toby's 'modesty of nature . . . , which, by the bye, stood eternal sentry
upon his feelings' (VI, xxix, 456) and thus shows that he too
recognizes the defensive nature of Toby's innocence.

Tristram Shandy contains other instances of passive good
nature's ability to wound. For example, Elizabeth Shandy's
desire to please her husband Walter only irritates him. He
wants her intellectual assent to his theories; her merely sympathetic acceptance of whatever he says torments him (VI,
xviii, 438–9). Of his uncle's attempts to relieve the distress of

Le Fever's son, Tristram concludes: 'The greatest injury could not have oppressed the heart of *Le Fever* more than my uncle *Toby*'s paternal kindness' (VI, xii, 431). Toby's most devastating blow, however, fells the woman towards whom he feels most tender.

Toby manages to wound Mrs Wadman in a manner so subtle that neither he nor she realizes a blow has been struck. His failure to violate her 'innocence' physically is played against his comical destruction of her morals. In a reversal of the story of Adam and Eve, Toby remains untempted by the evil fruit, while the temptress herself is tantalized by his modesty. If Toby is Adam, his modesty is the snake; if Mrs Wadman is Eve, her curiosity and lust play the devil with her. When Mrs Wadman asks directly about the exact location of Toby's wound in the groin, Sterne suggests the Old Testament analogy and the basis of her temptation in the medical and mental make-up of Toby:

> There is an accent of humanity in an enquiry of this kind which lulls SUSPICION to rest — and I am half persuaded the serpent got pretty near it, in his discourse with Eve; for the propensity in the sex to be deceived could not be so great, that she should have boldness to hold chat with the devil, without it — But there is an accent of humanity — how shall I describe it? — 'tis an accent which covers the part with a garment, and gives the enquirer a right to be as particular with it, as your body-surgeon. (IX, xxvi, 637)

Humanity means here what it means in Hume's *Enquiry* — the sentiment of benevolence that reason assists. Sterne sees that 'an accent of humanity' does not guarantee the speaker's benevolent motives. It may indeed camouflage some ulterior purpose and become a weapon for achieving it — in this case, the conquest of Toby and the knowledge of his wound. Sterne, however, goes beyond this stage of analysis. Mrs Wadman asks Toby about the wound:

'– Was it without remission? –
'– Was it more tolerable in bed?
'– Could he lie on both sides alike with it?
'– Was he able to mount a horse?
'– Was motion bad for it?' et caetera, were so tenderly
spoke to, and so directed towards my uncle *Toby*'s heart,
that every item of them sunk ten times deeper into it than the
evils themselves – (IX, xxvi, 637)

In this progression of questions from sympathy for pain to concern for sexual performance, we see the skilful temptress tempted. Her innocence falls to his modesty, but her weapons of
attack prove 'ten times' more effective than physical battering
because they are forged out of sentiment and sympathy – the
armament that has worked so well in Toby's behalf. Mrs
Wadman wields her weapons with apparent success, for she

> went round about by *Namur* to get at my uncle *Toby*'s
> groin; . . . – and then with tender notes playing upon his
> ear, led him all bleeding by the hand out of the trench, wip-
> ing her eye, as he was carried to his tent – Heaven! Earth!
> Sea! – all was lifted up – the springs of nature rose above
> their levels – an angel of mercy sat besides him on the sopha
> – his heart glow'd with fire – and had he been worth a
> thousand, he had lost every heart of them to Mrs *Wadman*.
> (IX, xxvi, 637)

She almost succeeds in her ploy, but the old soldier survives
unscathed. His survival is assured, however, only through the
further sacrifice of Toby's innocence. Toby has to sustain the
shock of Trim's revealing the true, sexual nature of Mrs Wadman's 'humanity'. His mental fortifications remain intact.
They have done their work for him, but they have also done
their work on others.

VI

Against a world of changing situations, Toby's mind, traumatized into stasis by his wound, throws up fortifications based on insensibility and sentimentality. These attributes turn Toby's tragic wounding into comedy. The threatened impotence yields real power. Furthermore, Toby lacks the self-consciousness and thus the doubts about the motives behind his own benevolence that animate Yorick's reflections in Sterne's last work, *A Sentimental Journey* (1768). Sterne instead gives *Tristram Shandy*'s readers the materials and opportunities for such reflections. Toby, however, need not think about himself nor justify his existence, perhaps because he feels that four years of agony from his wound and its treatment have validated his complacent retirement from active life. Thus, he is often led to another kind of impotence – of feeling without reflection and so without useful application except in the set-piece Story of Le Fever and in his unchanging relationship to his servant Trim.

Such apparently mindless feeling and Toby's horseplay at war on the bowling-green provide targets for Sterne's gentle satire. This satire is dwarfed, however, by the larger implications of Sterne's portrayal of Toby and by Sterne's exploration of widely used and misunderstood terms like 'sympathy', 'sentiment', and 'benevolence'. Tristram himself reacts to current misconceptions about human nature when he warns that the contradictory mixture of elements in Toby and himself will baffle the scientific, rational, systematizing mind. He condescends to 'those, who, when coop'd in betwixt a natural and a positive law, know not for their souls, which way in the world to turn themselves' (VI, viii, 423), and he apostrophizes: 'Vain science! thou assists us in no case of this [i.e., the human] kind – and thou puzzlest us in every one' (VI, xxix, 455).

Science, system, and positive laws are as hobby-horsical as Toby's bowling-green and fortifications. They are all playthings, illusory means to a man's character, and defences against a chaotic, fluid world. But as surely as we defend ourselves against the changes inherent in the life of the world, we appear foolish in its eyes. In *Tristram Shandy* the great source of laughter is the collision of hobby-horses, and the point of impact often occurs in the space created by misunderstood words. Such comic clashes may, however, produce unexpected results. Words such as 'sympathy' and 'sentiment' undergo changes as their moralistic and physiological meanings first clash with and then interpenetrate one another. The Whytt–Haller controversy and Sterne's fiction provide evidence that both science and literature play a part in these changes. By the century's end Dugald Stewart, another in the line of Scottish moral philosophers, could write that sensibility, the simple first principle of the mid-century materialists, 'depends in great measure, on the power of the imagination' (Radner, 1979, 193). By insisting that imagination is a necessary part of sensibility, philosophers such as Stewart carried on the battle against mechanistic explanations of moral life. Sterne, however, insinuates that a moral philosophy based on an ideal of pure benevolence was, like mechanistic materialism, one of the grand, collective hobby-horses of his century.

FURTHER READING

De Porte, 1974   Rodgers, 1980
Hagstrum, 1980   Rousseau, 1976
Moravia, 1978   Rousseau and Porter, 1980
Rather, 1965   Tuveson, 1967

The Scientific Muse: The Poetry of Erasmus Darwin

MAUREEN McNEIL

EDITOR'S INTRODUCTION

*I*n *Tristram Shandy*, Sterne poked fun at medical practice and, in particular, at midwifery, which was at that time a fashionable subject for satire. Medical practitioners themselves were frequently active as literary figures, sometimes writing about their occupation in verse (Lonsdale, 1984). The pre-eminent example of this eighteenth-century trend was Erasmus Darwin (1731–1802), Charles Darwin's grandfather. Like many other medical practitioners of the century Darwin wrote verse, and McNeil's paper is concerned with his long, didactic poems rather than with his prose works. This is the only part of the book where the relationship between science and poetry is examined. McNeil shows how important Darwin's style of writing was for the content, both explicit and implied, of his works. She draws attention to the devices Darwin employed, such as personification, the pathetic fallacy and anthropomorphism, to illustrate his larger vision of science, technology and English society.

The wealth of available material about Darwin's milieu makes him an especially fruitful case to study, for we can document with some precision his links with the burgeoning industry of the Midlands, and with the middle-class, often Nonconfor-

mist entrepreneurs who were its leaders, and were active in all
aspects of provincial social and cultural life. McNeil argues
that Darwin's allegiances were precisely with this self-con-
sciously modernizing, efficient group of industrialists, rather
than with those who actually carried out the productive processes. Darwin's poetry extolled the achievements of head (en-
trepreneurial innovation) not hand (labour). He must also be
located in a quite precise political context: Darwin's friends
were radical in their leanings, generally sympathetic to the
American Revolution, to the abolition of slavery and, when it
came, to the French Revolution, especially in its early stages.
On its publication in 1796 Richard Payne Knight's poem *The
Progress of Civil Society*, which McNeil compares with Darwin's poetic work, was widely condemned, especially by
Tories, as pro-Jacobin, and dangerously subversive. The
context in which Darwin lived and worked was one with a
heightened sense, especially during the 1790s, of the potential
threats to the social order. The activities of natural philosophers and medical practitioners were frequently regarded
with suspicion, as the riots in which Joseph Priestley's
house was attacked bear witness.

Darwin's attempt to transcend the division between mind
and matter by developing a unified science of life derived from
a radical epistemology which underlay his whole outlook.
McNeil also shows how Darwin denied some very important
elements of real human existence by omitting labour from the
picture he painted of industry. She sharpens this point by contrasting Darwin with Blake, whose social affinities lay not
with an educated, comfortably off middle class but with the
economically marginal autodidact craftsmen and artisans of
the printing and engraving trades who constituted his milieu.
Viewed from this perspective, Darwin's silences become as
eloquent as his statements, since poverty, unemployment, food
prices and large families are never mentioned in his verse,

although he was composing his main works at a time of unparalleled crisis in the poor-relief system.

Nor should we be surprised by this if we consider McNeil's thesis that the Industrial Revolution must be understood as a *cultural* transformation. Presenting science, technology and medicine to an audience which was socially central – the bourgeoisie – was an essential element in the transformation which could only take place if the far-reaching social, economic and political changes were accepted by those *not* directly involved in manufactures. In this light Darwin's synthesis of science and poetry can be viewed, not as a weird quirk, but as standing at the heart of English intellectual life. It welded together a number of disparate elements. The novelty of using technological and industrial terms in a poetic context was tempered by the use of traditional literary devices and by the wealth of classical allusions and strategies Darwin employed. At the same time as he celebrates the coming of a new age, he conjures up images of magic, myths and heroes. 'Polite' literature was combined with the celebration of modern life. The poems were published complete with lengthy, descriptive footnotes whose didactic purpose was to inform, once the reader had been entertained. Darwin's writings thus functioned at a number of different levels.

In order to entertain the reader, Darwin painted vivid word pictures, appealing especially to the visual imagination. McNeil shows how this emphasis on visual information was part of Darwin's theory of knowledge; the theory that seeing was knowing was widespread in the period. This visual epistemology was closely linked to physiological preoccupations with the mechanisms of vision. The well-known eighteenth-century debates about 'taste' and about the relationships between art and nature were part of a larger cultural preoccupation which ranged from aesthetics, through psychology, epistemology and physiology, to the politics of poetry.

Poetry was of course deeply political in the sense that poets espoused strongly held positions about the most important issues of the day. The different ways in which Newton was treated in verse were hardly innocent of political implications (Nicolson, 1946). These principally hinged on the question of what kinds of rights and powers human beings had in and over nature. The treatment of social, moral, political and philosophical questions within a single domain was thus well-established long before Erasmus Darwin. McNeil argues, however, that social, moral and natural categories were *increasingly* blurred as the century wore on, culminating in Malthus's *Essay on the Principle of Population* (1798), which treated poverty, charity and population in terms of natural laws. The means by which these categories were merged were, of course, linguistic, hence the historical importance of a project to decode literary devices. The coalescence of categories which McNeil found in Malthus also illuminates the fervour of Blake's reaction to Enlightenment science and philosophy (Frye, 1966). He sought to keep some things separate – spurious knowledge from true understanding, for example – but his urge to distinguish had nothing in common with conservative attempts to maintain the separation between mind or soul on the one hand and body or matter on the other. Politically conservative and theologically traditional thinkers were agreed on the importance of these divisions because they symbolized other distinctions which were central to the social order: God and 'man', monarch and subjects, and in France, Pope and Catholic masses.

Darwin's poetry illuminates a far-reaching historical change – the Industrial Revolution – from the perspective of a specific social group: the middle-class entrepreneurs who promoted an ideology of social and scientific innovation. Darwin wrote for a 'polite' audience, and with an ability to command recognized literary devices. The content of his verse, while not entirely unique, was notable for the detailed vision of industrial production it evoked. The detail was carefully constructed to induce amazement at the *intellectual* innovation embodied in the new industries, that is, at the powers of human domination over nature. The reader was informed about the abstract processes of production, but discouraged from drawing any conclusions about the *human* material conditions of production, i.e. the work force.

The contrast with Sterne is apparent. Where Sterne, as a cleric and literary man, writing a generation earlier in the 1750s and 1760s, played with the concepts of the new life sciences and with the imaginations of his readers, Darwin, medical practitioner and natural philosopher, does no such thing. He, by contrast, painted an authoritative *picture* for his readers to admire. The implied analogy with the visual arts is of course not fortuitous, but reflects Darwin's epistemology. In the end it is the intricate intertwining of science, literature and ideology which makes Darwin such a fascinating figure who can emerge with great historical vividness in his role as a member of the radical Midlands intelligentsia at a time of social consolidation as well as of political crisis.

The second half of the eighteenth century witnessed a flourishing of provincial culture in Britain. Erasmus Darwin (1731–1802), who, amongst other things, was a medical writer and practitioner, a poet, an inventor, and a theorist of education and agriculture, was a central figure in this blossoming. He was a founder of some of the provincial societies which were generating this activity: the Botanical Society of Lichfield, the Derby Philosophical Society, and the Lunar Society of Birmingham.

The Lunar Society was particularly important and has been described as 'the chief intellectual driving force behind the Industrial Revolution' (King–Hele, 1977, 13). This was a circle of provincial men whose major interest was science, particularly as applied to industry. The group functioned between 1765 and 1791, but its most active phase was in the period 1781 to 1791. Besides Darwin, the best-known members of the group were: Matthew Boulton (1728–1809), the Birmingham manufacturer and James Watt's business partner; Thomas Day (1748–89), author of the children's classic *The History of Sandford and Merton* (1783–89), reformer and experimenter in Rousseauesque modes of education; Richard Lovell Edgeworth (1744–1817), reforming landlord in Ireland and designer of carriages and other mechanical inventions; Samuel Galton (1753–1832), manufacturer and scientific experimenter; James Keir (1735–1820), industrial chemist; Joseph Priestley (1733–1804), leader of the dissenting community, and an experimenting naturalist known for his work on air and phlogiston; James Watt (1736–1818), the steam engine inventor; Josiah Wedgwood (1730–95), the potter; John Whitehurst (1713–88), geologist and clock constructor; and William Withering (1741–99), a medical practitioner who was associated with the early medical use of digitalis.

The lively provincial culture of this period was outward looking, and Darwin's network extended beyond the Lunar

Society. It included Joseph Banks (1743–1820), the botanist and President of the Royal Society; Thomas Beddoes (1760–1808), experimenter in pneumatic medicine and chemistry; Benjamin Franklin (1706–90), the American statesman and man of science; and William Hutton (1726–97), the geologist. Like his more famous grandson Charles Darwin (1809–82), Erasmus theorized about the development of the natural world.

'The first *literary* character in Europe, and the most original-minded man' (Logan, 1936, 12) – this was Coleridge's description of Darwin. Perhaps the most distinctive feature of the work of this *'literary* character' was his attempt to bring together science and poetry. In the Advertisement to *The Botanic Garden* (1791), he expressed his ambition to 'inlist Imagination under the banner of Science; and to lead her votaries from the looser analogies which dress out the imagery of poetry, to the stricter ones which form the ratiocination of philosophy'.

This ambition to 'inlist Imagination under the banner of Science' characterized all of Darwin's poetry. His first major work was the lengthy didactic poem *The Loves of the Plants* (1789). This was followed by *The Economy of Vegetation*, a poetic exploration of the features of nature, which was published with a second edition of *The Loves of the Plants* in 1791. The two works comprised *The Botanic Garden*, which established Darwin as a popular poet of his day. This combined volume was also an unusual contribution to scientific knowledge in that its copious footnotes and additional notes were primarily designed to enhance the contemporary understanding of nature.

After the appearance of *The Botanic Garden*, Darwin published substantial treatises on educational, medical and agricultural theory: *A Plan for the Conduct of Female Education in Boarding Schools* (1793); *Zoonomia; or, The Laws of Organic Life* (Part I, 1794, Parts I–III, 1796); *Phytologia;*

or, *The Philosophy of Agriculture and Gardening* (1800). *The Temple of Nature; or, The Origin of Society* was his final work, and it appeared posthumously in 1803. In *The Temple*, he returned to the poetic form, employing it to unveil the progressive operations of nature, from the beginning of microscopic life to society.

This essay explores the roots and character of Darwin's project of bringing together science and poetry. I will argue that Darwin's attempt to integrate the worlds of science and poetry was neither fortuitous nor eccentric. Hence, my first premise is that the Darwinian project was an historically significant one which deserves explanation. My second premise is that the Industrial Revolution was not only an economic and social transformation but also a cultural transformation and that this facet of the Revolution merits more consideration. I shall indicate how Erasmus Darwin's poetry embodied part of this cultural transformation. My examination of Darwin's ambition to bring together science and poetry begins by situating him in the eighteenth-century poetic debate concerning science. From there I shall move to a consideration of Darwin's own picture of industrialization, suggesting the social and political roots of his poetic presentation of science and technology. The third part of my analysis consists of an examination of how Darwin's poetic form complements his political perspective on science and technology. In particular, I consider his view of the imagination and his use of poetic devices. My overall aim will be to demonstrate how Darwin's poetry represents the cultural face of the economic, social and political transformation of the Industrial Revolution.

I

Erasmus Darwin has been described as 'the first English poet to interpret modern science' (Logan, 1936, 147). Darwin celebrated various scientific and technological accomplishments including Wedgwood's innovations in pottery production, Boulton's coining machinery, the engines of Newcomen, Savery, and Watt, Franklin's experiments on electricity, and Arkwright's transformation of cotton processing. Science and technology were the recurring themes of his poetry as he wrote of fire, steel, tools, steam engines, philosophical bellows, lightning rods and countless other similar topics. Despite claims concerning Darwin's vanguard position, his poetry can be considered as part of a poetic debate concerning science and technology which spanned the eighteenth century in Britain.

Not all the participants in this debate shared Darwin's enthusiasm for contemporary science and technology. A less favourable interpretation was taken earlier in the century by Henry Brooke (1703–83) and Alexander Pope (1688–1744). Brooke wrote in *Universal Beauty* (1735):

> For deep, indeed, the ETERNAL FOUNDER lies,
> And high above his work the MAKER flies;
> Yet infinite that work, beyond our soar;
> Beyond what Clarkes can prove, or Newtons can explore.
>   (Brooke, 1778, 42, lines 319–22)

A similar scepticism about science pervaded Pope's *Essay on Man* (1733–4). Pope suggested that there were definite limits to what science could teach humanity about nature:

> Superior beings, when of late they saw
> A mortal Man unfold all Nature's law,
> Admir'd such wisdom in an earthy shape,
> And shew'd a Newton as WOULD shew an Ape.
>   (Pope, 1753, Epistle II, lines 31–4)

While recognizing Newton's achievement, he felt strongly that this accomplishment was only remarkable within the boundaries of the human perspective of nature. For both Brooke and Pope the limitations of the human mind were concretely manifested in science.

However, eighteenth-century science (particularly Newtonianism) did receive a good deal of positive poetic attention
(Nicolson, 1946). James Thomson (1700–48) offered one of
the many poetic effusions over the accomplishments of science
in *The Seasons* (revised edition, 1746):

> Here, awful Newton, the dissolving clouds
> Form, fronting on the sun, the showery prism;
> And to the sage-instructed eye unfold
> The various twine of light, by thee disclosed
> From the white mingling maze.
>   (Thomson, 1901, 11, lines 208–12)

The chief distinction between the earlier, more negative
approach to science (in the work of Brooke and Pope) and the
enthusiasm for science expressed by poets such as Thomson
and Mark Akenside (1721–70) resulted from two different
estimations of the significance of the human perception of
nature. For Brooke and Pope, science was restricted precisely because it was the tool of a finite creature, the human
being. It was a limited tool employed to explore the infinite
magnitude of God's creation, nature. For Akenside and
Thomson, however, *only* the human comprehension of nature
mattered. For them the accomplishments of Newton and other
scientists should be celebrated as extensions of the human
perspective of nature. Accordingly, Akenside contended that
Newton's description of the rainbow actually intensified the
human experience of this part of nature (Akenside, 1744, 50–
1). Thomson's eulogy of Newton is noteworthy in this regard:

> When Newton rose, our philosophic sun!
>   ('To the Memory of Sir Isaac Newton',
>   line 90 in Thomson, 1901, 439)

For Thomson, Newton's role in natural philosophy was equivalent to that of the sun in vision. Emphasizing the intrinsic
and exclusive importance of human awareness of nature,

Thomson's metaphor created the impression that human knowledge was a sort of universe of its own with Newton at the centre.

A third poetic approach to science in the eighteenth century brought together the scepticism of the first wave and the sense of the primacy of the human mind that characterized the second variety. D. J. Greene has sketched the dynamics of this third poetic school as manifested in the attacks on Newtonianism by Christopher Smart (1722–71) and William Blake (1757–1827) (Greene, 1953). The necessary primacy of the human mind in any science was one of the central tenets of both Smart and Blake. This commitment is obvious in Blake's *Vision of the Last Judgement*:

> The Last Judgement is an Overwhelming of Bad
> Art & Science. Mental Things are alone Real;
> what is call'd Corporeal, Nobody Knows of its
> Dwelling Place; it is in Fallacy, & its
> Existence an Imposture. Where is the Existence
> Out of Mind or Thought?
> (For the year 1810, in Blake, 1972, 617)

Greene has shown that for both Smart and Blake the passivity of the mind in relation to the physical world, implicit in the Newtonian and Lockean dualistic and materialistic cosmology, was unacceptable. Locke (1632–1704) considered the mind to be a *tabula rasa* upon which sensations made their impressions. This was the primary source of ideas. In reworking Locke's analysis of mental operations, Berkeley (1685–1753) had insisted upon the impossibility of anything existing independently of perception. This led him to the radically sceptical position of denying the existence of all matter. Greene considers that these poets explored the central problem of Newtonianism, identified by Berkeley, of metaphysical pretensions which evaded the crucial issue of *how* one moves from individual sensations to objective statements regarding

an external nature. As I have outlined above, the poetic effusions over Newtonianism (especially in the works of Thomson
and Akenside) shared the presumption that there were no
problems in this area.

The poetic accounts of science and technology took a fourth
direction in the final decade of the eighteenth century. The
optimism of Richard Payne Knight (1750–1824) and Erasmus Darwin regarding contemporary science and technology
created an affinity between their work and that of Akenside
and Thomson. Nevertheless, Knight and Darwin were sensitive to many of the issues raised by Smart and Blake. In *The
Progress of Civil Society* (1796) Knight set the tone of his
poem with his initial query about the key epistemological issue
of the era:

> Whether primordial motion sprang to life
> From the wild war of elemental strife;
> In central chains, the mass inert confined
> And sublimated matter into mind? –
> Or, whether one great all-pervading soul
> Moves in each part, and animates the whole;
> Unnumber'd worlds to one great centre draws:
> And governs all by pre-establish'd laws? –
>
> (Knight, 1796, 3)

He concluded that such questions were unanswerable and that
his poem should deal with the accessible:

> Let us less visionary themes pursue,
> And try to show what mortal eyes may view.(3)

Thus, this poem became a graphic display of the progress of
human inventions:

> Still one invention to another leads,
> And art to art, in order slow, succeeds. (50)

And,

> Thus more effective implements were found
> To raise the building, and to till the ground
> Labour by art was methodized and fed;
> And man's domain over nature spread. (51)

Knight implied that there was an organic relationship between men and their inventions in one section of the poem:

> Each bright invention rear'd its infant head:
> Science and art their various powers combined,
> To polish, charm, and elevate mankind. (82)

This image also recalls the image of nature as the child of God conveying both the organic and divine facets of human creativity in invention.

Although Knight's treatment of human progress as reflected in technology was close to Darwin's, there were crucial differences between the two poets. Darwin, unlike Knight, did not shy away from the epistemological problems which they both recognized as fundamental. For Darwin, the only method whereby human claims to knowledge of nature and natural laws could be validated must involve a monistic account of a common origin for nature and mind. The Creator had 'stamped a certain similitude on the features of nature', he claimed in *Zoonomia*, 'that demonstrates to us, that *the whole is one family of one parent*. On this similitude is founded all rational analogy' (Darwin, 1801, I, Preface). He thus pinned his hopes on the possibility that a science of life would overcome the epistemological problems regarded by Smart and Blake as the fundamental shortcomings of Newtonian natural philosophy.

Darwin's expectations for the unifying effect of a science of life were set out in the first lines of *The Temple of Nature*:

> By firm immutable immortal laws
> Impress'd on Nature by the GREAT FIRST CAUSE,
> Say, Muse! how rose from elemental strife

Organic forms and kindled into life;
How Love and Sympathy with potent charm
Warm the cold heart, the lifted hand disarm;
Allure with pleasures, and alarm with pains,
And bind Society in golden chains.

Darwin sought to provide a framework which would incorpo-
rate all social, intellectual, and moral developments into the
operations of nature. 'The laws of motion therefore are the
laws of nature', he observed in the first page of his medical
treatise *Zoonomia*, before outlining those laws as they related
to the human body and mind. *The Temple of Nature* sketched
the progressive operations of these laws of motion, from the
first appearance of primitive life to the most sophisticated
technological and moral achievements of Darwin's society.

The project was unique. For Darwin the verification of the
organic unity of mind and nature through a science of life
offered the only possible solution to the epistemological dilem-
mas plaguing eighteenth-century natural philosophy and
poetry. The reaction to Darwin's solution was typified by the
Edinburgh Review's charge that one of his most serious errors
in *The Temple of Nature* 'arises from constantly blending and
confounding together the two distinct sciences of matter and of
mind' (II, No. I July 1803, 449). The Newtonian version of
Descartes's duality was too firmly entrenched to be shaken by
Darwin's gropings towards a science of life.

The foregoing discussions show how distinctive Darwin's
poetic handling of scientific and technological themes was. His
juxtaposition of descriptions of inventions with poetic portraits
of the vegetable world in *The Loves of the Plants* was not
anomalous or bizarre. This striking move paralleled the life,
experience, and happiness of plants with human life, experiences, and perpetuation through technology. For Darwin, the
loves of plants and the achievements of eighteenth-century sci-

ence and technology were two equally important aspects of the operations of nature.

II

The preceding section described Darwin's optimistic view of science and technology. This section will suggest that his perspective was rooted in his social and political position within the Industrial Revolution. Thus, to grasp the cultural and political significance of Darwin's view of science and technology, it is necessary to turn to his poetic portraits of production.

The excerpts from Darwin's lengthy poems which are most pleasing to the twentieth-century reader are those which describe mechanized production in the early Industrial Revolution:

> — Quick wheels the wheel, the ponderous hammer falls,
> Loud anvils ring amid the tumbling walls,
> Strokes follow strokes, the sparkling ingot shines,
> Flows the red flag, the lengthening bar refines;
> Cold waves, immersed, the glowing mass congeal,
> And turn to adamant the hissing steel.
>
> (*The Economy*, Canto II, lines 187–92)

Other machines also captured his poetic imagination. This industrial muse sang of pumps, the printing press, Boulton's coining apparatus, and of the mechanical processing of cotton:

> — First with nice eye emerging Naiads cull
> From leathery pods the vegetable wool;
> With wiry teeth *revolving cards* release
> The tangled knots, and smooth the ravell'd fleece;
> Next moves the *iron-hand* with fingers fine,
> Combs the wide card, and forms the eternal line;
> Slow, with soft lips, the *Whirling Can* acquires

> The tender skeins, and wraps in rising spires;
> With quicken'd pace *successive rollers* move,
> Then fly the spokes, the rapid axles glow; –
> And slowly circumvolves the labouring wheel below.
>   (*The Loves*, Canto II, lines 93–104)

The footnotes accompanying these lines describe cotton production in considerable detail. Darwin provides his readers
with a vivid picture of the mechanical operations identified
with the Industrial Revolution.

There is a second kind of industrial poetry in *The Botanic
Garden* and *The Temple of Nature*, praising the products
of the new mechanical production and new factories.
Wedgwood's pottery, Boulton's coin and medals, steel, and
steam itself are celebrated by Darwin:

> Hail, adamantine STEEL! magnetic Lord!
> King of the prow, the plowshare, and the sword!
> True to the pole, by thee the pilot guides
> His steady helm amid the struggling tides,
> Braves with broad sail the immeasurable sea,
> Cleaves the dark air and asks no star by Thee –
>   (*The Economy*, Canto II, lines 201–6)

The preceding selections are representative of Darwin's
industrial poetry. They present certain features of industry:
raw materials, the mechanical inventor or factory owner,
machinery, and products. However, the labourer's role in the
production process was totally ignored. Hence, except for the
initial creativity of the inventor or the entrepreneur, Darwin
conjured the image of purely mechanical industrial production.

A particularly striking example of this disembodied picture
of industrial work is found in one of Darwin's descriptions of
cotton processing:

> So Arkwright taught from Cotton-pods to cull,

And stretch in lines the vegetable wool;
With teeth of steel its fibre-knots unfurl'd,
And with silver tissue clothed the world.
(*The Temple*, Canto IV, lines 261–4)

The verb 'taught' has no object here. Whom did Arkwright
teach? This picture implies that those who learned from
Arkwright were irrelevant to the process or that the knowledge which Arkwright conveyed was embodied in the
machine itself which can 'cull and stretch . . . the vegetable
wool . . . [and] . . . its fibre-knots unfurl'd'. The manufacture
of cotton and the great achievement of clothing the world were
shown as the result of the interaction between the inventor and
the machinery. The workers and the labour process which
integrated work, raw materials, and the means of production
are given no place in this sketch of the marvels of industrial
production.

Darwin's salute to that bastion of freedom, the printing
press, provides even starker evidence of his failure to acknowledge the labourer and the labour process in industry:

enlighten'd realms possess
The learned labours of the immortal Press;
Nursed on whose lap the birth of science thrive,
And rising Arts the wrecks of Time survive.
(*The Temple*, Canto IV lines 269–72)

Here it is *'the Press'* that 'labours' (my emphasis). Darwin
had used a similar construction in *The Loves of the Plants*
when, in reference to cotton processing, he wrote of 'the
labouring wheel' (Canto II, line 104). Within his poetry,
machinery completely usurps the role of living labour. For
Darwin, it was the *press* and *not* those who operated it which
guarded precious social liberties.

Darwin gave poetic expression in his silence to two features
of the Lunar Society involvement with industrialization: the

preoccupation of members with mechanical inventions, and their difficulties with living labour. He and the other members of the Lunar Society were prolific inventors and among the leaders in the mechanization of production in Britain (Schofield, 1963; King-Hele, 1977). So, it is necessary to turn to their interactions with the industrial labour forces.

Those members of the Lunar Society who were in direct contact with workers were repeatedly reminded of the 'refractoriness' of labour. Matthew Boulton was convinced that the quality and quantity of production could only be improved through large-scale machine production (Smiles, 1865, 173). Watt lamented 'the incapacity and unsteadiness of his workmen' (Smiles, 1865, 226, 251–3; Muirhead, 1859, 262–3). He complained in his letters to Boulton about this unreliable component within industry. Wedgwood shared these grievances. As Smiles put it, 'he had considerable difficulty with these workmen, who were wedded to their own ways, and could scarcely be brought into conformity with their new master's modes of workmanship' (Smiles, 1894, 42). The nineteenth-century philosopher of 'self-help' estimated that 'the management and discipline of his workmen' were Wedgwood's principal difficulties. The pottery industry remained one of hand manufacture well into the twentieth century. Nevertheless, in Wedgwood's resolve to 'make such machines of *Men* as cannot err' (McKendrick, 1961, 34), there is an indication of how machinery exercised its dominion over the labour process even in a non-mechanized factory.

Wedgwood confronted his labour force both ideologically and actively armed with Lunar Society visions of 'industrial progress'. In 1783 while he was on a trip to London, a food riot broke out at Etruria. In response to the uprising, Wedgwood published *An Address to the Young Inhabitants of the Pottery* to convince the young members of the community of the error of their elders' ways. He described the transformation undergone by the community and concluded that 'Industry has been the parent of this happy change' (Wedgwood, 1783, 22). Thus, he did not handle this riot by addressing himself to the causes of discontent, fears of hunger and unemployment among the labour force. Rather, Wedgwood used the occasion to expound on the merits of industrialization. Like Darwin's, his vision of industrialization completely ignored the labourer's experience.

Darwin's poetry was thus strategically related to Lunar Society ideology and practice during the early phases of the Industrial Revolution. The Society's experience was indicative of how the worker ceased to be the centre of the productive process with the coming of large-scale industry. Marx analysed theoretically, as a stage in the development of capitalism, the displacement of the labourer within production which was recorded in Darwin's poetry:

> The full development of capital, therefore, takes place — or capital has posited the mode of production corresponding to it — only when . . . *the entire production process appears as not subsumed under the direct skilfulness of the worker, but rather as the technological application of science.* [It is,] hence, the tendency of capital to give production a scientific character; direct labour [is] reduced to a mere moment of this process. (Marx, 1974, 699, [my emphasis, editor's interjections bracketed])

Darwin's poetry was not the only cultural expression of this fundamental shift occurring during the Industrial Revolution. Raymond Williams has traced how the very word 'industry' and its derivatives assumed new meanings during the last decade of the eighteenth century. He explains that, prior to this period, industry 'was a name for a particular *human* attribute' (my emphasis). In the 1790s, 'it became a collective word for our manufacturing and productive institutions, and for their general activities' (Williams, 1963, xiii, and 1983, 165–8). Williams also claims that it was in the nineteenth cen-

tury that the adjective 'industrious' describing persons was
supplemented by 'industrial' describing institutions. This is
one in a conjunction of vocabulary changes which he sketches
and which relate directly both to Darwin's industrial poetry
and to the transformations involved in Britain's industrialization.

There are three facets of industry as described in Darwin's
poetry: the intellectual achievement of the industrial designer,
the operation of the machinery, and the product. The labour
process and manual labour have been completely sifted out of
his vision of work and production. On some occasions this is
expressed in a glorified picture of the labour involved and the
attribution of such labour to the inventor or the entrepreneur:

> So with strong arm immortal BRINDLEY leads
> His long canals, and parts the velvet meads
> Winding in lucid lines, the watery mass
> Mines the firm rock, or loads the deep morass.
>
> (*The Economy of Vegetation*,
> Canto III, lines 349–52)

It is important to note that it was *not* Brindley who 'Mines the
firm rock, or loads the deep morass' and who did the physical
labour involved in such a project. Moreover, phrases such as
'parts the velvet meads' and 'winding in lucid lines, the watery
mass' obscure the hard physical labour involved in canal building. Similarly, in his description of pottery production, the
labour is attributed to 'Gnomes' who magically perform the
work required. This focuses attention on Wedgwood as the
person who assembled these magical forces:

> GNOMES! as you now dissect with hammers fine
> The granite-rock, the nodul'd flint calcine;
> Grind with strong arm, the circling chertz betwixt,
> Your pure Ka-o-lins and Pe-tun-tses mixt:
> O'er each red saggars burning cave preside,

The keen-eyed Fire-Nymphs blazing by your side;
And pleased on WEDGWOOD lay your partial smile,
A new Etruria decks Britannia's Isle.

(*The Economy*, Canto II, lines 297–304)

In his last poetic work, *The Temple of Nature*, Darwin's separation of mental and manual labour and his celebration of the former are most obvious. In his presentation of Arkwright's accomplishments quoted previously (p. 173) Darwin used a pedagogical verb, thereby emphasizing that the ideas and knowledge of inventors and entrepreneurs, rather than the physical labour of workers, were the important factors transforming the contemporary environment.

Darwin's poetic works praised his heroes of the industrial era: entrepreneurs, inventors, and scientists. These were the men whose ideas, rather than whose physical labour, propelled large-scale manufacture. He employed several devices which further aggrandize their achievements. He juxtaposed mythological heroes and gods with contemporary scientists and industrialists, which creates the impression that the latter are the modern equivalent to the former. He associated these modern heroes with futuristic visions of technological triumphs and attributed magical powers to them:

So SAVERY guided his explosive steam
In iron cells to raise the balanced beam;
The Giant-form its ponderous mass uprears,
Descending nods and seems to shake the spheres.

(*The Temple*, Canto IV, lines 249–52)

Darwin's heroes of the modern world include Watt, Boulton, Priestley, Arkwright, Newcomen, Franklin, Wedgwood, and Brindley. Their stature was highlighted by his references to 'immortal Brindley', or 'immortal Franklin'. He conjured images of men with Faustian powers over nature.

This respect, verging on reverence, for the industrial

innovators and men of science of his day did not manifest itself
only in his poetry. Darwin was doubly fascinated by machines
and mechanical genius. He kept abreast of the mechanical
innovations of his day to such an extent that he could write to
Boulton about the many improvements that had been made in
Arkwright's machinery, confidently asserting 'all which I am
master of, and could make more improvements myself' (King-
Hele, 1981, 141).

Darwin captured the increasing separation of mental from
manual labour which Marx regarded as the foundation of
large-scale industry:

> The separation of the intellectual faculties of the production
> process from manual labour, and the transformation of
> those faculties into powers exercised by capital over
> labour, is, as we have already shown, finally completed by
> large-scale industry erected on the foundation of machin-
> ery. The special skill of each individual machine-operator,
> who has now been deprived of all significance, vanishes as
> an infinitesimal quantity in the face of the science, the
> gigantic natural forces, and the mass of social labour,
> embodied in the system of machinery, which, together with
> these three forces, constitute the power of the 'master'.
> (Marx, 1976, 548–9)

Darwin's poetry highlighted the achievements of science, and
celebrated the powers of scientists, industrialists, and machines over nature. But, as Marx demonstrated, these powers
implied new power over labourers.

While Darwin acknowledged the technical domination of
nature realized by industrialists, he was largely silent about
their social domination over their workers. While describing
the mode of production, he neglected the social relations of
industrialization. This becomes obvious when his pictures of
industry are contrasted with other contemporary judgments.
About the same time that Darwin offered his poetic descrip-

tion of the mechanical processes of Arkwright which 'with silver tissue clothed the world', Sir Thomas Bernard (1750–1818), a contemporary philanthropist, presented a very different, albeit paternalistic, perspective on cotton manufacture:

> Our national individual increases of wealth, from the manufacture of cotton, has been attended with so much injury to the health and morals of the poor, and is so utterly destructive of that which constitutes the essential and fundamental virtue of the female character; that if I am not permitted to suggest a doubt, whether it would not have been better for us *that cotton mills had never been erected in this island,* I may at least express an anxious wish, that such regulations may be adopted and enforced, as shall diminish, if not entirely remove, the injurious and pernicious effects, which must otherwise attend them. (Bernard, 1805, II, 362, his emphasis)

In his *Political Register*, the champion of political reform, William Cobbett (1762–1835), alluded to similar unpleasant features of this industry:

> Some of these lords of the loom have in their employ thousands of miserable creatures. In the cotton-spinning works, these creatures are kept, fourteen hours in each day, locked up, summer and winter, in a heat from *eighty* to *eighty-four degrees*. The rules which they are subjected to are such as no negroes were even subject to. (Cobbett, 1824, 458, his emphasis)

For Cobbett, domination of nature went hand in hand with domination of labourers. Looking at cotton manufacture from the perspective of labourers, his picture of this mechanized industry was altogether less glowing than Darwin's.

Darwin's focus was on technological innovations as individual achievements. His acknowledgment of only the mental component involved in inventions caused him to view

technological triumphs as the product of a specific mind or
genius rather than of a social process. However, the history of
eighteenth-century technology shows that seldom was any
innovation the exclusive creation of an isolated individual
(Marx, 1976, 493; Fitton and Wadsworth, 1958, 76).
Furthermore, the realization of inventions required skilled
craftsmanship, as Marx recognized:

> the inventions of Vaucanson, Arkwright, Watt and others
> could be put into practice only because each inventor found
> a considerable number of skilled mechanical workers avail-
> able, placed at their disposal by the period of manufacture.
> (Marx, 1976, 503)

At least three members of the Lunar Society and heroes of
Darwin's poetry – Wedgwood, Boulton, and Watt – were
dependent on craftsmen. Indeed, Watt had originally been a
craftsman himself. Nevertheless, Darwin conveyed no sense
of this dimension of technological history, because he took for
granted that the impetus for innovation came exclusively from
mental labour.

Darwin's demarcation of the spheres of mental and manual
labour reflected the very character of the Lunar Society. The
group was a loosely bound conglomerate of men of ideas. For
the most part, they concentrated on generating ideas which
were executed by others. Darwin, for example, had local car-
riage-makers build the vehicles which he designed. Likewise,
Wedgwood conceived of the scheme of making copies of the
Portland vase, and his labourers realized his ambition.

The first section of this article situated Darwin within the
poetic debate concerning science and technology in eighteenth-
century Britain. I then considered the social and political roots
of Darwin's optimism concerning science and technology.
This industrial muse sang of the machines, the products, and
the entrepreneurs and scientists of the new era. Although
mechanization was slow and piecemeal, the production pro-

cess shifted from one which was labour-orientated to one which was machine-orientated. I have shown how Darwin's poetry captures this transformation both in what it celebrates and in its silences. He also presented poetically the growing division between mental and manual labour realized with industrialization. His view of technological production was part of a new and powerful industrial image of society and culture.

III

Watching the dawn of industrialization in Britain, Erasmus Darwin sang of a new humanity which could re-create both itself and its world. Hence, he expressed the specific experience of the industrial bourgeoisie as the universal expansion of human powers. The imagination was the crucial instrument which Darwin invoked in his project. In addition, his use of certain devices – particularly personification and the pathetic fallacy – was strategic to his poetic vision. Thus, I shall now turn to the poetic modes employed by Darwin in his celebration of science and technology.

In the Preface to *The Temple of Nature*, Darwin simply stated his aim as 'to amuse by bringing distinctly to the imagination the beautiful and sublime images of the operations of Nature'. It is significant that he addressed his poem to his readers' imagination, the faculty which intrigued investigators of human nature at this time. Furthermore, he labelled his task as the production of 'the beautiful and sublime images of the operations of Nature', thereby invoking the visual emphasis that predominated in his poetic work. Ernest L. Tuveson has described the centrality of the conception of imagination in eighteenth-century British thought. He traced the development of an interpretation of the relationship between God and humanity in which nature became the mediator and imagination the faculty which facilitates salvation (1960). The contributions of Hobbes, Locke, Addison, Shaftesbury, and

Hutcheson to this tradition are highlighted in Tuveson's account. Even from the perspective of a less explicitly religious framework, imagination tended to be regarded by most eighteenth-century philosophers as a bridging mechanism. It was seen as a mediator between human sensory faculties and intellectual and higher faculties. Alexander Gerard (1728–95) was one of the many exponents of this view: 'those internal senses from which taste is formed, are commonly referred to the *imagination*, which is considered as holding a middle rank between the bodily senses, and the rational and moral faculties' (Gerard, 1780, 143). Mark Akenside took a similar stand in 'The Design' of *The Pleasures of Imagination:* 'There are certain powers in human nature which seem to hold a middle place between the organs of bodily sense, and the faculties of moral perception: they have been called by a very general name, the Powers of Imagination' (1744, 5).

By addressing his poetry to the imagination Darwin also seemed to recognize the mediating potential of this faculty. His Advertisement to *The Botanic Garden* suggested his endorsement of such a role for the imagination:

> The general design of the following sheets is to inlist Imagination under the banner of Science; and to lend her votaries from the looser analogies, which dress out the imagery of poetry, to the stricter, ones which form the ratiocination of philosophy. While their particular design is to induce the ingenious to cultivate the knowledge of botany, by introducing them to the vestibule of that delightful science, and recommending to their attention the immortal works of the celebrated Swedish Naturalist, LINNAEUS.

The familiar eighteenth-century instrumentalist view of the imagination as a vehicle to a higher state is secularized here. The imagination is invoked as mediating between sensual poetic images and 'the ratiocination of philosophy'. In this scheme, science replaces God as the telos of human struggle.

The phrase 'immortal works' plays on the eighteenth-century religious tradition described by Tuveson while locating its dynamics in a new, entirely human setting.

Darwin's poetry appealed not just to a mediating but also to a visually orientated imagination. In the Proem of *The Loves of the Plants*, he beckoned his readers: 'Lo, here a CAMERA OBSCURA is presented to thy view, in which are lights and shades dancing on a whited canvas, and magnified into apparent life!' He then explained that he had tried to restore plants to their original animality in his poem with portraits, 'Which thou may'st contemplate as diverse little pictures suspended over the chimney of a Lady's dressing-room'. This poem was presented as a series of portraits of plants. The Preface to *The Temple of Nature* indicated a similar intention to bring before the imagination 'images of the operations of nature'. The content of these works realized their author's intention. Thus, after his invitation to 'walk and view the wonders of my INCHANTED GARDEN', Darwin led his readers through his poetic garden of portraits of various plants in *The Loves of the Plants*. Similarly, in *The Temple of Nature*, he provided his readers with a panorama of nature. Nature, as a visible goddess, appears in the successive settings of the production of life, the reproduction of life, and the moral sphere. He characterized his own poetry as *'pure description'* (*The Loves*, 40).

This poetic practice was reinforced by theory. In the first Interlude of *The Loves of the Plants*, Darwin argued that poetry should use few words denoting abstract ideas: 'And as our ideas derive from visible objects of our other senses, the words expressive of these ideas belonging to vision make up the principal part of poetic language. That is the Poet writes principally to the eye, the Prose-writer uses more abstracted terms.' He contended that personification and allegory were eminently suitable poetic devices because of their ability to appeal to the visual sense. In the second Interlude of this poem he extended his analysis, explaining that the simile 'should

have so much sublimity, beauty, or novelty, as to interest the
reader; and should be expressed in picturesque language, so as
to bring the scenery before the eye'. In the third Interlude, he
expounded on the similarities between the sister arts of painting and poetry. The poet should provide pictures of the operations of both nature and human nature. The artist and the
poet should both busy themselves 'making sentiments and passions visible . . . this is done in both arts by describing or por-
traying the effects or changes, which those sentiments or passions produce upon the body'. Thus, Darwin endorsed the
long-standing 'ut pictura poesis' tradition which extolled the
similarities between painting and poetry (Cohen, 1964;
Hagstrum, 1958; Praz, 1970; Spacks, 1967; Graham,
1973). This concern with the visual dominated not only Darwin's poetic theory, but also his epistemology. His definition
of ideas in *The Temple of Nature* indicated that he regarded
them as the product of the interaction between the visual and
tactile senses as the 'successive trains of the motions, or
changes of figure, of the extremities of the nerves of one or
more senses' (Canto III, fn. 398). He gave ideas a physiological definition as provoking a visible change in body figure.
This notion of ideas was captured poetically:

> As the pure language of sight commands
> The clear ideas furnished by the hands.
>
> (Canto III, lines 163-4)

Hence, his entire epistemology was founded on a visual
framework.

Darwin's interest in vision, was rooted in his own
physiological work. He devoted a large section of *Zoonomia*,
his medical treatise, to a detailed explanation of vision, and he
considered various problems of visual distortion and illusion.
His son, Dr Robert Darwin, had investigated the degree of
pleasure and pain experienced by the eye when exposed to
various stimuli, and the son's treatise on this topic was

included in *Zoonomia*. Erasmus Darwin pursued this investigation with speculations about the possibility of 'luminous music' drawing on Newton's ideas of the spectrum of colours.

The background to this emphasis on the visual sense is important. Newton's *Opticks* (1704) had launched the physiological investigation of vision and the exploration of the problems of vision, light, and colour which came to preoccupy many eighteenth-century minds. Thus, Darwin participated in the scientific investigation of vision by natural philosophers which began with the *Opticks* and Berkeley's *Essay Towards a New Theory of Vision* (1709). This scientific response to the *Opticks* was accompanied by a poetic response to which Darwin also contributed and which Marjorie Nicolson has explored in *Newton Demands the Muse* (1946).

The visual sense was also central to eighteenth-century speculations about ideas and knowledge. This development stemmed from Locke's highly visual epistemology. He described the process whereby the mind acquired simple ideas in *An Essay Concerning the Human Understanding* (1690):

> Whatsoever is so constituted in nature, as to be able, by affecting our senses, to cause any perception in the mind, doth thereby produce in the understanding a simple idea; which, whatever be the external cause of it, when it comes to be taken notice of by our discerning faculty, it is by the mind looked on and considered there, to be a real positive idea in the understanding. (Locke, 1706, 73)

Locke's use of a verb of vision was in line with his general interpretation of the mind as a 'mental eye'. Joseph Addison (1672–1719) used Locke's notion of visual ideas to posit a visually stimulated imagination. In his influential essay in the *Spectator* in 1712 (entitled 'The Pleasures of the Imagination'), Addison established the basis for the subsequent exploration of this faculty with his claim that all the pleasures of the imagination 'arise originally from sight' (Addison, 1854, 270).

The poetry of Enlightenment Britain reflected the Lockean and Addisonian emphasis on the visual sense. Darwin joined Thomson, Collins, Gray, Smart, and Cowper in this tradition. Thomson, the most renowned nature poet of eighteenth-century Britain, specialized, like Darwin, in the production of panoramas of the operations of nature. Thomson's most famous work, *The Seasons*, can be 'taken from the beginning to be a triumph of vision in the literal sense' (Spacks, 1967, 46).

The push towards visually orientated poetry came from several directions. Painting exerted considerable influence on English poetry during this period (Hagstrum, 1958). On a more theoretical level, this trend was reinforced by specific aesthetic concepts, particularly the vogue for the 'picturesque' (the fashion for objects 'which please from some quality capable of being illustrated in painting') (Gilpin, 1792, 3; Hipple, 1957). Finally, the various styles of gardening were indicative of the attention given to visual experience during the century. Fashions in gardening, in turn, often influenced the nature poetry of the era (Paulson, 1971). Darwin had his own botanic garden in Lichfield which provided part of the inspiration for his poetic *Botanic Garden*. In his last, uncompleted letter, written on the day he died, to Richard Lovell Edgeworth, Darwin compared his garden to that of William Shenstone (1714–63), a minor eighteenth-century poet who created picturesque gardens (King-Hele, 1981, 338–9). For many of the nature poets of his century, the poet's verbal tour of nature offered visual sensations comparable to those experienced in a stroll through an English garden.

The legacy of Locke and Addison combined two strains: the identification of the visual sense with the faculty of reason (with knowledge and 'clear ideas') and the association of that sense with the faculty of imagination. Samuel Johnson (1709–84) captured these two kinds of vision in his dictionary of 1755. The entry for Imagination offered four definitions: two pertaining to the physical sensation and perception involved in vision, and two alluding to the imaginative experience denoted by the term.

Darwin was very much influenced by these developments. He drew on the dual affinities of the visual sense with reason and with imagination. His confidence that he could 'Inlist Imagination under the banner of Science' through his highly visual poetry was based on his recognition of the visual orientation of eighteenth-century natural philosophy. Furthermore, Darwin's strategy was instrumentalist not only in relation to the faculty of the imagination, but also in relation to the visual sense itself. He tried to use this sense to reorientate his readership towards the aims of his peers in the industrial Midlands, in particular towards the pursuit of science. Joseph Wright brought similar ambitions to the visual arts (Klingender, 1975, 43–64). The realization of the goals of eighteenth-century men of science and industry of understanding the natural world and of employing that knowledge within industry was transcribed into a poetic project by Darwin.

This project was undermined by the emergence of critiques of Enlightenment presumptions. There was a growing awareness of the limitations of the faculty of reason (Jones, 1961; Petit, 1963). Francis Hutcheson (1694–1746) and his followers had argued that human behaviour was determined by the desire to maximize pleasure and minimize pain. For them, pleasure and pain were crucial aids for functioning with a limited reason in the universe. M. H. Abrams (1971) has shown that the century witnessed progressive moves towards the conception of a truly creative imagination.

The increasing awareness of the expansive powers of the imagination demanded a recognition of that faculty's involvement with all senses or even its potential to carry human beings beyond the limitations of their senses. In this light, the exclusive reliance on appeals to the visual sense came to be regarded as a weakness rather than as a strength in poetry. Edmund Burke (1729–97) claimed as early as 1757: 'Indeed, so little does poetry depend for its effect on the power of raising sensible images, that I am convinced it would lose a very considerable part of its energy if this were the necessary result of all description' (Burke' 1803, 195). Late in the eighteenth century, Archibald Alison (1757–1839) compared the powers of the poet and of the painter from a similar vantage point: 'The Painter addresses himself to the Eye. The Poet speaks to the Imagination. The Painter can represent no other qualities of Nature, but those which we can discern by means of the sense of sight. The poet can blend with those all the qualities which we perceive by means of our other senses' (Alison, 1790, 91). Both Burke and Alison were moving away from Addison's conception of the imagination as an exclusively visually orientated faculty.

On the basis of this broadening of the dimensions of the imagination, many of Darwin's critics found his preoccupation with visual images the most unsatisfactory feature of his poetry. The *Edinburgh Review* deplored this aspect of his work, explaining that 'it is surely a very unjust limitation of the natural range of poetry, to consider it as solely or ultimately employed in the production of such picturesque effects' (II, No. IV, July 1803, 502). Working within the Addisonian interpretation of the imagination, Darwin had restricted the appeal of his poetry to the visual sense.

The natural philosophy of Darwin's century also came under attack for its preoccupation with visual images. The first lines of Coleridge's critique of David Hartley's (1705–57) theory exemplify this:

> Of Hartley's hypothetical vibrations in his hypothetical oscillating ether of the nerves, which is the first and most obvious distinction between his system and that of Aristotle, I shall say little. This, with all other similar attempts to render *that* an object of sight which has no relation to sight, has already been sufficiently exposed. (Coleridge, 1817, I, 106)

Hartley's work had been one of the most important influences on Darwin's theorizing about the natural world. Thus, Coleridge's criticism undermined one of the lynchpins of Darwin's natural philosophy. Burke and Alison had challenged the association of the imagination and poetry with the visual sense. Coleridge aimed his assault from the other direction, criticizing natural philosophy which was supported by a Lockean epistemology that regarded the mind as an 'internal eye'.

The full implications of the Lockean–Addisonian tradition for eighteenth-century science and imagination were explored by William Blake, who also did some of the engravings for the illustrations of Darwin's books (Keynes, 1971, 59–61). Blake regarded Newton as the dominant figure of the century, and he recognized the particular potency of 'the picture-language quality of Newton's system' (Ault, 1974, 50). For him it was precisely its visual orientation which made Newton's cosmology equally appealing to the faculties of reason and imagination. Newton's system played on the duality of the visual, its inroads to reason and imagination.

Blake's explorations of the visual stood in direct opposition to Darwin's poetic project. The basis of this opposition is described in the following account of this facet of Blake's work:

> Because Newton's system and Descartes' before him, submerged such powerful metaphors of vision under a logically consistent structure of reality, it is no accident that Blake, looking at them as a 'visionary' could appreciate the threat these powerful images posed to the human imagination. It was incumbent on him, then to appropriate many details from these systems and transform these supposedly 'visualizable' concepts into images in his poetry to operate symbolically, drawing their *critical* aspect from their oblique reference to scientific doctrines and their *positive* aspects from their independent operation in the poetry as metaphor. (Ault, 1974, 50)

Blake was determined to rescue the imagination, which he felt
had been threatened by Newtonianism. Hence, he stood
steadfast against an instrumentalist view (such as Darwin's) of
that faculty. To this end, he inverted the tradition of the visual
orientation which dominated Darwin's poetry. While Darwin
used the visual sense as a vehicle for scientific knowledge,
Blake gave the visual image an independent status. He set
about his task of liberating the imagination from the fetters of
Newtonianism by freeing the metaphor of vision from its
mediating role within eighteenth-century poetry and natural
philosophy (Beer, 1969, esp. 260–3). Blake thereby imbi-
bed the century's emphasis on vision, criticized it (as it was
expressed in the Newtonian cosmology), and transformed it in
his own use of 'perspective' and optical analogies:

> The nature of infinity is this: That everything has its
> Own Vortex; and when once a traveller thro' Eternity
> Has pass'd that Vortex, he perceives it roll backward
> behind
> His path, into a globe itself unfolding like a sun,
> Or like a moon, or like a universe of starry majesty,
> While he keeps onwards in his wondrous journey on the
> earth
> Or like a human form, a friend (with) whom he liv'd
> benevolent.
> ('Milton: A Poem in 2 Books' (written and etched
> 1804–8), pt 15, lines 21–7, in Blake, 1972, 497)

The intimate relationship between the intellectual forces of the
Enlightenment and the social dynamics of industrialization
were manifest in the tensions between Blake's and Darwin's
poetic projects. While these poets took opposing stands on
such issues as the role of imagination and of reason, they both
recognized that the British natural philosophy of the
eighteenth century went hand in hand with a complementary
set of social and literary conventions and values. For both,

industrialization marked the culmination of the development of these forces.

Their disagreement was based on a difference in both social and literary perspective. Darwin was riding high on the triumphs of the industrial and scientific bourgeoisie. Buoyed by their success, he offered the century's most confident poetic testimony to their values: science as the avowed goal of poetry, exclusive reliance on the visual sense and an instrumentalist use of the imagination. For Blake, the impoverishment of the lower orders and the impoverishment of the imagination were part of the same process (Larrissey, 1982, esp. 103). In identifying with this segment of society, he saw the need to wage battle on their behalf against the entire heritage of the Enlightenment. Hence, Blake's mythical struggle against 'Urizen' was an effort to guarantee that Darwin's goal of enlisting 'the imagination under the banner of science' would not be realized. Urizen represented reason. As a tyrannical figure who threatened to dominate and destroy the universe, Urizen symbolized Blake's fears about the increasing reverence for reason in his period.

While Darwin employed an eighteenth-century view of a mediating imagination, he had a more innovative relationship to the forms of nature poetry characteristic of that century. The introduction of a poetic account of the struggle for existence constitutes his most important contribution to this literary form. He did have one predecessor in this new direction for nature poetry. In 1796, Richard Payne Knight published this poetic sketch of the struggle for existence within the animal kingdom:

Progressive numbers without end increase,
While nature gives them safety, food, and ease;
Whence, through the whole the balance to sustain,
And in proportion'd bounds each race restrain,
Each stands opposed to some destructive power,

By nature form'd to slaughter and devour;
And still, as each in greater numbers breeds,
More foes it finds, and more devourers feeds.

(Knight, 1796, 27)

Darwin extended the view of this struggle to include humanity:

So human progenies, if unrestrain'd;
By climate friended, and by food sustain'd
O'er seas and soils, prolific hordes! would spread
Erelong [sic], and deluge their terraqueous bed;
But war and pestilence, disease, and death
Sweep the superfluous myriads from the earth.

(*The Temple*, Canto IV, lines 369–74)

For both Darwin and Knight the interaction between human beings and their natural environment as portrayed in the 'climate and civilization' poems was specified into the biological struggle for survival. Darwin incorporated 'war', 'pestilence', and 'disease' into this framework as the most prominent natural forces operating within the human environment. He does not discriminate between social and natural forces: 'war', 'pestilence', and 'disease' are all portrayed as natural. Nevertheless, they are personified, conveying the impression that nature is purposeful. In addition, the pathetic fallacy is used in reference to climate, suggesting that the sort of relationship that exists between the individual and the climate is equivalent to one of friendship. The total effect of the passage is a blurring of the boundaries between the human and the natural.

Darwin's poetry on this theme of the struggle for existence echoed the ideas popularized by T. R. Malthus in *An Essay on the Principle of Population* (1798). In that essay, Malthus argued that 'A man . . . if he cannot get subsistence from his parents on whom he has a just demand, and if the society does not want his labour, has no claim of *right* to the smallest portion of food, and, in fact, has no business to be where he is. At nature's mighty feet there is no vacant cover for him' (Malthus, 1803, 531). Just as some environmental poets of late eighteenth-century Britain envisaged social and moral characteristics as natural, Malthus regarded the political and economic forces operating in industrializing Britain as natural. Unemployment and starvation were the equivalents in Malthus's vision to 'war', 'pestilence', and 'disease' in Darwin's poetic descriptions. They were regarded as sets of natural forces.

A closer appraisal of the preceding quotation from Malthus reveals how he played on the merger of social, moral, and natural categories. He begins with a description of a *social* situation — that of a man unable to get subsistence from his parents and unable to find work. He then interjects a *moral* evaluation of that social situation: this man has no right to food, or to a place in his society. Finally, Malthus reinforces this moral evaluation by presenting it as *nature's* judgment on this individual's condition. The personification of 'nature' in the last sentence is the final ingredient in the subtle play on the categories of the social, moral, and natural. This personification parallels Darwin's use, as noted previously, of personification and the pathetic fallacy in a similar way.

Malthus and Darwin, through their play on the categories of the social, moral, and natural, lent legitimacy to the poverty and suffering of the lower orders during the early stages of industrialization in Britain. So, for example, it has been suggested that there were 'ideological advantages' in Malthus's appeal to an 'authoritarian nature', rather than to an 'authoritarian ruling class' (Copley, 1982, 160–2). This is not to say that they set such legitimization as their goal. Malthus's *Essay* was intended as a protest against the concept of perfectibility as espoused by Condorcet (1743–94) and Godwin (1756–1836) — a protest against their view that humanity was automatically progressing by virtue of the growth of scientific knowledge (Young, 1969; Flew, 1970; Passmore, 1970). Darwin, on the other hand, was preoccupied with the benefits of industrialization. His commitment to it as a progressive agent was so total and his identification with those gaining most in its wake was so unquestioned that he presumed that the destructive forces which he saw operating about him originated in nature rather than in his industrializing society.

William Blake, a contemporary of Malthus and Darwin, was not of the same opinion. He satirized Malthusian attitudes:

> Compell the poor to live upon a Crust of bread, by soft mild
> arts.
> Smile when they frown, frown when they smile; & when a
> man looks pale
> With labour & abstinence, say he looks healthy & happy;
> And when his children sicken, let them die; there are
> enough
> Born, even too many, & our Earth will be overrun
> Without these arts.
> ('The Four Zoas', written and revised 1795–1804,
> 'Night the Seventh', lines 17–22, in Blake, 1972, 23)

Blake's use of the imperative – 'Compell', 'Smile', 'let die' – and his recurrent references to 'arts', convey his belief that the problems observed by Malthus were matters of social responsibility. The so-called natural forces of unemployment and hunger (discussed in Malthus's *Essay*) and disease (described in the quotation from *The Temple*) are portrayed vividly and personally. In fact, these lines have been considered as directly referring to Pitt's Malthusian policies (Erdman, 1977, 366–7). Blake, like Darwin and Malthus, also played on the merger of moral, social, and natural categories. However, he reversed the tendency inherent in the ideas of Malthus and Darwin. Rather than projecting the social problems of industrializing Britain onto nature, Blake telescoped these problems onto the individual conscience. For him, there were no abstract natural forces controlling society; there were only concrete, tragic social problems created by callousness and irresponsibility.

On a more general level, the development of the nature poetry of eighteenth-century Britain revealed the growing intimacy of the relationship between humanity and nature. Pope's *Essay on Man* (1733–4) was a forceful statement concerning the human position within the total framework of nature, in 'The Great Chain of Being' (Lovejoy, 1961). However, Pope's nature poetry (*The Pastorals* and *Windsor Forest*) indicates that his main interest was in a *schema* of human location within nature. From this perspective, Thomson's *Seasons* (first completed version 1730) represented a new direction for nature poetry. Its main concern and presumption was that each individual's relationship with nature was vital. For Thomson, nature was the primary focus of human life and of poetry: 'I know no subject more elevating, more amusing, more ready to evoke the poetical enthusiasm, the poetical reflection and the moral sentiment, than the works of Nature' (Preface to the second edition of 'Winter' in Thomson, 1901, 240). He regarded all aspects of human life, from the intellectual and artistic spheres to the moral, as directly affected by this fundamental relationship to nature. In a later work, *The Castle of Indolence* (1748), he explicitly sketched a picture of nature as created for humanity. Patricia Meyer Spacks has shown that Thomson used 'description of nature as a method for approaching discussion of man' (Spacks, 1967, 23).

This intimate relationship between humanity and nature was intensified and personalized towards the end of the century, particularly in the writings of William Cowper (1731–1800). In Cowper's poetry the generalized relationship between humanity and nature found in Thomson's or Akenside's work was transformed into the very personal interactions bet-

ween individuals and nature. In *Retirement* (1782), for example, he described an individual who seeks 'the refuge of some
rural shade' where

> He may possess the joys he thinks he sees,
> Lay his old age upon the lap of ease,
> Improve the remnant of his wasted span;
> And having liv'd a trifler, die a man.
>
> (Cowper, 1782, 259)

Rather ironically, only by retreating from society to nature
can the individual be restored and 'die a man'.

The most concrete expression of the projection of human
characteristics onto nature was the dominance of certain poetic
devices. The most frequently used devices in the British
poetry of this period were personification and the pathetic fallacy (the 'attribution of human feeling to the natural world').
Josephine Miles and Earl Wasserman have produced detailed
studies of the use of the pathetic fallacy and personification
respectively (Miles, 1965; Wasserman, 1950). Both give
well-documented accounts of the various functions of the two
devices, and of the context which made them particularly suitable techniques. However, neither Miles nor Wasserman discussed in any detail the implications of the widespread use of
these devices during the eighteenth century for the humanity/
nature relationship.

Erasmus Darwin's friend and fellow-member of the Lunar
Society, Joseph Priestley, described some of these implications in his account of the suitability of the device of personification:

> As the sentiments and actions of our fellow-creatures are
> more interesting to us than anything belonging to inanimate
> nature, or the actions of brute animals, a much greater var-
> iety of sensations and ideas must have been excited by them
> and consequently adhere to them by the principles of associ-

ation. Hence it is of prodigious advantage in treating of inanimate things, or merely of brute animals, to introduce frequent allusions to human actions and sentiments, where any resemblance will make it natural. This converts everything we treat of into thinking and acting beings. We see *life, sense, intelligence everywhere.* (Priestley, 1777, 247, my emphasis)

Priestley's is a telling account of the appeal of the poetic devices of personification and pathetic fallacy. The desire to convert 'everything we treat of into thinking and acting beings' assumes the legitimacy of such a transformation. Moreover, this desire is distinguished from primitive anthropomorphism by the fact that it involved a *conscious* attempt to read human characteristics into nature.

Priestley's literary strategy paralleled other Lunar Society activities. Situated on the leading edge of the Industrial Revolution, the members of the society increasingly intervened in the natural world through science and technology. The growth of their economic and social powers during industrialization increased their confidence that the natural world was not a foreign realm but an appropriate sphere for human activities. Accustomed as he was to this form of intervention in the natural world, Priestley had no reservations in advocating an equivalent metaphorical intervention. The increasing dominion over the natural world realized by the Lunar Society found its literary expression in Priestley's advocacy of, and Darwin's use of, the pathetic fallacy and personification.

Given their situation at the leading edge of industrialization, Darwin and Priestley found the human dominion in the world unproblematic. Again, it must be emphasized that it was the unique situation of their class which fostered this presumption. Their literary strategy complemented their ambitions for science and industry. Thus, Priestley had no reservations about advocating the projection of human features onto nature through the use of the pathetic fallacy and personification. Likewise, Darwin depended on these devices and described a natural world which assumed human traits in all his poetic works.

If there was a general movement in eighteenth-century English poetry towards the merging of the categories of the human, the natural, and the divine, Erasmus Darwin's poetry represents the culmination of this movement. He used both personification and the pathetic fallacy frequently:

> New woods aspiring clothe their hills with green,
> Smooth slope the lawns, the grey rock peeps between;
> Relenting Nature gives her hand to Taste,
> And Health and Beauty crown the laughing waste.
> (*The Economy*, Canto III, lines 197–200)

Nature, in all its forms and manifestations, behaved very humanly in Darwin's poetry. Nature was also portrayed as a goddess in both of his poetic books:

> – Till o'er the wreck, emerging from the storm,
> Immortal NATURE lifts her changeful form,
> Mounts from her funeral pyre on wings of flame,
> And soars and shines, another and the same.
> (*The Economy*, Canto IV, lines 377–80)

Despite the fact that many contemporary literary critics were sceptical about the use of machinery in poetry, he seemed convinced that it was appropriate to use it in his panoramas of nature and human nature. The attribution of divine characteristics further aggrandized nature and humanity.

Darwin's use of the pathetic fallacy, personification, and machinery can be seen as the continuation of the general tendency to coalesce humanity, nature, and God in the poetry of his era. However, his use of an industrial metaphor to describe the operations of nature was a unique contribution to this trend:

In earth, sea, air, around, below, above,
Life's subtle woof in Nature's loom is wove,
Points glued to points in living line extend,
Touch'd by some goad approach the binding end.

(The Temple, Canto I, lines 251–4)

Hence, he explicitly described nature as a machine and life as the product of an industrial process. The use of this industrial metaphor reveals the vantage point of Darwin's poetic studies of nature. Enlightenment natural philosophy and industrial processes were brought together through the metaphor of the machine, the loom. Priestley had observed that, in looking at nature, it was appropriate that human beings should project their characteristics onto nature so that 'We see life, sense, intelligence everywhere'. For Darwin, 'life, sense, intelligence' were quintessentially embodied in the industrial machine. This identification was by no means fortuitous. It related directly to his affiliation with the industrialists of the Midlands and to his allegiance to mechanical innovators such as Arkwright, Watt, and Boulton. Thus, Darwin's vision of nature and his peculiar expression of the coalescing of divine and natural powers in industrialization were directly influenced by his social setting.

The social roots of this vision become more obvious when Darwin's use of the metaphor of weaving is contrasted with that of William Blake. Writing a few years later, Blake drew on similar associations in constructing his metaphor: the mechanistic natural philosophy spearheaded by Locke and Newton, and mechanized industrial processes. Like Darwin, Blake depicted the meshing of industrial production and natural philosophy:

I turn my eyes to the Schools & Universities of Europe
And there behold the Loom of Locke, whose Woof rages
dire,
Wash'd by the Water-wheels of Newton: black the cloth

In heavy wreathes folds over every Nation; cruel Works
Of many Wheels I view, wheel without wheel, with cogs
                                                  tyrannic
Moving by compulsion each other, not as those in Eden,
                                                  which
Wheel within Wheel, in freedom revolve in harmony &
                                                  peace,
('Jerusalem: The Emanation of the Giant Albion', written
and etched 1804–20, Plate 15, lines 14–20 in Blake,
1972, 636)

Darwin, excited by the God-like powers involved in industrial
production, used the loom as an analogue for God's functioning within nature. His perspective was that of the inventors of,
and controllers of, the machinery of production, Blake's
perspective was that of labourers within 'cruel works'. From
this vantage point, appalled by the destructive consequences
of industrialization, he used the same metaphor to condemn the
philosophy which fostered industrialization and concomit-
antly, he felt, social tyranny.

CONCLUSION

This essay has examined Erasmus Darwin's attempt to bring
together science and poetry. The first part of the analysis
situated Darwin within the eighteenth-century poetic debate
concerning science in Britain. His contribution to this debate
can be characterized as an optimism about science and
technology pinned to his hopes of establishing a science of life.
Section II identified the roots of Darwin's optimism in the
political and social experience of the Lunar Society during the
Industrial Revolution. His industrial technological poetry
represented the cultural face of the industrial transformation
experienced in Britain at this time. His focus on machinery
rather than living labour and on mental rather than manual
labour were cultural expressions of crucial political and

economic shifts in production and work during the Industrial
Revolution. Finally, the third segment of the analysis described Darwin's view of the imagination and use of poetic devices. His instrumentalist use of the imagination, his visually orientated poetry, his employment of the poetic devices of personification and pathetic fallacy and of industrial metaphor, complemented the position of the Lunar Society during the early stages of British industrialization. Here Darwin's poetry contrasted sharply with that of William Blake. Viewing the Industrial Revolution from an opposite vantage point, Blake, unlike Darwin, wrote from the perspective of those for whom industrialization meant less not greater power.

FURTHER READING

For Darwin's biography, see King-Hele, 1977. For a description of the activities and concerns of the Lunar Society, see Schofield, 1963. Reviews of the political significance of much of the literature of Darwin's period can be found in Williams, 1963, and Butler, 1981. For a fuller account of Darwin's ideas in their historical context, see McNeil, 1986.

PART 2

The Nineteenth Century

'The Face of Nature': Anthropomorphic Elements in the Language of The Origin of Species

GILLIAN BEER

EDITOR'S INTRODUCTION

*T*he intellectual as well as the familial kinship between Erasmus Darwin and his grandson Charles Darwin has often been mentioned. Loosely speaking, both were evolutionists and hence faced the shared challenge of recounting in an intellectually convincing manner the long and complex history of nature, both living and inert. Erasmus Darwin's French contemporary, the transformist Lamarck, encountered similar problems, and his prose fell into many of the pitfalls discussed by Beer in relation to Charles Darwin. Yet the differences between *On the Origin of Species* (1859) and earlier evolutionary writings are of fundamental importance, especially the style of argument. In Lamarck's *Philosophie Zoologique* (1809) and later in Robert Chambers's *Vestiges of the Natural History of Creation* (1844), we are presented with an abstract overview of cosmic change, generalized developmental mechanisms, and relatively sparing examples. Darwin, by contrast, offers, as Beer points out, a rich, full narrative, replete with lengthy descriptions of the natural world packed with sensual detail, in a conversational tone which invites the reader in. Part of Darwin's success thus lay in his capacity to tell a convincing story, his masterly command of language, and his sophisticated approach to his own linguistic practices.

Yet Darwin, like all other writers, revealed far more than his conscious thoughts in his writings — a situation which enables us to unpack some of the deep complexities of his thought by a close reading of his prose. Beer takes the presence of 'man' in *The Origin* as a case study in a larger inquiry into the nature of what she calls 'evolutionary narrative'. Darwin was certainly aware of the problems man posed for him in *The Origin* and made what seems like a conscious decision to remain silent as far as he could on the question. Yet, as Beer says, readers were quick to seize the implications of Darwin's argument for man's place in nature. But she also shows how man appears in the language of *The Origin*, in the metaphors, in the personifications, in the very terminology.

Nature, Beer stresses, was always feminine for Darwin, enabling her to appear benevolent and maternal. In the long history of the personification of nature as female, other implications have also surfaced: Nature may be a virgin, to be raped or more gently penetrated, a goddess to be worshipped, a woman whose full nakedness should be revealed, a mother who is above all fecund, and so on. Furthermore, several scholars have suggested that on the precise way in which nature as woman is imaged hangs our whole sense of human rights over nature (Easlea, 1983; Merchant, 1980). This question of the identification of woman with nature is also discussed by Huss in relation to the French historian Jules Michelet. Different notions of nature and of science are at issue here, and also different definitions of the feminine. The full implications of linking woman and nature have yet to be explored, and further work on this topic will certainly demonstrate the potential fruitfulness of studying science and literature together.

Beer further shows that Darwin never treated natural selec-

tion as gendered, conceiving it rather as a sexless force. Yet
the language he used in connection with natural selection did
often suggest intention. One of the main problems to have dog-
ged evolutionary writers is how to describe adaptation and
purpose in nature without implying conscious intentions. Critics were quick to see impiety in a language which seemed to
devalue divine power and the human will by endowing other
parts of nature, such as simple animals, with intention. Beer
compares Darwin with William Paley (1743–1805), the
most widely read natural theologian of the nineteenth century,
for whom any intention that existed in the universe must be
referred back ultimately to the Creator.

The vital point about metaphor, Beer argues, is that it can
contain contradictions. It adds significantly both to the richness of the language and to the author's difficulties in controlling the ways in which his text is read. For Beer this accounts
for the prodigious number of interpretations of Darwin, especially among so-called social Darwinists. Darwin's dense language allows us to 'read between the lines' for beliefs which are
not overtly articulated. For example, she points to Darwin's
'levelling' language which implies a common ground shared by
all organisms and so undercuts the hubris he perceived in
people's behaviour, their tendency to treat beings such as
slaves or natives as 'other' in order to justify their own
privilege.

The equalizing language Darwin uses evokes a sense of kinship, not just among human beings but between them and other
living beings. It is of course precisely this point which was felt
to be most threatening by his critics. Beer shows how *The Origin* is in fact permeated by images of kinship, genealogy,
inheritance, family and descent, for instance in the use of trees
and webs as powerful metaphors. These terms were fundamental to evolutionary thinking, which proclaimed that it was
in terms of production (a natural process) rather than creation

(a supernatural one) that the natural world must be comprehended. Lamarck had also insisted on this distinction between production and creation as a necessary foundation of a historical science of life half a century before *The Origin* appeared (Jordanova, 1984, 85). For him the distinction was a pledge to explain nature in its own terms, having recourse only to directly observable processes or to those closely analogous to them. Such a pledge carried a heavy linguistic burden, to find a language in which nature's productive powers could be conveyed without implying intention or will, qualities associated with creative rather than productive acts. This emphasis on production indicates why the vocabulary Darwin used was so fraught with the associations of human reproduction — the most immediately available experience of production.

Beer's paper is the only one in the book which treats a major text in the history of science, and it shows how such texts can repay literary analysis. This involves breaking down the spurious distinction between style and content, and examining scientific writings as texts to be analysed at many different levels. Beer's article shows how this heightens our awareness of Darwin's arguments, and also enables us to see him in a much fuller context, both social and intellectual. It would be a mistake to draw a rigid distinction between being a scientist engaged in acts of 'discovery' and being a writer. Like so many scientists and medical practitioners Darwin was both a writer *and* an interrogator of nature. The two pursuits went hand in hand. To ask questions of nature, these have to be formulated in language, as do the answers, even before the job of constructing a narrative giving a connected account of a specific aspect of nature has begun. Beer's approach should be applied to many other scientific texts, and, at a more specific level, the theme of 'evolutionary narratives' is a useful one in understanding nineteenth-century culture. The idea of progress assumed general importance, pervading all aspects of thought, and what is 'progress' if not a term for a story of development, the story which the vast majority of nineteenth-century scientists aspired to tell, whether in relation to the earth, organisms, the cosmos or civil society?

———————

Man is a determining absence in the argument of *The Origin of Species* (1859). He appears only once in the first edition as the subject of direct inquiry: that appearance is in the Conclusion of the work and is cast in the future tense. The whole paragraph reads:

> In the distant future I see open fields for far more important researches. Psychology will be based on a new foundation, that of the necessary acquirement of each mental power and capacity by gradation. Light will be thrown on the origin of man and his history. (Darwin, 1968, 458)

The prophetic mode of the last sentence distances into an authoritative but as yet unknown future the matter of the past: origins and history. The vatic opening, 'In the distant future I see open fields', retains, in a manner typical of Darwin's style, an allegorical undertow in a word (here 'fields') working within a scientific discourse. (Langland's Piers Plowman at the beginning of his dream saw 'a faire felde full of folke'.) The poetic and scientific senses are fused by means of the double grammatical function of 'open', primarily verbal but also with an adjectival relationship to 'fields' implied. 'Tomorrow to fresh woods and pastures new', Milton, one of Darwin's most loved writers, ends his elegy *Lycidas*. Any inquiry into the implications for humankind of Darwin's ideas is held beyond the bounds of present knowledge and beyond the bounds of the text. That holding off is accomplished partly by the visionary style with its literary and biblical references ('a new foundation') and partly by the implicit narrative positioning of Darwin (1809–82) at the end of his work in a role like that of Moses — seeing from afar off the promised land.

The style within which Darwin here makes his direct reference to man sustains a vague and noble distance, and thus avoids offence to man's pride. When in 1857 Wallace asked him whether he would discuss man in *The Origin*, Darwin

replied: 'I think I shall avoid the whole subject, as so surrounded with prejudices; though I fully admit that it is the
highest and most interesting problem for the naturalist' (Darwin, 1887, II, 109). And just after the appearance of *The
Origin* he wrote to Jenyns: 'With respect to man, I am very far
from wishing to obtrude my belief; but I thought it dishonest to
quite conceal my opinion. Of course it is open to every one to
believe that man appeared by a separate miracle, though I do
not myself see the necessity or probability' (Darwin, 1887, II,
263–4). So the avoidance of the topic of man is, according to
Darwin, tactical in a wordly sense, or as Ellegård (1958) puts
it, 'diplomatic'. Darwin feared that he would have injured the
success of his book if he had 'paraded, without giving any evidence, my conviction with respect to his origin' (Darwin,
1887, I, 94). Yet it is manifest from the reception of the book
that the exclusion of any discussion of man did *not* prevent his
readers immediately seeing its implications for 'the origin of
man and his history'. Many indeed appear simply to have
ignored the lack of open reference to man and to have grasped
the argument forthwith as centrally concerned with man's descent. In doing this, of course, they were manifesting again precisely the overweening pride which Darwin in his 1830s
notebooks saw as typical of man's ordering of experience:
'Mayo (Philosophy of Living) quotes Whewell as profound
because he says length of days adapted to duration of sleep in
man!! whole universe so adapted!!! and not man to Planets –
instance of arrogance!!' (Gruber and Barrett, 1974, 455).

However much Darwin may have represented to himself
and his correspondents the absence of man from the text as a
matter of diplomatic restraint, the exclusion had an immediate
polemical effect: it removed man from the centre of attention.
An act of will by the reader was required to restore him to his
centrality. This transaction in itself problematized the centrality of man to the natural order. The absence of any reference
to man as the crowning achievement of the natural and super-

natural order made the text subversive: it was – as at some
level it must have been known to be – deeply disquieting. One
question which needs examining is how far Darwin re-endows
his mankind with a special status through linguistic activity,
such as the personification of 'Nature' as female person.
Another problem is to judge the degree of awareness which
Darwin possessed concerning the theoretical implications with
which his style was freighted. Is the sub-text of *The Origin*
simply unavoidably full of human reference (because cast in
human language) or is it knowingly, even strategically, so?

Though Marx oversimplifies Darwin's use of the 'struggle
for existence', his account is valuable for its caustic specifica-
tion of the anthropomorphism embedded in the text. Malthus
emphasized the gap between human numbers and the means of
their support. Marx exactly sees how Darwin diverges from
Malthus, though he interprets as Darwin's *mis*-reading or
insufficient reading of Malthus what was in fact Darwin's
determined re-reading and riposte to him.

> Darwin . . . amuses me when he says he is applying the
> 'Malthusian' theory also to plants and animals, as if with
> Mr. Malthus the whole point were not that he does not
> apply the theory to plants and animals but only to human
> beings – and with geometrical progression – as opposed to
> plants and animals. It is remarkable how Darwin recog-
> nizes among beasts and plants his English society with its
> division of labour, competition, opening-up of new mar-
> kets, 'inventions', and the Malthusian 'struggle for exis-
> tence'. It is Hobbes's *bellum omnium contra omnes*, and one
> is reminded of Hegel's *Phenomenology*, where civil society
> is described as a 'spiritual animal kingdom', while in Dar-
> win the animal kingdom figures as civil society. (Marx and
> Engels, 1965, 128)

Darwin had initially in the 'Big Book' he was writing before
he heard that Wallace also had thought of Natural Selection

used the Hobbesian phrase 'the war of nature' and had quoted Hobbes directly. His later substitution of the word 'struggle' was an attempt to move away from the human into a word which lacked the organized force of war and expressed instead the interpenetration of energies. Moreover, in his account of the 'struggle for existence' he insists on using the term in a 'large and metaphorical sense', and he takes trouble to articulate the varying senses in which he uses it, and to grade the degrees of fictive or metaphoric appropriateness the term possesses. One may argue that his trouble went for nothing, since so many of his contemporaries ignored such velleities and approximated 'the struggle for existence' with Spencer's 'survival of the fittest'. Marx's brief critique is striking for the clarity with which he discriminates the social analogy underlying Darwin's description of the natural order. Darwin, however, did take considerable pains — not always successfully — to avoid legitimating current social order by naturalizing it.

Darwin rejected the pervasive anthropocentrism of natural theology with its assumption of special providence and creation. Instead he imaged a world of infinite interconnection, an 'inextricable web of affinities'. He refused to set man over against the rest of the natural world. In this he concurred with Lyell (1797–1875) who points out how man's preoccupation with himself distorts the records of past natural events:

> It is only within the last century and a half, since Hooke first promulgated his views respecting the connexion between geological phenomena and earthquakes, that the permanent changes effected by these convulsions have excited attention. Before that time, the narrative of the historian was almost exclusively confined to the number of human beings who perished, the number of cities laid in ruins, the value of property destroyed, or certain atmospheric appearances which dazzled or terrified the observers. The creation of a new lake, the engulphing of a city, or the raising of a new island, are sometimes, it is true, adverted to, as being too

obvious, or of too much geographical interest, to be passed over in silence. (Lyell, 1830–3, I, 399)

Darwin concurred also with the theologian Feuerbach, who in the 1840s analysed man's tendency to separate himself equally from the natural order and from the potentialities of his own nature: from the natural order by rejecting the constraints of the physical world; from his own nature, by projecting onto God, and thereby alienating, all those attributes most valued by mankind. Feuerbach saw man's assertion of a special providence as a hubristic claim for dominance and for freedom from natural order:

> Providence is a privilege of man. It expresses the value of man, in distinction from other natural beings and things; it exempts him from the connection of the universe. Providence is the conviction of man of the infinite value of his existence – a conviction in which he renounces faith in the reality of external things; it is the idealism of religion . . . Man distinguishes himself from Nature. This distinction of his is his God. (Feuerbach, 1854, 105–6)

Darwin shared Feuerbach's respect for the material world. Throughout *The Origin* he attempts to subdue the hierarchical nature of man's thought which places himself always at the pinnacle or centre. Even at the celebratory culmination of the work man is not named, not distinguished from the other higher forms of life: 'Thus, from the war of nature, from famine and death, the most exalted object which we are capable of conceiving, namely, the production of the higher animals, directly follows' (Darwin, 1968, 459).

When man does appear, it is to serve as the second term in metaphors – for example, illuminating the social behaviour of ants by an ironic glance at man's class-organization, or as an exterminated tribe whose monuments lie beneath the forest trees. He is the 'artifical selector' whose efforts are disparagingly compared with the power and extent of nature's 'natural selection'. And in later editions Darwin makes it clear that man can neither originate nor obliterate selection. He is disqualified from observing the great movements of natural law by the shortness of his life-span, and he is recalled in a language like that of Ecclesiastes:

> How fleeting are the wishes and efforts of man! how short his time! and consequently how poor will his products be, compared with those accumulated by Nature during whole geological periods. Can we wonder then, that Nature's productions should be far 'truer' in character than man's productions . . . (Darwin, 1968, 133)

Man is less favoured than other species in his progenitive powers, 'even slow-breeding man'. He is a newcomer to history whose social antecedents are brief in the extreme.

A reading of his earlier notebooks reveals the exultant pleasure which Darwin felt in restoring man to an equality with other forms of life and in undermining that hubristic separation which man had accorded himself in all previous natural history:

> Animals whom we have made our slaves we do not like to consider our equals – (do not slave holders wish to make the black man other kind). Animals with affections, imitation, fear of death, pain, sorrow for the dead – respect. (Gruber and Barrett, 1974, 447)

The image of master and slave which Darwin uses suggests the intensity of his distaste for man's tyrannical self-aggrandizement and for the licence which this had led him to feel towards other species. Darwin emphasizes the relativism of the value accorded to diverse properties of consciousness: 'People often talk of the wonderful event of intellectual man appearing – the appearance of insects with other senses is more wonderful. Its mind more different probably and introduction of man nothing compared to the first thinking being, although hard to draw line' (Gruber and Barrett, 1974, 446). The ant's brain, he claims, is a more amazing instrument than that of man, and though man gives the highest value to reason, a bee would do so to instinct.

The early works reveal an exuberant liberation from the constricting separatism of the religious idea of man as specifically created, set apart by soul, and dedicated to a relationship with God – inhabiting essentially a supernatural order which sets him at odds with his natural peers and leads him to scorn his natural inheritance. Adam had the power of naming – and by naming rendered all other forms of life subservient to himself, and to his language and his progeny. As early as 16 August 1838 Darwin notes: 'Origin of man now proved – metaphysics must flourish – he who understands baboon would do more for metaphysics than Locke.' The work of Gruber (Gruber and Barrett, 1974) has demonstrated the continuity of Darwin's interest in psychology and anthropology as aspects of his theory. Gruber's study has made it clear that the absence of man from the text of *The Origin* was not a neutral absence nor one resulting from a lack of concern with human psychology. The enterprise of the present essay is to analyse the ironic counterpoise of Darwin's language in relation to man in nature.

Darwin was in dispute with Max Müller (1823–1900) over Müller's view that language divided man from 'the brutes'. In 1861, without naming Darwin, Müller responded to the implications of *The Origin of Species* in this way:

It might seem, after all, as if the great problems of our being, of the true nobility of our blood, of our descent from heaven or earth, though unconnected with anything that is commonly called practical, have still retained a charm of their own – a charm that will never lose its power on the mind, and on the heart of man. Now, however much the frontiers of the animal kingdom have been pushed forward, so that at one time the line of demarcation between animal and man seemed to depend on a mere fold in the brain, there is *one* barrier which no-one has yet ventured to touch – the barrier of language.

Language is something more palpable than a fold of the brain, or an angle of the skull. It admits of no cavilling, and no process of natural selection will ever distill significant words out of the notes of birds or the cries of beasts. (Müller, 1861–4, I, 357)

Darwin in his notebooks disputed the idea that man alone had a coherent language. Indeed, he considered music to be antecedent to language, and this idea persists throughout the 1830s notebooks and into *The Descent of Man* in the 1870s. He claims that the flute and the epic are two points on the same spectrum. Thus he considered the rhythmic and sensory properties of language to be older and more enduring than its argumentative and sequentially reasoned properties. He links the idea of music to the second great means of evolution after natural selection – that of sexual selection.

Despite his decision to exclude man from his discussion, the tendency of his argument is to range man alongside all other forms of life. The multivocal nature of metaphor allows him to express, without insisting on, kinship, and in his reliance on metaphor he is running counter to Comte, who insisted on the need for single meaning in scientific language. Moreover, man is a familiar in *The Origin* though concealed in its interstices. The activities of planting crops and breeding selected animals allow Darwin to transpose and extend these concepts into the idea of 'natural selection'. Genealogy, with its insistence on 'breeding' and 'inheritance', provides another node of meaning between the values and organization of his own society and those which he infers to be general in the natural order beyond man. The absence of any reference to man as the crowning achievement of the natural and supernatural order made the text disquieting; but the entire absence of man as a point of reference or a point of conclusion would have rendered it nihilistic. Darwin did not reach so extreme a position, though his insistence on the free play of interactions between organism and environment, and his resistance to absolute origins, is expressed both in the multivocality of his metaphors and his argumentative insistence on metamorphosis. It places him and his work equivocally within the debate between 'freeplay and history' described by the French structuralist philosopher Derrida:

> As a turning point toward the presence, lost or impossible, of the absent origin, this structuralist thematic of broken immediateness is thus the sad, *negative*, nostalgic, guilty, Rousseauist facet of the thinking of freeplay of which the Nietzschean *affirmation* — the joyous affirmation of the freeplay of the world and without truth, without origin, offered to an active interpretation — would be the other side. *This affirmation then determines the non-center otherwise than as loss of the center.* And it plays the game without security. For there is a *sure* freeplay: that which is limited to the *substitution* of *given and existing, present*, pieces. In absolute chance, affirmation also surrenders itself to *genetic* indetermination, to the *seminal* adventure of the trace.
>
> There are thus two interpretations of interpretation, of structure, of sign, of freeplay. The one seeks to decipher, dreams of deciphering, a truth or an origin which is free from freeplay and from the order of the sign, and lives like an exile the necessity of interpretation. The other, which is no longer turned toward the origin, affirms freeplay and tries to pass beyond man and humanism, the name man being the name of that being who, throughout the history of metaphysics or of ontotheology — in other words, through the history of all of his history — has dreamed of full pre-

sence, the reassuring foundation, the origin and the end of the game. (Derrida, 1970, 264)

Darwin was a man, writing for men, aware of his own species-characteristics and using a mode of communication permeated with humanistic assumptions – if not supernaturalist ones. He had one specific problem. He could not create a new language peculiar to his discovery. He had to work within a language imbued and active with natural theological assumptions. Presumptions about creation and design had constantly to be contested, yet this contest must, as it were, be dramatized, enacted, within a received language weighted towards that which he seeks to controvert. It is possible that he was freed from some of the difficulties he experienced in expressing the relation of man to the rest of the natural order by his reading of Dickens, whose style insists upon the recalcitrance of objects – their way of mimicking the human order without yielding their own 'thisness', their 'haeccitas'. The theme of hidden yet all-pervading kinship is one which their narratives share. Darwin shares with other Victorian writers, such as Ruskin and Gerard Manley Hopkins, the feeling for the thisness of things which signals both their full presence and their impenetrability, their freeplay, their resistance to interpretation in terms of man's perceptions and needs, and yet man's profound need to join himself to them which may be expressed liguistically through metaphor.

THE PROBLEM OF KINSHIP

Darwin sought to restore man to his kinship with all other forms of life. In that sense Darwin was bent on an enterprise which seemed to accord with the surface ideals of his society and its literature. He sought the restoration of familial ties, the discovery of a lost inheritance, the restitution of pious memory, a genealogical enterprise.

As it is difficult to show the blood relationship between the numerous kindred of any ancient and noble family, even by the aid of a genealogical tree, and almost impossible to do this without this aid, we can understand the extraordinary difficulty which naturalists have experienced in describing, without the aid of a diagram, the various affinities which they perceive between the many living and extinct members of the same great natural class. (Darwin, 1968, 413)

The factor of irony in such a passage, however, is that all these themes, so familiar in the novels and dramas of the time, are here displaced from the class structure of his society. In wishful Victorian literature, working-class heroes and heroines, inheritors restored to their kingdom, prove usually to have aristocratic blood, as in Disraeli's *Sybil*. A concealed aristocratic lineage lies behind them, just as in terms of Bible myth it does for man – the son of God, cast out of his inheritance by his forebears' sin and restored to it by the intercession of the immediate heir. Instead, in Darwinian myth, the history of man is of a difficult and extensive family network which takes in barnacles as well as bears, an extended family which will never permit the aspiring climber – man – quite to forget his lowly origins. In terms of the class organization of his time this is clearly a deeply unpalatable view. Ruskin (1819–1900) denounced 'the vile industries and vicious curiosities of modern science' . . . 'deciphering the filthy heraldries which record the relation of humanity to the ascidian and the crocodile' (1873, 59). Without his analysing or needing to analyse his reasons, therefore, there seem to have been as good social as there were religious reasons for Darwin to attempt to conceal man in the interstices of his text – or to permit him almost to escape beyond its parameters. Moreover, the emphasis on kinship changed the status of words such as 'inhabitants' or 'beings' into a far more egalitarian form: 'When I view all beings not as special creations, but as the lineal descendants of some few beings which lived long before the first bed of the Silurian system was deposited, they seem to me to become ennobled'

(Darwin, 1968, 458). Lineage escapes from class and then from kind: 'We possess no pedigrees or armorial bearings; and we have to discover and trace the many diverging lines of descent in our natural genealogies, by characters of any kind which have long been inherited.' 'Characters' shifts here from heraldic semiology to living characteristics. The utopian drive in Darwin's thinking declares itself in the levelling tendency of his language, which always emphasizes those elements in meaning which make for community and equality and undermines the hierarchical and the separatist.

> When we can feel assured that all the individuals of the same species, and all the closely allied species of most genera, have within a not very remote period descended from one parent, and have migrated from some one birthplace; and when we better know the many means of migration, then, by the light which geology now throws, and will continue to throw, on former changes of climate and of the level of the land, we shall surely be enabled to trace in an admirable manner the former migrations of the inhabitants of the whole world (Darwin, 1968, 457)

In this passage writer and reader are held in comradeship by that initiating 'we'; individuality and community are, equally, promised ('individuals', 'closely allied species', 'one parent', 'one birthplace'); continuity is assured 'the light which geology now throws, and will continue to throw'; affirmation and hope – something rhetorically both beyond and just short of certainty – are expressed: 'we shall surely be enabled to trace in an admirable manner', and history and fullest community are conjoined in 'the former migrations of the inhabitants of the whole world'. 'The inhabitants of the whole world' and their migrations include man, without setting him apart from all the other inhabitants of the whole world: animals, plants, fishes, insects – the whole of animate nature – become one moving and proliferating family. Words like 'parent' and 'birthplace', so often reserved for humankind, are here set at the service of all living forms.

The levelling of man with other species is not, then, in Darwin's thinking a necessarily punitive enterprise. Only man's own hubris makes him feel it as such. To Darwin the multitudinous fecundity and variety of life had more than enough room for man among all other living beings. Whereas Müller sees 'the great problems of our being, of the true nobility of our blood, of our descent from heaven or earth', Darwin emphasized rather the problems of relationship. Where then does Darwin place himself within the text and where does he place the reader?

Though Darwin does not use literary allusions in the way that Lyell does, by direct reference, his style is instinct with biblical organizations and psalmic apostrophe. It is also freighted with a Wordsworthian confidence in the feasible congruence of mind and world, language and referent. Lyell found a place for man within his geological texts through his constant references to literature and through his lyrical praises of man's imaginative powers, which generate the possibility of interpretation and backward understanding even of those great tracts of time before man came to be, in this 'theatre of re-iterated change'. Darwin was more distrustful of man's imaginative powers. Even that sentence 'Thus, from the war of nature, from famine and death, the most exalted object *which we are capable of conceiving*, namely, the production of higher animals, directly follows' has a double meaning. The limits of our conception tend to confirm man as the highest product, but this is not necessarily the case. Although the text is permeated with human references, these are not granted a special attention. They function rather as means of illustration elucidating other forms of life than ours. When human beings enter, they are present in the guise of observers – scientists patiently recording, collecting, and considering: for example on page 338 (Darwin, 1968) Mr Clift, Professor Owen,

Messieurs Lund and Clausen, Mr Woodward and himself: 'I was so much impressed with these facts that I strongly insisted, in 1839 and 1845, on this "law of the succession of types".' Nor is the non-scientific reader excluded from observation: 'a similar relationship is manifest, even to the uneducated eye, in the gigantic pieces of armour like those of the armadillo, found in several parts of La Plata'.

Darwin appears in the text as a speaking voice; his style is active, poised on verbs with their power to generate change. He alludes to his own experiences and acknowledges his debt to other observers. He had frequent recourse to the first person plural and to sentence structures which draw attention to occasion: 'When we' is a typical sentence opening. The reader is drawn into a relationship which appears socially reliable with the persona generated by the discourse of the text. Lyrically expressive exclamation and questioning – which suppose inquiry and reply from the reader – are frequent. The author presents himself not as abstract authority, but as arguer, interpreter of observations, as companion. The effect of this is primarily reassuring, even emollient. The text is very like a travel book – it moves from place to place across the world, flattering the armchair traveller, the reader: 'We see the full meaning of the wonderful fact, which must have struck every traveller, namely, that on the same continent . . .'. His hope is that 'scientific and common language will come into accordance', through a proper respect for specificity, and his movement of mind is always away from essentialism to the variety of substance: 'It is quite possible that forms now generally acknowledged to be merely varieties, may hereafter be thought worthy of specific names, as with the primrose and cowslip; and in this case scientific and common language will come into accordance . . . we shall at least be freed from the vain search for the undiscovered and undiscoverable essence of the term species' (Darwin, 1968, 456).

Being specific is necessary both to the tone and to the argument of *The Origin of Species*. His son Francis Darwin commented on the humility of the style – the first person pronoun is quite frequently used, and often with an edge of humour which calls attention to Darwin as a man writing, and as a man experiencing: 'Systematists will be able to pursue their labours as at present; but they will not be incessantly haunted by the shadowy doubt whether this or that form be in essence a species. This I feel sure, and I speak after experience, will be no slight relief.'

The language of *The Origin* emphasizes the element of address – and implies the presence of both addresser and addressee. Conversation rather than abstraction is the predominant mode, and the emphasis is upon things individually seen, heard, smelt, touched, tasted. The individual presence of the observer in the language is a necessary methodological control, supplementing the work's imaginative history. The exotic instances are brought home for the reader by analogies with our own native landscape and wildlife – these analogies' functions are both loosely illustrative, alerting the reader's own image-making powers, and also more precisely furthering the inquiry into the relationship between habit and environment in bringing about variation:

> I have often watched a tyrant flycatcher (Saurophagus sulphuratus) in South America, hovering over one spot and then proceeding to another, like a kestrel, and at other times standing stationary on the margin of water, and then dashing like a kingfisher at a fish. In our own country the larger titmouse (Parus major) may be seen climbing branches, almost like a creeper; it often, like a shrike, kills small birds by blows on the head; and I have many times seen and heard it hammering the seeds of the yew on a branch, and thus breaking them like a nuthatch. (Darwin, 1968, 215)

The tone of a single man speaking, the presenter of the evidence, the creator of the theory, is a necessary counterpoise to that speculative extension back through time and change which is also crucial to the argument. And the emphasis upon sense experience, particularly colour and touch, means that our medium of experience is not simply necessarily, but warmly, human.

Darwin's delight in the process of discovery and in the material with which he is working, sometimes makes him represent as benign, processes which are not necessarily so. He is generous in his use of intensives; indeed, his children laughed at some of his descriptions as being too like an advertisement. It is at this point that disturbances in his language become registrable. His grandfather had written of mountains that they 'Are Mighty Monuments of Past Delight', representing past pleasure and the felicity of organic life. One strain in Darwin's temperament – and indeed one major premise of his theory – emphasized the tendency towards happiness in living creatures. But in his recognition of 'the appetite for joy' Darwin saw also the extent of suffering which any individual organism might at any one time have to undergo. This was one of his reasons for rejecting the idea of a benign orderer, and this recognition brings about a disturbing oscillation between anthropomorphic and abstract senses within a word. Perhaps one also needs a pair of other terms – anthropocentric and anthropofugal? A word like 'inhabitant' can liberally expand without strain to denote all denizens of an environment – as indeed, of course, it had done already in the writing of biologists well before Darwin. But a word like 'face' has a strong and specific human sense, that of visage, as well as the sense of 'surface' or 'plane' – and in expressions such as 'the face of a mountain' and particularly 'the face of nature' the human presence is hard to expunge. St George Mivart, writing on instinct and reason, complains of Darwin's 'biological anthropomorphism', by which he means 'the attribution of human qualities to brutes', for example 'maternal tenderness' (1875, 773).

PERSONS AND PRODUCTION

In the first edition of *The Origin* both nature and natural selection have grammatically the function of agents – and, moreover, despite his later exasperation with the issue, Darwin does endow them in his language with a latent activity. If one examines a sentence like the one that occurs on page 219 (1968), there is a noticeable difference between the apparently parallel functions (both grammatical and ideological) accorded to variation, generation, and natural selection: 'In living bodies, variation will cause the slight alterations, generation will multiply them almost infinitely, and natural selection will pick out with unerring skill each improvement.' Variation causes, generation multiplies, but natural selection 'picks out with unerring skill'. The implication of an active and external agent is far stronger in the last term. It would be a mistake, though, to dwell upon the animistic qualities of this metaphor in isolation. In part Darwin is suffering simply the recalcitrance of human language, which is permeated with intention. But the argument about the eye, of which this sentence is a part, is one passage where he turns back worsted from an attempt to describe an unintended order and complexity and has recourse instead to a language which draws heavily on that of Paley (1743–1805): 'May we not believe that a living optical instrument might thus be formed as superior to one of glass, as the works of the Creator are to those of man?' Paley had used a comparison of telescope and eye to point out that 'in comparing the eyes of different kinds of animals, we see in their resemblances and distinctions, one general plan laid down' (Paley, 1830, 22). Examination of the eye, Paley said, was a cure for atheism.

The passages in which he personified nature and natural selection are some of those with which Darwin most often struggled in later editions. One problem he faced was the tendency of readers to personify natural selection and to see it as an active, intentionalist force ('Some have even imagined that natural selection induces variability . . .'), or as representing immanent intention ('others have objected that the term selection implies conscious choice in the animals which become modified'). Darwin's answer is to point out the metaphorical nature of language in other scientific propositions — and strikingly he points to terms which had already been taken up and recast in literary language by Goethe in the title of his novel *Die Wahlverwandschaften*: elective affinities. In the third edition Darwin writes:

> In the literal sense of the word, no doubt, natural selection is a misnomer; but whoever objected to chemists speaking of the elective affinities of the various elements? — and yet an acid cannot strictly be said to elect the base with which it will in preference combine. It has been said that I speak of natural selection as an active power or deity; but who objects to an author speaking of the attraction of gravity as ruling the movements of the planets. Everyone knows what is meant and is implied by such metaphorical expressions; and they are almost necessary for brevity. So again it is difficult to avoid personifying the word nature; but I mean by nature, only the aggregate action and product of many natural laws and by laws the sequence of events as ascertained by us. With a little familiarity such superficial objections will be forgotten. (Darwin, 1959, 165)

Elsewhere Darwin himself used powerfully the phrase 'the inextricable web of affinities'. In it he combines the space-free language of chemistry 'affinities', the genealogical language of the table of affinities, and the space-and-sight-bound language of 'weaving' and the spider's web.

His grandfather Erasmus Darwin had already noted the speed and ease with which personification takes place in English. Since English is an ungendered language one need only add a 'his' or 'hers' to turn a word into a personification. With personification enters intention. Darwin expands further

on the problem of intention which lurks in all language, drawing as it does upon human experience and human ordering of
experience. He notes the latent metaphor in 'ruling' – the
notion of order and intention – and then he appeals to general
usage as his authority: 'every one knows'. The problem, of
course, for the reader was that everyone did *not* know what
was meant by natural selection – the term was a neologism and
therefore stood forth with full metaphorical expressiveness and
personifying power.

> It may be said that natural selection is daily and hourly
> scrutinising, throughout the world, every variation, even
> the slightest; rejecting that which is bad, preserving and
> adding up all that is good; silently and insensibly working,
> whenever and wherever the opportunity offers, at the
> improvement of each organic being in relation to its organic
> and inorganic conditions of life. (Darwin, 1968, 133)

In the second edition he varies this to 'may metaphorically be
said'.

The sense of a brooding presence was perhaps reinforced
by the way in which he distinguished the gender of nature and
natural selection. Nature is always 'she', whereas natural
selection is neuter – the neuter becomes a form of sex, a sexless
force. In the third edition he parallels it to the 'survival of the
fittest', a natural process, whose terminology he borrows from
Huxley and which falls dangerously in with the Spencerian
notion of an accord between moral fitness and the ability to
survive. But in the early editions natural selection cannot
avoid a personified presence in his text. In the mythological
order of his language it appears as an aspect or avatar of the
more general 'nature', whose maternal ordering is contrasted
with the egocentric one of Man. She tends and nurses with
scrupulous concern for betterment. The word 'Man' in this
polarization achieves a masculine rather than a fully inclusive
use of the word, and this effect is reinforced by the working

world with which he is associated: a world of inadequate discrimination, lacking refinement of attention.

> Man selects only for his own good; Nature only for that of
> the being she tends. Every selected character is fully exer-
> cised by her; and the being is placed under well-suited con-
> ditions of life. Man keeps the natives of many climates in the
> same country; he seldom exercises each selected character
> in some peculiar and fitting manner. (Darwin, 1968, 132)

In later editions Darwin attempts to deconstruct the mythological personage Nature — sometimes equating her with natural
selection, sometimes with the complexity of interpenetrating
laws. Are the objections to his use of Nature superficial, as he
suggests? Certainly, his usages do not invalidate his attempt to
find a non-teleological language. But the struggle he has,
comes in part from his relations to natural theology, and from
the need to expand the material order rather than to leave a
metaphysical void. He has to put something in the space left
by God. He is determined to avoid a creationist language,
though even here he had difficulties with passive forms, for
example, 'the preservation of favoured races in the struggle for
life'.

Description tends always to create its own metaphysic, and
we see this process at work in this text. For example, when he
writes that 'the natural system is a genealogical arrangement',
it is still possible to substitute 'obvious' for 'natural' in that first
form, 'the obvious system is a genealogical arrangement'. In
the fifth edition this becomes the Natural System. It has the
authority of a nominated system rather than of simple description.

He is seeking to transform the occult into the natural, to
substantiate metaphor. His world is the fertile profuse creativity of generation, and he specifically formulates his theory as a
means of discovering the fullness of life as it is, has been, and
will be on this earth. His is no sidereal study. The same

emphasis upon materiality, upon physical experience, tends to allow for the renewed presence of the personified and the person.

Darwin's personification of nature as female was, of course, part of a long tradition. In Ovid's proto-geological account in the fifteenth book of the *Metamorphoses* which Lyell cites in the first chapter of *The Principles of Geology*, Deucalion is instructed to throw behind him the bones of his great mother. It is a usage which can be found both in contemporary literature and in other scientific writing of the period: for example Alexander Combe in 1836 writes that 'Nature is more willing to do her part than we are to do ours', and John Tyndall in 1860 remarks that 'In the application of her own principles, Nature often transcends the human imagination'. Gerard Manley Hopkins (1844–89) in 'That Nature is a Heraclitean Fire and of the Comfort of the Resurrection' emphasizes equally the maternal and the reckless in nature's nature:

> Million-fuel'd, nature's bonfire burns on.
> But quench her bonniest, dearest to her, her clearest-selved
>   spark
> Man, how fast his firedint, his mark on mind, is gone.
>   (Hopkins, 1967, 105)

Kingsley's (1819–75) Tom in *The Water Babies* – a book written under the immediate influence of Darwin's ideas – discovers the creative principle at the end in the guise of a woman dreaming on a rock in the middle of the sea, from which all creatures seethe and flow:

> He expected, of course – like some grown people who ought to know better – to find her snipping, piecing, fitting, stitching, cobbling, basting, filing, planing, hammering, turning, polishing, moulding, measuring, chiselling, clipping, and so forth, as men do when they go to work to make anything.

> But, instead of that, she sat quite still with her chin upon
> her hand, looking down into the sea . . . (Kingsley, 1863,
> 313)

The effects of personifying nature as female are manifold: but
for the purposes of this argument there are two particularly
important effects — one is to distinguish nature from God, the
second is to ascribe a benign surveillance to the natural world.
Emerson in his essay on 'Nature', which Darwin read, spoke
of it as the secularization of nature. In a more popular work
like J. G. Wood's *Nature's Teachings: Human Invention
Anticipated by Nature* (1877), science is gendered as female in
a way that tends to equate science reassuringly with nature: 'It
is, therefore, partially true that science does destroy romance.
But, though she destroys, she creates, and she gives infinitely
more than she takes away . . .' (Wood, 1877, 2). In Darwin's
use of the word 'nature', vulnerability and suffering are also
emphasized.

FACES AND WEDGES

How to control the emotional force of words becomes a
specific difficulty for Darwin's argument in the case of 'faces'
and, curiously, 'wedges'. Recently, both Gruber (1980) and
Colp (1979) have discussed Darwin's imagery of wedging
and wedges. They point out that despite the appearance of the
'wedge' metaphor in Notebook 3 (1838), and in the 1842 and
1844 essays and in the 'Big Book' on natural selection, Darwin removed it from *The Origin of Species* after the first edition. Colp speculates on the sexual and unconscious significa-
tion of wedging for Darwin. He links its appearance in Darwin's thought to his imminent marriage and also to his feelings
towards his *Wedgwood* relations, and he considers that it 'may
have come to symbolise Darwin's assertion of himself in the
areas of work, sex, money, and resistance to opposition'
(Colp, 1979, 1627). Gruber writes: 'It would be interesting
to know why Darwin dropped it, since it does convey dramat-

ically the way in which variation and struggle continuously dis-equilibrate the natural order at almost every point in space and time' (Gruber, 1980, 513). This is exact, but, like all Darwin's major metaphors, 'wedging' holds in counterpoise contradictory or divergent implications, signifying equally, holding, splitting, stabilizing and destabilizing. This multivocality may have been one reason for Darwin's later withdrawal of the image, since the movement of later editions is away from language whose implications cannot be contained.

One can understand some of the problems created for Darwin by the anthropomorphic tendency of metaphor by looking in more detail at the particular relationship between the image of the wedge and wedging and Darwin's image of nature. Comte had written scornfully of 'the imaginary law of the imaginary being, Nature' and had pointed to the dangers of introducing intent through metaphor. In later editions Darwin struggled to control the personification, in the second edition by changing lower-case nature to Nature, and then in the third edition inserting a demurring and specifying description of what he means by Nature. So we move from 'Man can act only on external and visible characters: nature cares nothing for appearances', with its suggestion of a higher morality in nature's concern for use rather than show ('she cares nothing for appearances' invokes a Jane Austen style of characterization), to 'Man can act only on external and visible characters: Nature (if I may be allowed thus to personify the natural preservation of varying and favoured individuals during the struggle for existence) cares nothing for appearances.' Throughout the first edition of *The Origin of Species* 'Nature' is closely related in attributes both to the Great Mother and to Athena. And even in later editions this passage still continues: 'She can act on every internal organ' and 'Every selected character is exercised by her'.

If we look now at the passages in which Darwin uses the wedge imagery we can see that anthropomorphic problems in language develop in two ways: one, in the implied presence of a figure wielding a hammer. The problem of an implied external agent, of course, beset Darwin at every turn in language, but was particularly acute in a workaday image drawing on human activity. Colp cites his description in 1831 of his geologist's hammer: 'a heavy hammer, with its two ends wedge-formed and truncated' (Barrett, 1977, I, 248). This suggestion of external agent can be subdued so long as the metaphor is focused strictly on the force of the wedges themselves. In 1838 Darwin writes in his notebook: 'One may say there is a force like a hundred thousand wedges trying [to] force every kind of adapted structure into the gaps in the economy of nature, or rather forming gaps by thrusting out weaker ones' (Gruber and Barrett, 1974, 135). In 1842 he writes: 'a thousand wedges are being forced into the economy of nature' (de Beer, 1958, 47). In 1844 this becomes 'Nature may be compared to a surface, in which rest ten thousand sharp wedges touching each other and driven inward by incessant blows', and he continues: 'reflect on the countless seed scattered by a hundred ingenious contrivances, year after year, over the whole face of the land' (de Beer, 1958, 118). In 1857 in the chapter of his unpublished major study called 'The Struggle for Existence' he describes the activity thus:

> Nature may be compared to a surface covered with ten-thousand wedges, many of the same shape representing different species, all packed closely together and all driven in by incessant blows: the blows being far severer at one time than at another; sometimes a wedge of one form and sometimes another being struck; the one driven deeply in forcing out others; with the jar and shock often transmitted very far to other wedges in many lines of direction: beneath the surface we may suppose that there lies a hard layer, fluctuating in its level, and which may represent the minimum amount of food required by each living being, and which layer will

be impenetrable by the sharpest wedge. (Stauffer, 1975, 208)

The description of vigorous and varying activity, the emphasis on blows, on jar and shock, give the reader the close sense of bodily experience. Yet the organization of the comparison is in terms of simile, not metaphor: 'may be compared to', 'representing', 'we may suppose', 'which may represent'. There is a discrepancy between the elaboration and immediacy of experience and the functional properties of the similes in the argument. The experiential here dominates, and may also confuse: what status in argument has 'the jar and shock' we feel? Is it descriptive of a natural process, or offering us an analogy based in our own experience?

In the chapter on 'The Struggle for Existence' in *The Origin*, Darwin opens with an admission of the sheer imaginative *difficulty* of bearing constantly in mind the struggle for life: 'We behold the face of nature bright with gladness, we often see superabundance of food.' This vivid passage, with its open personification of nature, its sense of joy checked by an apprehension of destructiveness – 'we do not see, or we forget, that the birds which are idly singing round us mostly live on insects or seeds, and are thus constantly destroying life' – is charged with that imaginative zest, the vitality of shifting forces, which epitomizes Darwin's relationship to the natural world. It is followed only two pages later by the following dark passage:

In looking at Nature, it is most necessary to keep the foregoing considerations always in mind – never to forget that every single organic being around us may be said to be striving to the utmost to increase in numbers; that each lives by a struggle at some period of its life; that heavy destruction inevitably falls either on the young or old, during each generation or at recurrent intervals. Lighten any check, mitigate the destruction ever so little, and the number of the species will almost instantaneously increase to any amount. The face of Nature may be compared to a yielding surface, with ten thousand sharp wedges packed close together and driven inwards by incessant blows, sometimes one wedge being struck, and then another with greater force. (Darwin, 1968, 119)

The wedge imagery is here summarized and placed in apposition to Nature – not 'the economy of Nature', or 'the surface', but 'the face of Nature'.

The drive towards actualization has created an image so grotesque, so disturbingly figurative of violence, in which the barriers between earth and body have so far vanished, that the wedge image has become shockingly sadistic in a way that effaces its argumentative usefulness. Emotionally, it does correspond to Darwin's most sombre sense of the individual within the natural order – 'The face of Nature may be compared to a yielding surface, with ten thousand sharp wedges packed close together and driven inwards by incessant blows' – but the progressive condensations of language over the various versions have here resulted in an image of uncontrollably intense and repellent anthropomorphism. The last sentence of the paragraph is excised in all future editions.

That Darwin was much beset by the tendency of metaphor to become more concrete than was intended – for the second term to achieve a dominant position in meaning – is made clear by the argument which intervenes between these two passages about 'the face of Nature'. Although scientists may often seek to substantiate their models, Darwin was sensitively and unusually aware of the spectrum of fictionality both within specific metaphors and between diverse metaphors in the context of an argument. So, though he seeks to show that 'metamorphosis' is a real process and not part simply of Ovid's mythical fictions, he is chary of the social implications of 'the struggle for existence'. It is immediately after that first mention of 'the face of Nature' that he remarks: 'I should premise that I use the term "Struggle for Existence" in a large and metaphorical sense', ranging from the actuality of dogs struggling for food 'in a time of dearth' to mistletoe which 'can only in a far-fetched sense be said to struggle with these trees'. This insistence on proper estrangement as well as proper congruity in the making of metaphor, shows Darwin's shrewd distrust of too close an approximation of other forms of life to foreknown human experience – which will always tend to take over and dominate our interpretation of material – as it does in the passage later excised.

METAPHOR AND THE PROBLEM OF CREATION

The quagmire of the metaphoric troubles Darwin, yet he needs it. He needs its tendency to suggest more than you meant to say, to make the latent actual, to waken sleeping dogs, and equally its powers of persuasion through lassitude, through our inattention. Analogy, suspect though it has always been to scientists, was one of the great tools of nineteenth-century evolutionary theory. Moreover, analogy was not simply a tool of theory, but was itself part of theory. There was an emphasis on analogous structures and movements, and these analogies are not a matter of coincidence, they are essential to the structural history of life on earth. Thus the biological evidence authenticated the linguistic method. Analogy and morphology are both concerned with discovering structures common to diverse forms. Analogy and metaphor express kinship, disturb hierarchy, make us look again at the orderings of our value systems (Hesse, 1966; Black, 1962). In his early essay entitled 'Are There Real Analogies in Nature' Clerk Maxwell insists upon the need for the 'excenterisation' of man. The images of the wedges and the face of nature which we have just been examining, demonstrate the problems in language and implication when anthropocentrism takes over.

All Darwin's metaphors have varying and often contradictory elements within their meanings – elements which point towards and away from man: for example, the tree is both genealogical, the tree of man, and the great tree of nature which has no particular regard for man. It is also both an oppressive colonial image and an organic image. In a poem published ten years before *The Origin of Species* these diverse connotations are spelled out. In A.H. Clough's (1819–61) *The Bothie* the following passage occurs:

> I don't myself feel always,
> As I have felt, more sorrow for me, these four days lately,
> Like the Peruvian Indians I read about last winter,
> Out in America there, in somebody's life of Pizarro;
> Who were as good perhaps as the Spaniards; only weaker;
> And that the one big tree might spread its roots and
> > branches,
> All the lesser about it must even be felled and perish.
> No, I feel much more as if I, as well as you, were,
> Somewhere, a leaf on the one great tree, that, up from old
> > time
> Growing, contains in itself the whole of the virtue and life of
> Bygone days, drawing now to itself all kindreds and
> > nations,
> And must have for itself the whole world for its root and
> > branches.
> No, I belong to the tree, I shall not decay in the shadow.
> > (Clough, 1968, 165)

Darwin, watching the oppression of the Indians by the Spaniards and recording it in the voyage of the *Beagle*, had also seen the implications of 'natural' selection in the human world.

The presence of man in metaphor, analogy and literary allusion in the text, together with his exclusion from its argument, has one profound and troubling effect. The suppression of the human means that man lurks as an uncontrolled element in the argument. The appropriation of Darwinian biological ideas to social Darwinism was made possible partly because of this evasion. Man's relationship to the description of the organization of life is not precisely delimited, and the metaphors which call on his activities outgo their status in the text and generate fresh consequences.

Darwin's copious use of surface metaphor as well as implicit model, and of analogy, encourages the acts of recognition by which we scan for the elements suppressed as well as expressed within an argument – and by that means glimpse the disanalogous within the activity of analogy. One of Darwin's most thoroughgoing invocations of analogy shows this procedure at work:

> I believe that animals have descended from at most four or five progenitors and plants from an equal or lesser number. Analogy would lead me one step further, namely, to the belief that all animals and plants have descended from some one prototype. But analogy may be a deceitful guide. Nevertheless all living things have much in common, in their chemical composition, their general vesicals, their cellular structure, and their laws of growth and reproduction. We see this even in so trifling a circumstance as that the same poison often similarly affects plants and animals; or that the poison secreted by the gadfly produces monstrous growths on the wild rose or oak tree. Therefore I should infer from analogy that probably all the organic beings which have ever lived on this earth have descended from one primordial type, into which life was first breathed. (Darwin, 1959, 753)

The 'progenitor', the 'prototype', 'one primordial form', the original parent, here takes a notably un-Adamic form, but the problem of the generation of the progenitor lurks in the analogy and is skirted in that final clause 'into which life was first breathed'. In the second edition Darwin succumbed briefly to the creationist implications and added 'by the creator' to the end of the sentence. It is a curious reversal after his scornful queries on the previous page. But he thought better of this again and simply deleted the whole clause from later editions, so that the sentence ends as his inquiry must with 'some one primordial form'. G. H. Lewes was perhaps the first to point out the residue of the theistic in that idea of the one form and to suggest instead that it would be possible to substitute a germinal membrane active throughout the whole world.

The problem of creationist language has been raised again recently, in terms that perhaps cast light on a hidden knot in Darwin's relation to theories of creation and generation. Pierre Macherey, the Marxist literary theorist, in *Towards a Theory of Literary Production* (1978) polemically substitutes the word 'production' for that of 'creation' to describe the formation of literary texts. With no apparent awareness that he is continuing an argument already broached by Darwin, he comments:

> Les diverses 'théories' de la création ont ceci de commun qu'elles traitent le problème de ce passage qu'est une fabrication en éliminant l'hypothèse d'une fabrication ou d'une production. (The various theories of creation have in common that they treat what is a made object by eliminating the hypothesis of making an object or of production.) (1974, 85)

These remarks come in the context of an argument concerning humanism as a merely superficial criticism of religious ideology. The humanist, Macherey says, simply places man at the centre where God used to be – and anthropology is nothing but an attenuated theology: 'à la place du Dieu-homme, est installé l'Homme' ([humanism] puts man in the place of God – incarnate) (1974, 83).

Darwin's major concern was to emphasize the workings of natural law and to avoid the issue of final causes, though Lyell wittily observed that he tended to deify secondary causes: 'the production and extinction of the past and present inhabitants of the world have been due to secondary causes'. But another aspect of his polemical enterprise was to undermine the pseudo-religion which placed *man* alternatively at the centre of the universe's attention and significance. The rhetorical means that he discovered for expressing his dissent from anthropocentrism was to exclude the figure of man from the text as a topic for debate, while at the same time he employs the human to serve the purposes of his argument — an argument whose attention was focused on all the other inhabitants, present and past, of the globe. Man is never the subject — he is subjected to ends that refer always out beyond him.

But there was another problem of position and of language for Darwin to solve which is also signalled by Macherey's more general argument. I do not think that Darwin would have recognized the terms in which Macherey proposes it, but I do believe that it is a difficulty inherent in his text and in its status in our culture. How far did Darwin figure himself as creating what he describes? He was producing a text certainly, creating an argument. Because of the nature of that argument he could not rely upon a fully experimental method. He was obliged to work in terms of an imaginative history. He moved outside the protecting terms of Baconian induction into a role more like that of a 'creative artist'. All his creative energy was concentrated on authenticating his account of the way in which species had been formed (the usual shortened form of the title loses both the element of narrative and of specific means in 'On the Origin of Species by Means of Natural Selection'). The 'great facts' which Darwin perceived were expressed through a profusion of example and through a profusion of metaphor. They demanded an imaginative re-ordering of experience. *The Origin of Species* was itself a work which could only too easily be cast by its critics as speculative and utopian, fascinated with its own ethnography in the style of Utopias from

Thomas More on. And although the dismissive edge of such criticism may have passed away, there is still a sense in which we hold Darwin *responsible* for his history of the world, as though he had created rather than simply observed the processes he records. There is some justice in that too, because the highly individualistic yet culture-bound language of *The Origin*, with its terms like 'the struggle for life', 'the great family' and 'natural selection', its ransacking of contemporary ideologies, has had consequences beyond the control or cognizance of the text which engendered them. So Darwin is in a creationist dilemma. He wishes simply to record orders which in no way depend upon him. But because of his highly charged imaginative language and the need to invent fresh terms and to forge new metaphorical connections, he appears to perform an individual creative act. His text has a progenitive power. He seeks to express the equivalence of man with all other forms of life, but the power and novelty of the text makes it appear that Darwin, man's representative, has as much created as described.

ACKNOWLEDGMENT
A shorter version of this essay is published as part of chapters 2 and 3 in *Darwin's Plots: Evolutionary Narrative in Darwin, George Eliot and Nineteenth-Century Fiction*, Routledge & Kegan Paul, 1983.

FURTHER READING

Brooks, 1984	Jones, 1980
Derrida, 1976	Manier, 1978
Foucault, 1970	Miller, 1963
Gillespie, 1979	Politi, 1977
Hesse, 1979	Young, 1969

Fairy Tale or Science? Physiological Psychology *in* Silas Marner

SALLY SHUTTLEWORTH

EDITOR'S INTRODUCTION

Georgetype Eliot participated in the same general intellectual culture as Darwin did, and was, indeed, much influenced by him, as she was by many other prominent scientific and philosophical writers. Educated Victorians were, in fact, preoccupied with a central, related set of issues (some of which have already been alluded to by Beer) which spread beyond narrow disciplinary boundaries. The nature of kinship, for example, of fundamental concern to Darwin, is also interrogated in *Silas Marner* (1861), which takes as one of its themes the conflict between the claims of a good adoptive father (Silas) and an inadequate biological father (Godfrey Cass). In this chapter Shuttleworth focuses on the interrelated social and psychological assumptions in *Silas Marner* and shows how these were part of larger evolutionary debates.

From the discussion of Darwin in the previous chapter, it emerged that metaphor and analogy were central to his task. Analogy, for instance, allowed him to move freely in his argument from the life of an individual to that of a species or race. One of the most potent aspects of nineteenth-century evolutionary theory was its capacity to draw different levels of natural or social phenomena together into a single synthesis.

Shuttleworth stresses that this flexibility applied particularly to psychology, where theorists extended the laws which governed matter and life to include the realm of the mind. This development of physiological theories of psychology was accompanied, however, by a growing scepticism towards the more settled and traditional notions of the continuity of mental activity. Such scepticism has a determining impact on the plot of *Silas Marner*, for the most decisive events of Silas's life occur whilst he is in a fit or trance, deathlike in his lack of awareness. His mental life and memory are not continuous but are subject to radical disruption.

Shuttleworth explores the reasons for Eliot's employment of this device, and suggests some of its more far-reaching implications. One of these implications concerns the importance attached to an individual's memory as a guarantee of a secure, seamless, continuous self. Shuttleworth indicates how Eliot links ideas of personal identity to those of social environment: the self is constructed through a process of constant interaction between the individual and the social medium. The spheres of social and psychological life are, for Eliot, inseparable. Her explorations of psychological continuity are thus directly related to her investigations into the bases of social community. In each case she is fundamentally concerned with the issue of integration.

Eliot's preoccupation with ideas of community and integration stems, in part, from her interest in organicist social theories which rose to prominence in the nineteenth century. Although the idea of comparing society to a natural organism was not a new one, the analogy acquired a greater range of meaning and a new seriousness and authority in this period. Raymond Williams (1963; 1983, 227–9) has demonstrated the significant breadth of meanings which can be contained by the notion of an 'organic' society, including agricultural, industrialized, conservative, traditional and planned, some of which, of course, are contradictory. In exploring the bases of

organic community in *Silas Marner*, Eliot investigated some of
these contradictions.

The Victorian use of the concept of an 'organic' society
helps illustrate two points which have been made earlier in this
book. The first is the importance of terms that can contain a
range of meanings, and so generate fruitful as well as more
troublesome ambiguities. The second concerns the social
implications of scientific terms. It may seem inappropriate to
designate 'organic' as a scientific term, but this course has been
followed in order to suggest the term's centrality in biological
and psychological work as well as in social thought, and also to
stress how nineteenth-century usage depended on a particular
way of understanding organisms as coordinated systems. It
should not be thought that we are discussing terms which come
up in one realm and are then applied to or borrowed by
another. On the contrary, as Shuttleworth shows, these terms
emerged in a context where a range of meanings was ascribed
to them from the first, precisely because people were
interested in how the individual and the social, the bodily and
the mental, functioned as different, or analogous, aspects of
the same natural phenomena. Movement between levels was
built into the language. An excellent example of this shift can
be found in the language of habit, repetition, channelling and
pathways which George Eliot used in *Silas Marner*. In
employing this vocabulary she drew on a well-established
tradition which sought to explain mental phenomena in
naturalistic terms and by analogy with other physical processes such as geological erosion. Shuttleworth argues, in fact,
that there was a single vocabulary which could be employed to
describe physiological, mental or social life. The idea of con-
tinuities between these different levels was thus encoded within
a common language. Without such a language, these relationships would, quite probably, have been conceptualized in
entirely different terms. The idea that language is constitutive
of scientific ideas was recognized in the eighteenth and

nineteenth centuries. For example, Shuttleworth points to Bichat's argument that the vocabulary of the physical sciences was taken as paradigmatic rather than that of biology since the former developed first. When Bichat was writing, the sciences of life were less well-established than in Eliot's day and their fragility heightened his sense that a robust science should have its own vigorous language. George Eliot's own intimate associates, George Henry Lewes and Herbert Spencer, were particularly involved with the life sciences, using them as the foundation for both their psychology and social philosophy. The dominance of biological language in nineteenth-century social thought, in fact, bears clear witness to the enhanced strength of the life sciences.

By writing fiction Eliot was able to endow biological and psychological ideas with a specificity more theoretical accounts lacked. Through the concrete world of her novels, which locates characters within very specific environments, Eliot is able to explore both the implications and limitations of contemporary theories. Her descriptions of Silas's fits offer a case in point. Eliot is here drawing on the growing interest in the unconscious elements in human nature during the mid-Victorian era. Her use of catalepsy in this novel suggests just one aspect of her wider concern with unconscious processes. Thus in *Daniel Deronda* (1876), for example, she chose to explore the role of dreams, and of mental associations which appear, superficially, inexplicable.

Whilst some critics have tended to view Silas's cataleptic trances at some of the most crucial moments of his life as a sign of weak plotting, Shuttleworth suggests that they actually highlight Eliot's uneasiness about continuous, progressive development, be it of individuals or societies. *Silas Marner* explores both the positive features of an organic community and its limitations. In both cases, memory, whether individual or collective, is one of the main keys to good social and natural relationships. Silas comes back to a full mental life, and actually achieves new depths of awareness as he raises the little girl, Eppie, who found her way to his cottage as her drug-addicted mother was dying in the snow nearby. The growth of the child stands as a metaphor for Silas's psychological development and also for his increasing social integration into the village community — a fine example of how the different levels of analysis are brought together. Growth is an important expression of continuity, whether within a single life or over generations. It is presumably because of the shared experience of growth and the closeness it brings that Eppie rejects her 'real', i.e. biological, father Godfrey Cass, in favour of Silas. Her whole sense of identity has been constructed around her adopted father and his social class, into which she also marries, so that George Eliot can draw clear social implications from the story about the barrenness of the early nineteenth-century squirarchy — another transition from the individual level of analysis to that of the moral and the social.

In *Silas Marner*, George Eliot employed a number of important, if controversial, ideas from contemporary social and psychological theory, never treating them uncritically but rather examining their weaknesses and limitations. Eliot's fictional explorations of these ideas can be clearly set within the wide context of general nineteenth-century scientific debates. Eliot's questioning of continuous psychological development parallels, for example, the nineteenth-century conflict in geological theory between uniformitarianism, which posited a continuous, law-governed history of nature, and catastrophism, which detected sudden, dramatic leaps and changes like the Flood. In turning to theories of physiological psychology to explain the actions of her characters, Eliot enters into the whole mind/body debate which took on both renewed significance and vehemence in the mid-century. The controversies surrounding hypnotism and mesmerism, for instance, represented only one aspect of a wider controversy concerning unconscious processes — elements of the mind which escaped the dominating control of the will. Eliot's analysis of the role of habit in determining behaviour links to one of the most hotly debated aspects of evolutionary theory, which was fully canvassed in discussions about the inheritance of acquired characteristics (Bowler, 1983). For Eliot, the crucial issue was a moral one: how far an individual may be held responsible for his or her actions. In exploring the ramifications of this question she engages centrally with contemporary scientific debate.

Silas Marner sheds considerable light on mid-Victorian science, philosophy and social thought. George Eliot's explorations of the complexity of the language of nature, and the contradictions and ambiguities it contained, reveal the profound implications for social relations of scientific discourse.

George Eliot's own account of the origins of *Silas Marner* has encouraged readers to view the novel as a simple fairy tale. 'It came to me first of all, quite suddenly', she wrote to her publisher, 'as a sort of legendary tale, suggested by my recollection of having once, in early childhood, seen a linen-weaver with a bag on his back' (Haight, 1954–78, III, 382). The novel's opening picture confirms this legendary vision: it speaks of pale 'alien-looking men [who] appeared on the upland, dark against the early winter sunset', weighed down by a mysterious burden. This evocation of mystery and the inexplicable, framed within the archetypal division between dark and light, provides a fit opening for a tale of 'natural magic', in which the weaver Silas's lost guineas are transformed into the golden curls of the child Eppie. Yet readers should not be misled by the apparent simplicity of the novel's form. Eliot's choice of the fairy tale mode for this novel does not suggest a retreat from the complexity of her earlier work, but rather an increasingly sophisticated use of her narrative medium. The narrative form of *Silas Marner* both reflects and comments upon one of the novel's dominant themes: the issue of social evolution or development.

Throughout *Silas Marner* Eliot interrogates ideas of social and psychological development current in mid-nineteenth-century social and scientific debate: the legendary form of the work, the magical aspects of the tale, and the study of the primitive superstitions of Raveloe life all contribute to her exploration of contemporary theories of social change and progress. Behind the structure of *Silas Marner* lie the theories of the mythic imagination promulgated by the radical theologians and philosophers David Friedrich Strauss and Ludwig Feuerbach, whose works *The Life of Jesus* (1837) and *The Essence of Christianity* (1841) the young Marian Evans had translated in 1846 and 1854. More importantly, perhaps, one can also detect the influence of the social philosopher Auguste Comte's (1798–1857) model of the three stages of human historical evolution, from the fetishism of the polytheistic stage, through to the rational thought of positivism. In her study of the primitive forms of thought and experience within the Raveloe community, Eliot is trying to place her analysis of the development of an individual life within the perspective of a wider evolutionary framework.

Eliot's concern with the processes of the mythic imagination forms only one aspect of her interest in theories of social development. In Comte's work, and in the writings of her close associates Herbert Spencer (1820–1903) and G. H. Lewes (1817–78), she was presented with a theory of social change which suggested that society, like a biological organism, followed a slow process of natural growth from simplicity through to complexity, which permitted change without disruption. All three figures believed that the evolution of society and the individual could be explained scientifically in accordance with the laws of organic life. Spencer and Lewes extended these principles one stage further, to the realm of physiological psychology, to show how the same laws governed the formation of the mind. The language and assumptions of these authors permeate *Silas Marner*, but the novel offers no simple endorsement of social progress.

Eliot sets *Silas Marner* in the pastoral world of 'Merry England', a social situation traditionally associated with images of harmony and organic integration, but then she deliberately highlights the *lack* of organic unity within the society. Furthermore, although the moral narration of the novel reinforces the idea of uniform laws governing the circumstances and results of individual behaviour, the plot itself is made to depend crucially on sudden, inexplicable disruptions and discontinuties. The novel, indeed, seems to offer two models of history: one based on chance and disruption, and the other on uniform, even development. While the former undercuts ideas of unity and continuity in the growth of the individual, or the larger social organism, the latter stresses ideas of uniform organic growth and progress. This duality, I would suggest, reveals Eliot's own ambivalent responses to theories of unified social and individual development. It also highlights, however, the internal contradictions that existed in nineteenth-century social and scientific theories of the organic. Eliot employs principles of physiological psychology both to challenge and to affirm conceptions of organic unity and continuity. In exploring the diverse, and often contradictory, ways in which Eliot employed scientific ideas in social argument, I hope to reveal the complex network of interrelationships which existed in nineteenth-century social and scientific theory. The apparent conflicts in Eliot's uses of physiological psychology cannot simply be dismissed as literary misappropriation of scientific argument. The divisions within her work both reflect and explore the internal conflicts within nineteenth-century social and scientific theories of the organic.

Like a true fairy tale, *Silas Marner* seems to move towards an unequivocal happy ending. As the 'four united people' (Silas, his adopted daughter Eppie, her newly-betrothed Aaron, and his mother) approach the fenced-in garden where 'the flowers shone with answering gladness', Eppie exclaims, in the concluding words of the novel, 'I think nobody could be happier than we are.' This Edenic conclusion does not, however, offset the far darker social vision offered earlier in the novel. Far from avoiding the harsher social realities, Eliot seems deliberately to confront them in this work. Her 'fairy tale' encompasses Godfrey's sordid backstairs marriage, his wife Molly's death from opium addiction, his brother Dunsey's theft, and Silas's experience of social alienation. The narrative seems at one and the same time to endorse the ideal of progress towards organic social unity whilst also presenting the social conditions that would undermine its validity.

The movement of the plot reinforces this ambiguity, for it shifts backwards, not forwards, in time. Expelled from his life in the industrial city, Silas is gradually incorporated into the world of 'Merry England', 'never reached by the vibrations of the coach horn, or of public opinion'. The village of Raveloe to which he retires stands 'aloof from the currents of industrial energy and Puritan earnestness' (Eliot, n.d., ch. III, 33). Against the march of history, the plot moves from industrialized city life to the pre-industrial setting of rural England, to a village which seems immune to historical change. The plot structure clearly challenges ideas of organic progress. At a deeper level, this structural disjunction is mirrored in the conflict between the ethical principles of action endorsed by the moral narration, and the causal principles actually shown to be in operation. The narrator draws on the uniformitarian principles of development, formulated in nineteenth-century geological theory, to stress the need for moral responsibility in human action. The narrative assumes that social processes, like the physical processes of the earth, are governed by the operation of uniform laws. Individuals must therefore always consider the consequences of their actions, since all conduct is subject to the uniform operation of linear principles of cause and effect. At crucial points in his history, however, Silas is not responsible for his actions. Cataleptic fits disrupt the continuum of conscious awareness. Chance, not uniform law, seems to govern his history. Significantly, it is on the random result of the casting o' lots that he is thrust out of Lantern Yard, the evangelical religious community which has, until this point, formed the basis of his entire life.

Silas Marner, as I suggested earlier, offers two models of social and psychological history: one which stresses continuity, moral order, and individual integrity and control, and another which stresses gaps and jumps in historical development, the operation of chance, and individual powerlessness and internal division. Both can be related to contemporary social interpretations of scientific theory, thus casting light on the diverse ways in which scientific ideas were actually appropriated and mediated within social thought. The latter model

finds a scientific parallel in Darwinian conceptions of randomness and chance and, as I will argue later, in Lewes's development of some of the psychological implications of organic
theory. Acceptance of this model was fuelled by increasing
fears of the actual disorder of industrial development which
appeared so resistant to individual control. In the 1860s,
however, when England was still in the midst of industrial
expansion and relative prosperity, it was the former model,
with its stress on order and continuity, which held the greatest
ideological power.

In all her earlier essays and reviews Eliot adhered to a
model of ordered development; she shared with Comte,
Spencer, and Lewes the conviction that science could illuminate the principles of social and ethical conduct. Positivism, as
Lewes remarked, 'aims at creating a Philosophy of the Sciences as a basis for a new social faith. A social doctrine is the
aim of Positivism, a scientific doctrine the *means*' (Lewes,
1853, 9). Turning from traditional orthodox religion, Eliot
found her articles of faith in the belief that the development of
the social organism was governed by the operation of the same
immutable laws of gradual growth that governed physiology.
In her 1851 review of Robert Mackay's *The Progress of the
Intellect* she communicated the excitement felt at 'the recognition of the presence of undeviating law in the material and
moral world', that 'invariability of sequence which can alone
give value to experience and render education in the true sense
possible' (Pinney, 1963, 31). Science could not only explain
the principles of moral action: observance of its laws constituted a true moral education.

The nineteenth-century celebration of the educative functions of scientific law did not simply arise from a loss of religious faith: it represented a direct response to transformations in
scientific practice. Once the science of natural history, which
described the static order of the earth's surface, was supplanted by the emerging sciences of geology, paleontology,

biology, or evolutionary biology, which studied the history, rather than the order, of nature, social theorists turned, for their confirmation of social order, to the idea of laws governing historical development. George Eliot draws explicitly, in her essay on 'The Progress of the Intellect', on Charles Lyell's uniformitarian principles of geology, observing that in the education of the human race, 'a correct generalization gives significance to the smallest detail, just as the great inductions of geology demonstrate in every pebble the working of laws by which the earth has become adapted for the habitation of man' (Pinney, 1963, 31). Uniformitarian theory, with its vision of the gradual transformation of the earth's surface through the unchanging operation of law, seemed to offer, for social theorists, a perfect model for a moral theory of the laws governing the consequences of human action, and a social theory of developmental progress. This social interpretation was, of course, one which was not necessarily shared by scientists themselves. Eliot's assumption that the earth has been adapted for man suggests the implicit link drawn, in social theory, between ideas of undeviating law and conceptions of social progress.

George Eliot perhaps avoided the worst excesses of her contemporaries' enthusiasm for the moral functions of scientific law exemplified, as J. S. Mill pointed out, in the tendency to confuse the idea of a 'Law of Nature', denoting observed uniformities in the occurrence of phenomena, with the ethical interpretation of 'Law' as expressing 'what ought to be' (Mill, 1854, 15). She shared, however, in the common mistake of covertly assuming that the unchanging operation of physical law actually guaranteed an unbroken process of social development. Thus the historian H. T. Buckle concluded his *History of Civilization* with the eloquent proclamation:

it shall clearly be seen that from the beginning there has been no discrepancy, no incongruity, no disorder, no inter-

ruption, no interference; but that all the events which surround us, even to the furthest limits of material creation, are
but different parts of a single scheme which is permeated by
one glorious principle of universal and undeviating regularity. (Buckle, 1857–61, II, 601)

The idea of undeviating regularity is shifted from a description
of the functioning of physical law, to a description of the
nature of the social change itself. Development will be
ordered, regular and uniform, revealing no disruption or
cataclysmic changes. Notions of universal physical law are
here associated directly with uniformitarian theory and assimi-
lated to the social perspective of gradual social progress and
organic growth.

Optimistic theories of social development were also reinforced by the social appropriation of the laws of the conservation of energy that were, in 1847, extended by Helmholtz to
the sphere of organic life. According to this perspective,
energy could be transformed, but never lost. Spencer, confusing the concepts of force and energy, saw in what he termed
'the persistence of force' a vindication of the uniformity of
nature and the doctrine of social evolution (for an exploration
of this point see Smith, 1970, ch. 5; 1973, 100). The literary
critic Edward Dowden, in an essay on 'The Scientific Movement and Literature', outlines the popular interpretation of
this theory, observing: 'not only is nature everywhere constant, uniform, orderly in its operations; all its parts constitute
a whole, an *ensemble*. Nothing is added, nothing can be lost'
(Dowden, 1878, 100). Ideas of energy conservation were
illegitimately assumed to guarantee a moral order in the universe. The physical law seemed, to these social philosophers,
to reinforce the social doctrine of organic unity. For George
Eliot it clearly confirmed her moral theory of what she termed
'that inexorable law of consequences'. Translating the scientific theory of the conservation of energy into a philosophical

and social principle, George Eliot assumes not only that uniform law will govern the consequences of action, but that in the morally unified social whole or *ensemble*, the consequences will necessarily return to plague the original perpetrator. Science reinforces the social doctrine of organic unity and the related conception of individual duty. Thus 'human duty', George Eliot concludes in her discussion of the 'inexorable law', 'is comprised in the earnest study of this law and patient obedience to its teachings' (Pinney, 1963, 31). Reified scientific law has taken the place of the theological word as the source of a prescriptive morality.

In *Silas Marner* the explicit moral narration is governed by assumptions drawn from uniformitarian theory and the principles of the conservation of energy. Young Godfrey Cass, who hopes to escape the consequences of his unfortunate marriage, is roundly castigated for his reliance on chance. 'Favourable Chance', the narrator gravely observes, 'is the god of all men who follow their own devices instead of obeying a law they believe in' (ch. IX, 112). Godfrey's model of history is one that allows for jumps or gaps. The severity with which he is dealt with suggests the strength of the mid-Victorian commitment to uniformitarian principles of ordered development. Even Darwin, whose model of change Godfrey's theory most closely resembles, showed his allegiance to uniformitarian principles by downplaying the role of chance in his theory. The term 'chance', he argued, was a 'wholly incorrect expression', though it served 'to acknowledge plainly our ignorance of the cause of each particular variation' it did not suggest the breakdown of uniform law (Darwin, 1968, 173). Eliot herself, in her first responses to *The Origin of Species*, saw Darwin's theories only as one more confirmation of the 'Doctrine of Development' (Letter to Mme Bodichon, 5 December 1859 [Haight, 1954–78, III, 227]). The mechanism of natural selection did not, at this stage, disturb her doctrinal faith in ordered progression.

Mid-Victorian science was too closely allied to conceptions of social order to admit readily the possibility of the arbitrary, of events or actions which did not conform to the operation of uniform law. Significantly, the doctrine of free will, held sacrosanct by earlier philosophers as it was seen to enshrine the principle which differentiated man from the animal kingdom, was now subject to scientific attack. The physiological psychologist Alexander Bain (1818–1903) and Herbert Spencer both maintained that the doctrine was fundamentally immoral, since it suggested that human action was not included in the reign of law. The idea of a 'free and uncaused will', Bain argued, disrupts the possibilities of education, for 'according as we reduce Will to law, we foster good habits; according as we withdraw it from regularity and prediction, we unsettle the pursuit of virtue' (Bain, 1876, 499). Spencer based his whole theory of social evolution on the premise that free will was impossible, for 'free will, did it exist, would be entirely at variance with the beneficent necessity displayed in the progressive evolution of the correspondence between the organism and its environment' (Spencer, 1855, 620). To admit the possibility of a free uncaused will would be to disrupt the idea of progressive evolution that was, for Spencer, inseparable from the uniform operation of physical law.

Ideas of 'regularity and prediction' are clearly not neutral but hold strong ideological overtones. Eliot's discussion of Godfrey's reliance on chance reveals how closely ideas of predictability were linked to conceptions of economic and social order. Let a man 'live outside his income', the narrator observes, 'or shirk the resolute honest work that brings wages, and he will presently find himself dreaming of a possible benefactor' (ch. IX, 112). The qualifying adjectives 'honest' and 'resolute' suggest, not simply a theory of uniform law, but a normative vision of economic practice. The narrator continues:

> Let him forsake a decent craft that he may pursue the gen-
> tilities of a profession to which nature never called him, and
> his religion will infallibly be the worship of blessed Chance,
> which he will believe in as the mighty creator of success.
> (ch. IX, 112–13)

A fixed model of social order is here implicitly identified with
natural law. Each individual is 'called' by nature to a specific
occupation. To believe in chance, or to forsake a craft for the
greater gentility of a profession, was to violate the laws that
governed social order. Referring to the worship of Chance,
the narrator concludes that 'The evil principle deprecated in
that religion is the orderly sequence by which the seed brings
forth a crop after its kind' (ch. IX, 113). Ideas of economic
and social order are grounded in a model of gradual, organic
historical growth.

This model of history is not sustained, however, either by
the structure of the plot, or by the model of psychology prop-
osed. Neither Silas's social nor his psychological life conforms
to the laws of orderly sequence. His expulsion from Lantern
Yard establishes a radical break in the historical continuity of
his life that is not resolved by his movement backwards in time
to the world of Merry England. The social and psychological
reasons for his expulsion further reinforce the idea of a breakdown in the principles of continuity. Silas is accused (albeit
falsely) of theft — an action which clearly suggests a disruption
of the orderly sequence of social life in which 'honest labour'
reaps a deserved harvest. The occasion for the false plantation
of evidence against him is provided by his cataleptic fit. This
fit, like the later seizure which permits the entry of Eppie into
his world, disrupts the psychological continuity of his life.
Unexpected and inexplicable, Silas's fits appear to belong
more to the realm of chance than to the operation of uniform,
constant law. Though the narrator's opposition to Godfrey's
reliance on chance was based on the ethics of moral responsi-

bility, at each crucial stage in his history Silas is not responsible for his actions.

These discrepancies in the novel were noted by an early reviewer, E. S. Dallas, future author of *The Gay Science* (1866), who was himself interested in the relationship between psychological theory and the novel. Dallas objected to the fact that Silas's trances 'render him a singularly unaccountable being' (unsigned review in *The Times*, 29 April 1861, in Carroll, 1971, 182). For Dallas, the pleasure of fiction 'depends mainly on our being able to count upon the elements of human character and to calculate results'. Thus if an 'imbecile' is brought forward 'it involves the introduction of chance and uncertainty into a tissue of events the interest of which depends on their antecedent probability' (Carroll, 1971, 182). On the surface, Dallas appears to be arguing simply for rational accountability of action, but behind his statements lie the psychological premises of utilitarian economic theory, and the related conception of linear historical development. The enjoyment of narrative, Dallas believes, is founded on the comforting rehearsal of rational history in which continuous order can always be discerned. Predictability is thus the key to social and psychological order. Unconscious trances constitute a threat since they clearly introduce elements not subject to control.

Silas's fits seem, to Dallas, to be inconsistent with the dominant moral of the tale:

> As in one fit of unconsciousness he lost his all, so in another fit of unconsciousness he obtained a recompense. In either case he was helpless, had nothing to do with his own fate, and was a mere feather in the wind of chance. From this point forward in the tale, however, there is no more chance – all is work and reward, cause and effect, the intelligent mind shaping its own destiny. The honest man bestows kindness upon the child, and reaps the benefit of it in his

own increasing happiness, quickened intelligence, and
social position. (Carroll, 1971, 183–4)

Chance and the unconscious are balanced against continuity
and control. Drawing on the same values that determined
Eliot's moral criticism of Godfrey's reliance on the favourable
workings of chance, Dallas equates psychological continuity
and predictability with economic order. Work and reward are
presented as synonymous with the scientific principles of cause
and effect. His model of social order is that of the capitalist
economy; each individual in control of his own destiny, freely
pursuing his self-interest. In personal life, as in the market-
place, honest investment will reap a merited reward. The idea
of orderly sequence within individual life stands as a model for
the larger movement of history.

The narrator's declared allegiance to the theory of orderly
sequence, and conscious moral control of action, is, as Dallas
points out, undermined by Silas's loss of rational control. On
the occasion when the child Eppie enters Silas's cottage, he
stands by the door 'arrested . . . by the invisible wand of
catalepsy . . . powerless to resist either the good or evil that
might enter there' (ch. XII, 169). The reference to the magic
wand highlights the disruptive function of Silas's disease. The
decisive events in his life occur when he is in a state akin to
death, existing apart from the linear continuity of social life.

George Eliot's use of this device of catalepsy, which is by no
means necessary for the development of the plot, suggests, like
the backwards movement of the story, her uncertain allegiance
to theories of uniform historical development. Her previous
novel, *The Mill on the Floss* (1860), had ended abruptly,
with the catastrophe of the flood sweeping the heroine Maggie
and her brother Tom to their deaths, returning them to the
state of unity they had experienced in childhood. Maggie's
psychological life did not conform to the uniformitarian principles of historical change; her adult experience was one of inter-

nal contradiction, not unified development. Although the
moral of the tale reinforced the theory of organic social
development, the story was only satisfactorily resolved by a
plot structure based on the outdated geological premises of
catastrophism, a geological theory which had, by the 1860s,
been supplanted by uniformitarianism. Faced with evidence of
the extinction of species, the catastrophists had tried to maintain their allegiance to the biblical notion of the fixity of species
by postulating a series of world disasters and successive creations. Their model of history was thus one of discontinuity and
disruption. The internal conflict between the two models of
history in *The Mill* is reproduced in *Silas Marner*. The abrupt
breaks in historical continuity signalled by Silas's expulsion
from Lantern Yard, and his cataleptic fits, dramatize George
Eliot's doubts concerning the necessary relation between
uniformitarian principles of causation, and optimistic theories
of social progress.

Once Silas's sensibility returns after the entry of Eppie he
remains 'unaware of the chasm in his consciousness' (ch. XII,
169). His catalepsy, like the flood that concludes *The Mill on
the Floss*, disrupts the uniform continuity of development. In
drawing attention to the idea of 'chasms' in consciousness
George Eliot seems deliberately to be challenging the idea of
the unified rational actor that sustained contemporary theories
of social progress. Mackay's *Progress of the Intellect*, Lecky's
*History of the Rise and Influence of the Spirit of Rationalism in
Europe*, which Eliot reviewed in 1865, and Comte's theory of
the three stages of human development, all associated social
progress directly with the increase of rational control. Herbert
Spencer, taking the theory one step further, placed these
evolutionary beliefs on a physiological basis, arguing that the
psychological processes of rationality exemplified the universal law of Progress: physiological homogeneity gave place to
heterogeneity, just as, in the social sphere, primitive organizations were supplanted by societies with a more complex divi-

sion of labour. In *Principles of Psychology* he concludes that 'in this organization of experiences which we call Intelligence, there must be that same continuity, that same subdivision of function, that same mutual dependence, and that same ever advancing *consensus*, which characterize the physical organization' (Spencer, 1855, 485). The stress placed on continuity and consensus in the mind reflects the contemporary social preoccupation with unity and historical continuity in the development of the social organism. Spencer's theory of the physiological bases of rational thought clearly reinforces dominant social ideology.

George Eliot's use of the device of catalepsy could be interpreted as a clear rejection of the associated social and psychological assumptions of unified, organic development. Such a reading, however, fails to take into account the complex responses to evolutionary theory suggested by the tale. The moral critique of Godfrey is, as I argued before, entirely dependent on assumptions of social and psychological continuity. Furthermore, in her analysis of Silas, George Eliot also uses concepts drawn from the physiological psychology of Lewes and Spencer that reinforce ideas of evolutionary development. Yet, the thrust to affirm a morally ordered conception of social development is deliberately balanced by a clear-sighted vision of the possible disorder of social and psychological life. The novel anticipates the later Victorian decline of faith in the capacity of science to offer a firm foundation for the principles of ethics or to confirm the onward progress of social development. The dualism of George Eliot's vision, however, was also contained within contemporary science. In the complex relations between social and psychological interpretations of organic theory, I will argue, one can find a clue to the structure of *Silas Marner*.

In employing the *idea* of catalepsy George Eliot was not departing too far from the premises of mid-Victorian psychology. Though social theorists associated evolution predominantly with the development of rational control, increasing attention was being paid to the idea of the unconscious (see Whyte, 1962). As the focus of the sciences shifted from the order of nature to its history, so, in psychology, there was a corresponding shift as attention was turned from the external order of rational thought to the inner history of the mind. The 1850s saw the first formulation of W. B. Carpenter's influential theory of 'unconscious cerebration' and the publication of works on physiological psychology by Spencer, Bain and Lewes that all examined the operation of mental processes beneath the plane of consciousness (Spencer, 1855; Bain, 1876; Lewes, 1859–60). In both the popular and the more academic periodical press of the mid-century articles on the strange functions of memory or the symptoms of insanity frequently appeared. The foundation of the *Journal of Psychological Medicine and Mental Pathology* in 1848 by Forbes Winslow was indicative of this new interest. George Eliot's own reference in her journal of 1869 to an article in the *Spectator* which had 'some interesting facts about loss of memory and double life' (Haight, 1954–78, V, 6) offers further evidence of the general speculation aroused by this issue. No rigid divisions can be drawn between the popular and the more scientific treatments, for Bain, Carpenter and Lewes all relied, in their analysis of aberrant mental phenomena, on anecdotal stories similar to those found in articles in the popular press.

Despite the increased attention paid to strange phenomena of the mind, belief in the uniform law governing social and psychological development was not diminished, but rather augmented. Science could explain all occurrences. Even the popular sciences of mesmerism and phrenology that swept England in the 1830s and 1840s were firmly grounded on this conviction. Thus Robert Macnish, proclaiming the merits of the phrenological system, argued in his best-selling work *The Philosophy of Sleep* that it 'appears to me the only one capable of affording a rational and easy explanation of all the phenomena of mind. It is impossible to account for dreaming, idiocy, spectral illusions, monomania, and partial genius in any other way (Macnish, 1835, 7). Phrenology and mesmerism not only offered inclusive systems of explanation for the functioning of the brain, they also reinforced optimistic theories of social progress. The mesmeric force could be channelled and the mental faculties developed in ways that would necessarily lead to individual advancement. (For an excellent analysis of the social functions of phrenology see Cooter, 1976 and 1985.)

Interest in the internal or unconscious process of the mind did not, as one might expect, undercut notions of historical continuity in nineteenth-century thought, but seemed actively to confirm them. Thus for German *Naturphilosophen* such as Hegel and Schelling, who based their theory of organic social evolution on a vitalist model of the organism, the unconscious was an expression of the vital force, or Will, that determined history. Eduard von Hartmann, in his popular work *Philosophy of the Unconscious* (1870, English trans. 1884), identified his conception of the unconscious with Hegel's shaping Idea and the unconscious logic or Reason within history (Hartmann, 1893, I, 28). In England, theorists chose a different biological model for their theory of organic historical development. Spencer rejected the vitalist, teleological notions of history contained within German philosophy, but his theories of the unconscious still confirmed his belief in social progress. He acknowledged the existence of the unconscious: 'Out of a great number of psychological actions going on in the organism, only a part are woven into the thread of consciousness' (Spencer, 1855, 495). Yet he believed that progress, for both the individual and the race, consisted in the evolution of rationality as a unified consciousness emerges: 'Gradually as the nervous system becomes more and more integrated, the twisting of these various strands of changes into one thread of changes becomes more complete' (Spencer, 1855, 496). The unconscious does not disrupt the operations of the conscious mind; it seems rather a pre-form of rationality, which, in accordance with Spencer's theory of social progress, actively contributes to the evolving unity of mind. Despite increasing interest in seemingly irrational phenomena, the dominant image of the mind in English psychology remained the traditional one espoused even by that pioneer of theories of the unconscious, W. B. Carpenter: that of a horse and rider in which the dominant Will enforces its desires on its steed, the physical body (Carpenter, 1874, 26).

It is precisely this control over his own mental processes or destiny that Silas lacks. The occurrence of catalepsy remained something of an enigma even to the self-confident scientists of the mid-Victorian era, but George Eliot clearly employs the device in a way that highlights both its inexplicable and disruptive nature (see Appendix, p.286). Silas's cataleptic fits function as one symptom of a more inclusive powerlessness. The breaks in his consciousness stand as an image of the discontinuity of his history. Powerless to control the functions of his own mind, or the machinations of others, he is thrust out of his familiar surroundings in Lantern Yard. Unlike other contemporary theorists, George Eliot associates the operation of unconscious processes with social discontinuity. Once expelled, Silas undergoes the Lethean experience of exile 'in which the past becomes dreamy because its symbols have all vanished, and the present too is dreamy because it is linked with no memories' (ch. II, 20). Displaced from his familiar surroundings and routines, he finds it difficult to orient himself in the world of Raveloe. Far from possessing a rational, controlling ego, his very conception of self seems to be based on his relationship to his environment. As the narrator observes:

> Even people whose lives have been made various by learning, sometimes find it hard to keep a fast hold on their

habitual views of life, on their faith in the Invisible, nay, on the sense that their past joys and sorrows are a real experience, when they are suddenly transported to a new land, where the beings around them know nothing of their history, and share none of their ideas – where their mother earth shows another lap, and human life has other forms than those on which their souls have been nourished. (Ch. II, 20)

Identity, it is suggested, is a social construction based on interaction with the environment. Silas loses the sense that his past experiences are his own once the surrounding society ceases to reinforce his learned conception of self.

The model of psychology implied in this passage conflicts with the theory of moral responsibility underlying the later castigation of Godfrey for his reliance on the workings of chance. If there is no continuous identity, there can be no necessary responsibility for action. Yet the two theories stem from the same root: the conflicts in the text in fact reveal the internal contradictions present in nineteenth-century organicist theory. The opposition to chance was based on the belief that, in an organically united whole, ruled by uniform law, all individuals would inevitably face the consequences of their actions. The analysis of Silas's loss of identity, however, is also based on organicist theory: specifically, on the psychological premises outlined by Lewes in his development of Comte's organicist theory of history.

In order to understand how organic premises could yield such conflicting results, it is necessary to trace Eliot's relationship to organic theories of history. Eliot first articulated her allegiance to organicist notions of historical development in her essay 'The Natural History of German Life' (1856), where she defined the process of history as that of a dynamic interchange between organism and medium:

The external conditions which society has inherited from

the past are but the manifestation of inherited internal conditions in the human beings who compose it; the internal conditions and the external are related to each other as the organism and its medium, and development can take place only by the gradual consentaneous development of both. (Pinney, 1963, 287)

The model outlined is that of Comte's image of history as the assimilation by the individual organism of the external forms of the surrounding social medium (Comte, 1853, I, 361–2). Spencer and Lewes adopted a similar theory. History for Spencer was a process of 'progressive evolution of the correspondence between the organism and its environment'. Psychology, he believed, could be defined by 'the continuous adjustment of internal relations to external relations' (Spencer, 1855, 620, 472). Spencer's model, however, assumes a constant environment. Though he goes beyond Comte in applying physiological theories of the organic to the workings of the mind, he does not allow for the transformation of the social medium. His commitment to the idea of social progress, and an evolving unity of rational consciousness, ensures that he does not take fully into account the implications of a dynamic theory of organic life. In the work of G. H. Lewes, however, George Eliot found an organic theory of history that not only posited a process of reciprocal interaction between organism and environment, but also extended these premises to the sphere of psychology.

In *The Physiology of Common Life*, Lewes follows Comte's biological and social challenge to the idea of individual autonomy, stressing the fact that 'Life is possible only under the necessary conditions of an *organism*, on the one hand and an external medium on the other. It is the mutual relations of organism and medium which determine the manifestations we term Life' (Lewes, 1859–60, II, 436). He extends his questioning of autonomy, however, to the sphere of consciousness, arguing that 'Mind is the psychical aspect of Life – that it is as much the sum total of the whole sensitive organism, as Life is the sum total of the whole vital organism' (Lewes, 1859–60, II, 344). Just as the idea of organic life expresses the whole process of interaction between the organism and medium, so mind itself cannot be dissociated from this continuous process. Lewes wished to extend, through his theories of physiological psychology, the reign of scientific law: to show that the principles of organic unity determined both social and psychical life. The actual function of his theory, however, is to undercut the idea of the rational actor that, in Spencer's work, sustained ideas of organic continuity in history.

Lewes's theories of physiological psychology were clearly distinguished from those of his contemporaries by his belief that there was no single, exclusive centre of consciousness. The brain was only one organ of the mind, for the term 'Mind', he argues, 'includes all Sensation, all Volition, and all Thought: it means the whole psychical Life; and this psychical Life has no one special centre, any more than physical Life has one special centre; it belongs to the whole and animates the whole' (Lewes, 1859–60, II, 5). There was, therefore, for Lewes, no rational ego directing the operations of consciousness.

Lewes's theories aroused widespread dissent amongst his fellow scientists; a dissent, one would suspect, that was stimulated not only by his physiological premises, but also by the social implications of his psychology. Alexander Bain, summarizing the objections, argued that 'what determines the unity of consciousness, as showing which local currents have found means to activate the collective currents, is the unity of the *executive*' (Bain, 1876, 591). It was precisely this unity of the executive that Lewes denied. His model suggested, not only that the operations of the mind were not unified and controlled, but that there could be many conflicting sensations in the mind. Mental history need not, therefore, constitute a linear continuum.

George Eliot's portrait of Silas Marner is clearly based on similar psychological premises. Silas loses his sense of self when displaced from his familiar surrounding social medium, and the social forms on which his soul has been 'nourished'. With no directing, executive ego to establish a continuity of consciousness, both the past and the present become 'dreamy' under the 'Lethean influence' of exile. In place of a theory of unified development, based on the premise of a controlling ego, Eliot offers a multi-levelled model of history. Her psychological theory, like that of Lewes, clearly challenged dominant conceptions of 'natural', social, and psychological order.

In the work of mid-Victorian psychologists a clear correlation can be traced between theories of the linear nature of the mind and assumptions of social order. Bain, in *The Emotions and the Will*, observes that 'The unbroken continuity of our mental life holds together the past and the present in a sequence that we term Order in Time. Yesterday's events are remembered as a past reality from their contiguity to the present reality' (1876, 534). This mental continuity was, for Bain, both a measure and guarantee of social order: in an interesting elision, which conflates physical sequence with a normative, social sense of order, he associates the linear nature of the mind with 'the sequences of nature, or the order of the world' (1876, 535). The experience of Silas, however, clearly disrupts this conception. On moving to Raveloe he loses what Carpenter termed the 'consciousness of agreement' between the present state of consciousness and past experience. 'Without this recognition,' Carpenter argues, 'we should live in the present alone; for the reproduction of past states of consciousness would affect us only like the succession of fantasies presented to us in the play of Imagination' (1874, 454). Unless the individual consciousness united past and present experience, there could be no sense of ordered progression in history. Silas, however, possesses no essential centre of self that could perform this task. His sense of identity is dependent on his interaction with the environment and, in Raveloe, there are no external forms that can evoke his sense of continuity with the past. Dolly Winthrop's kindly attempt to explain her views of life to him was 'only like a report of unknown objects, which his imagination could not fashion' (ch. X, 132).

With the loss of his money, Silas is locked into an obsessional grief:

> Nobody in this world but himself knew that he was the same Silas Marner who had once loved his fellow with tender love, and trusted in an unseen goodness. Even to himself that past experience had become dim. (Ch. X, 132)

He loses not only his earlier modes of behaviour, but also his sense of a continuous identity. As Carpenter observed, 'this Consciousness of Agreement between our present and our past Mental experiences, constitutes the basis of our feeling of *personal identity*; for, if it were entirely extinguished, there would be nothing to carry on that feeling of identity from one moment to another' (1874, 455). Yet Carpenter's argument is only hypothetical. The only case he offers is one of physical infirmity, so his observation in no way undercuts his sense of the normal, continuous rational order. George Eliot accepts neither Carpenter's sense of psychological continuity, nor the divorce between the social and psychological realms that his theory implies. In accordance with Lewes's theory that individual psychology could only be understood in terms of a dynamic relationship between the organism and the social medium, she is examining not a purely psychic disorder, but the psychological effects created by social dislocation. Lewes, in his later work *Foundations of a Creed* (1874), takes psychological theorists to task for their belief that they could understand the operation of mind without examining its relations to the social organism: 'The psychologist, accustomed to consider the Mind as something apart from the Organism, individual and collective, is peculiarly liable to this error of overlooking the fact that all mental manifestations are simply the resultants of the conditions external and internal' (I, 128).

In her exploration of the relationship between Silas's social experience and his sense of personal identity, Eliot effectively challenges dominant assumptions of both social and psychological continuity. Silas's faith in a benign, God- given order was shattered when the drawing of lots declared him guilty. Eliot's analysis of his ensuing experience suggests that ideas of essential order in the social and psychological realms are also open to doubt. The role played by chance in the novel looks forward to the later *Daniel Deronda* (1876), where the gaming table stands as an image of the confusion and disorder that characterize Gwendolen Harleth's life and the conflict-ridden society to which she belongs. The separation between the English and Jewish worlds in this novel plays out on a larger-scale the difference between the two models of order examined in *Silas Marner*.

Eliot's determination to adhere to an organic theory of historical development in *Silas Marner* is confirmed by a letter to the critic R. H. Hutton in which she explains:

> It is the habit of my imagination to strive after as full a vision of the medium in which a character moves as of the character itself. The psychological causes which prompted me to give such details of Florentine life and history as I have given, are precisely the same as those which determined me in giving the details of English village life in *Silas Marner*, or the 'Dodson' life, out of which were developed the destinies of poor Tom and Maggie. (Haight, 1954–78, IV, 96–7)

Eliot clearly constructed *Silas Marner* in the light of the Comtean model of dynamic interaction, but in tracing the psychological implications of this theory she undercuts

Comte's determining social and moral assumptions. Her image of the relationship between the individual and surrounding society is not one of simple reflection, where psychological continuity reflects social continuity. Neither the individual nor society possesses intrinsic coherence. For the traditional psychological notion of an autonomous, unified entity, George Eliot substitutes a model of the individual as process: a continuous series of possibly conflicting streams of sensation. With this multi-levelled theory of individual history she is able to explore a complex series of relations between the individual and society: the growing *disjunction* between Silas and the surrounding world of Raveloe, and the effects of his increasing alienation.

Silas Marner also anticipates *Daniel Deronda* in its pessimistic vision of the conflict that can characterize social interdependence. Comte, Spencer and Lewes based their theory of history on the premise that the moral constitution of society would necessarily improve as the social organism evolved from homogeneity to heterogeneity. As the division of labour increased, and social interdependence developed, sentiments of altruism would necessarily supplant the more primitive emotion of egoism. Eliot's analysis of Raveloe life, however, does not reinforce this moral vision. Though Silas's presence in Raveloe signals a new increase in the division of labour, it does not create a growing solidarity in the community. He evokes hostility, not altruism, from his neighbours, and he himself is precipitated into isolation and egoism.

George Eliot's study is far from confirming organicist theories of social or economic development. The psychological theory she employs in fact allows her to show how Silas is reduced in Raveloe from human status to a 'spinning insect', until he finally takes on the qualities of an object:

> he had clung with all the force of his nature to his work and his money; and like all objects to which a man devotes himself, they had fashioned him into correspondence with

themselves. His loom, as he wrought in it without ceasing,
had in its turn wrought on him, and confirmed more and
more the monotonous craving for its monotonous response.
His gold, as he hung over it and saw it grow, gathered his
power of loving together into a hard isolation like its own.
(Ch. V, 63)

Eliot dispenses with the traditional hierarchical view of a
rational actor governing the realm of the senses, or a rider
dominating his steed. In tracing the process by which Silas, in
his increasing subjection to the loom and his gold, endows
these alienated self-images with his own active powers, she
reveals how his actual mode of experience is one in which there
is no necessary hierarchy within human, animal and object life.
It is not the Comtean evolution from fetishism to rationality
that Silas enacts but rather the 'fetishism of commodities'
described by that other great nineteenth-century historian,
Marx. In the monetary system, Marx observes, 'gold and
silver, when serving as money, did not represent a social relation between producers, but were natural objects with strange
social properties' (Marx, 1977, 442). For Silas, his relations
with his fellow villagers are a mere function through which he
can acquire more gold. Reduced into a 'constant mechanical
relation to the objects of his life' (ch. II, 29), he looks, for the
last vestiges of human contact, towards his gold. Lavishing his
loving attention on his piles of coins he 'thought fondly of the
guineas that were only half earned by the work in his loom, as
if they had been unborn children' (ch. II, 31). Social relations
are displaced into the realm of objects.

The powerful analysis of Silas's growing alienation inverts
the organicist categories of social continuity and growing
altruism. Departing from the traditional hierarchical view of
the rational actor, Eliot challenged the optimistic social
theories founded on that conception. It is not the rational play
of intelligence, but rather external, material forms, that domi-

nate the life of Silas and determine his conception of identity.

Yet it must not be forgotten that *Silas Marner* is a divided text. The analysis of Silas's alienation is balanced by a final affirmation of the values of organic community. Though the ultimate implications of Lewes's theories undercut ideas of ordered social or psychological development, his original impetus was to affirm the reign of order throughout the physical and social realms. Eliot's work is characterized by a similar duality. As I suggested earlier, she employs principles of physiological psychology both to challenge and to affirm conceptions of organic unity and continuity.

The dual functions fulfilled by physiological psychology in *Silas Marner* will be illuminated by an analysis of the relationship between this science and contemporary social theory. For both Lewes and Spencer, the great attraction of physiological psychology lay in the fact that it allowed them to extend to the mind the principles they saw operating in the social and physiological organism. They employed in their work a single vocabulary of channelled energy to describe the three different spheres of physiological, mental and social life. The unity of a shared vocabulary permitted easy transposition from one level to another, as physiology and social analysis became fully intertwined. This integrated vocabulary enabled Eliot in her novels to shift between intricate physiological analysis and wider social and moral conclusions. In doing so, however, she was not departing too far from the scientific practice of her day. In analysing the history of theories of the organic it is hard to dissociate the social and physiological components, to assign priority to either field. Lewes, for instance, in his *Seaside Studies* employed the image of the social division of labour to explain the physiological differentiation of functions (Lewes, 1858, 59–60). The role played by language and existing conceptions in the evolution of a scientific discipline was pointed out as early as 1800 by the physiologist Bichat who observed:

> If men had cultivated physiology before physics, I am con-
> vinced that they would have applied much of the former to
> the latter; they would have seen the rivers flowing because
> of the tonic effect of their banks, crystals uniting because of
> the excitation of their mutual sensitivity, the plants moving
> because they irritated each other at great distances.
> (Bichat, quoted in Jacob, 1973, 90)

Physiological psychology in the nineteenth century did not
create an entirely new vocabulary but drew on existing terms
like 'current', 'channel' or 'groove', which often carried with
them concealed assumptions concerning the formation of the
natural and social worlds.

George Eliot unites social and physiological theory in her
analysis of Silas. In an observation which unifies the concepts
of external cultural channels, and internal pathways of the
mind, she remarks that 'culture had not defined any channels
for his sense of mystery, and so it spread itself over the proper
pathway of inquiry and knowledge' (ch. I, 11). The image of
the force of mystery irresistibly spreading, once aroused, over
the 'proper pathway of inquiry and knowledge' is in accordance with Lewes's 'Law of Sensibility' that 'No sensation
terminates in itself . . . A self-terminating sensation is as
inconceivable as a self-terminating motion' (Lewes, 1859–
60, II, 55). A sensation once aroused must necessarily receive
issue. The image of channelled energy which George Eliot
adopted here is one that is crucial to the psychological theory
of Lewes. In *The Physiology of Common Life* Lewes
describes the ease of accustomed action, and the difficulties of
acquiring new skills in terms of the creation of mental channels
of discharge:

> Habits, Fixed Ideas, and what are called Automatic
> Actions, all depend on the tendency which a sensation has
> to discharge itself through the readiest channel. In learning
> to speak a new language, to play on a musical instrument,

or to perform any unaccustomed movements, great difficulty is felt, because the channels through which each sensation has to pass have not become established; but no sooner has frequent repetition cut a pathway, than this difficulty vanishes. (Lewes, 1859–6, II, 58).

Eliot applies this theory of blocked channels on both a social and psychological level. For Silas, the customs of Lantern Yard had been 'the channel of divine influences'. His social expulsion from these accustomed channels of expression is replicated internally in the physiological structure of his mind:

Thought was arrested by utter bewilderment, now its old narrow pathway was closed, and affection seemed to have died under the bruise that had fallen on its keenest nerves. (Ch. II, 23)

The sensitive description of Silas's psychological confusion is based on the physiologically precise idea of energy diverted from its usual defined channels of discharge.

The vivid metaphorical images Eliot employs did not represent a departure from scientific precision, but rather an extension of the principles of linguistic analogy that lay behind the development of physiological psychology. Thus Silas's lack of interest in the hedgerows he had once loved is expressed in the following terms:

these too belonged to the past, from which his life had shrunk away, like a rivulet that has sunk far down from the grassy fringe of its old breadth into a little shivering thread, that cuts a groove for itself in the barren sand. (Ch. II, 31)

From the hedgerow banks, which offer both a literal and a symbolic image of the changes in Silas's life, George Eliot moves to the idea of a shrunken current of life. The striking natural image expresses the physiological theory that streams of sensation, once displaced from their accustomed channels, only with difficulty carve a new pathway. It is the 'peculiar characteristic of vigorous intellects', Lewes notes, 'that their thoughts are ever finding new pathways instead of moving amid old associations' (Lewes, 1859–60, II, 59). Silas, however, has not the vitality to affect this change. Thus, in a variation on the earlier image, 'his soul was still the shrunken rivulet, with only this difference, that its little groove of sand was blocked up, and it wandered confusedly against dark obstruction' (ch. X, 132). The 'foundations of human love and faith' in his mind are locked up, unable to find a channel of release. The terms are still those of physiological psychology, but with the inclusion of 'soul' the physical description takes on both moral and social implications.

George Eliot's masterly study of Silas's growing isolation and alienation in Raveloe is based on the imagery of physical force. The effect of the movement of pity he had felt towards Sally Oates was not to increase his membership of the community. Instead it 'heightened the repulsion between him and his neighbours, and made his isolation more complete' (ch. II, 26), where the term 'repulsion' is used in its precise physical sense. Silas's growing subjection to the numbing activity of weaving and the counting of gold is explained in terms of the ease felt in a habitual action, for 'Do we not wile away moments of inanity or fatigued waiting by repeating some trivial movement or sound, until the repetition has bred a want, which is incipient habit?' (ch. II, 27). The suggestion conforms to Lewes's theory that once frequent repetition has cut a pathway, actions become so automatic that 'if once commenced, they must continue' (Lewes, 1859–60, II, 58). In hoarding his gold, marking the periods of his existence only by the acquisition of his guineas, Silas's life was 'narrowing and hardening itself more and more into a mere pulsation of desire and satisfaction that had no relation to any other being' (ch. II, 28). While the physical image of pulsation accurately portrays the nature of Silas's life, it also suggests, in moral terms, its inadequacies: Silas's reduction from a social to a purely physical being.

Physiological psychology allows George Eliot to explore the disjunction between Silas's experience and that of the surrounding village life. The physical terms in fact reinforce the moral point of his social isolation. Ultimately, however, George Eliot employs the unified vocabulary of social and psychological analysis to reaffirm the ideals of organic continuity. Though Silas's social experience has been that of disruption, discontinuity and growing isolation, his life is radically transformed by the sudden appearance of the child Eppie, who stimulates forgotten channels of his mind, thus operating as a catalyst to release his energy. Eliot is careful to make Silas's first response one of memory:

> Could this be his little sister come back to him in a dream . . . ?
>
> . . . It was very much like his little sister. Silas sank into his chair powerless, under the double presence of an inexplicable surprise and a hurrying influx of memories. (Ch. XII, 170)

This crucial analysis is based upon physiological principles of directed force. It conforms both to Lewes's conception of the mind as an 'aggregate of forces' and to his theories of unconscious association. The sight of the child stimulates 'a vision of the old home and the old streets leading to Lantern Yard — and within that vision another, of the thoughts which had been present with him in those far-off scenes' (ch. XII, 170). Silas's sequence of memory illustrates the 'law of attraction' defined here by Spencer: 'that when any two psychical states occur in immediate succession, an effect is produced such that if the first subsequently recurs there is a certain tendency for the second to follow' (Spencer, 1855, 532). The physical processes of unconscious association establish continuity in personal life, a continuity which Spencer believed was then passed on to

future generations through the physiological inheritance
of 'modified nervous tendencies' (Spencer, 1855, 526).
Spencer's theories of progressive social evolution were in fact
founded on the premise that unconscious association formed
the basis of the individual's adaptation to the environment,
and thence of the race's progressive development as these
'forms of thought' were transmitted to offspring. Since relations to the environment, once established, are, he argues, 'uniform, invariable, incapable of being absent, or reversed, or
abolished, they must be represented by irreversible, inde-
structible connections of ideas' (Spencer, 1855, 580). The
physiological unity of mind is taken as a guarantee of essential
social continuity and development.

Though George Eliot does not share Spencer's ebullient
optimism, it is undoubtedly the physiological unity of Silas's
mind, represented by his unconscious association of ideas, that
allows him to heal the breach in his social experience, to grow
once more into union with his neighbours, and into a sense of
continuity with his past. Eppie's gradual progressive development is mirrored in Silas as the underlying continuity of his history is revealed:

> As the child's mind was growing into knowledge, his mind
> was growing into memory: as her life unfolded, his soul,
> long stupefied in a cold narrow prison, was unfolding too,
> and trembling gradually into full consciousness. (Ch.
> XIV, 193–4)

The term 'full consciousness' is here replete with meaning: it
implies not only an integrated sense of self based on continuous
memory, but also an open, accepting awareness of surrounding social life. Under the influence of Eppie, Silas moves
beyond the 'ever-repeated circle' of thought established by his
gold to look for links and ties with his neighbours. He learns to
channel his previously inert feelings into 'the forms of custom
and belief which were the mould of Raveloe life; and as, with

reawakening sensibilities, memory also reawakened, he had begun to ponder over the elements of his old faith, and blend them with his new impressions, till he recovered a conscious-ness of unity between his past and present' (ch. XVI, 213). Social isolation and personal disruption are replaced by integ-ration.

Silas's change appears a dramatic transformation. In an unexpected reversal, he acquires both a coherent identity and membership of the social community. George Eliot carefully ensures, however, that his development does not violate uniformitarian principles. Eppie's appearance does not radi-cally alter Silas's psychic make-up, it merely reawakens dor-mant fibres. Though Eppie is compared to the angels who led men away from the city of destruction (ch. XIV, 101), there are no miracles involved in Silas's restoration: the natural chain of causation is not broken. As Strauss argued in his *Life of Jesus*, 'no just notion of the true nature of history is possible without a perception of the inviolability of the chain of finite causes, and of the impossibility of miracles' (1846, 64). Where the scientific principles of physiological psychology had earlier underpinned the analysis of Silas's alienation, they now endorse his growth into unity. His change confirms the principles of organic social evolution. Apparent discontinuity is discounted by the stable physiological structure of his mind. History, as the moral critique of Godfrey implied, is cumula-tive.

Like Spencer, George Eliot believed that the key to social evolution lay in physiology. She was vehemently opposed to Buckle's theories in his *History of Civilization in England* for he held that 'there is no such thing as *race* or hereditary trans-mission of qualities' (Haight, 1954–78, II, 415). Without this physiological transmission of experience, she believed, there could be no intrinsic moral advance in history. Though she is dealing in *Silas Marner* only with the individual life, the same belief — that moral action, once imprinted on the physiological structure of the mind, will never be destroyed – reinforces the structure of the tale. The satisfying conclusion of Silas's life is only possible, however, because the vocabulary of physiological psychology allowed George Eliot to analyse both his social and psychological life in terms of the direction of energy, thus eliding different levels of analysis. Ultimately, his isolation therefore appeared to be less a product of the structure of social relations in Raveloe than an accident of personal circumstance. The appearance of a figure who could release his blocked emotion and reopen the channels of his mind leads inevitably to the restoration of social and psychic organic unity in his life.

After the arrival of Eppie the novel appears to move swiftly towards a happy ending. The wedding of Eppie and Aaron Winthrop is set in the season of eternal renewal 'when the great lilacs and laburnums in the old-fashioned gardens showed their golden and purple wealth above the lichen-tinted walls' (Conclusion, 270). Confirmed by the, for once, unanimous approval of the Raveloe chorus, the wedding certainly seems to validate the organic social ideal. This forward movement of the plot is balanced, however, by a less positive image of historical development. Godfrey Cass, whose sorry history always puts into question the idea of Raveloe as a fully integrated organic community, is noticeably absent from the concluding scene. His absence functions as a reminder of the fact that Eppie, in an ideologically significant gesture, chose her nurturing parent over her natural parent, thus violating the chain of biological continuity. Also excluded from the conclusion is any reference to Silas's Lantern Yard past. *Silas Marner* appears, at one and the same time, to endorse the moral values of organic continuity, and to question their social validity. Such significant omissions point to another, competing, model of historical development.

Silas, after the arrival of Eppie, turned once more to a belief in providential government of history. Inspired by her to a sense of 'presiding goodness' (ch. XVI, 213), he comes to believe that his earlier expulsion from Lantern Yard must have been due to some error. He returns with Eppie to Lantern Yard to see Mr Paston, 'a man with a deal o' light', in the hope that he will be able to illuminate the historical process: why the 'drawing o' the lots' did not vindicate Silas's belief in an ordered universe but rather seemed to endorse the rule of chance. He does not find light and order, however, but rather darkness and destruction: 'Here and there a sallow, begrimed face looked out from a gloomy doorway at the strangers' (ch. XXI, 268). Into this gloom, so reminiscent of Eppie's origin, Lantern Yard has vanished, to be replaced by a factory, symbol of the industrial changes which, like Molly's dark history, had no discernible impact on Raveloe life. Silas fails to find order or meaning in history. Lacking historical illumination, he is left in darkness: 'It's dark to me Mrs. Winthrop, that is; I doubt it'll be dark to the last' (ch. XXI, 269). Through Eppie he finds 'light enough to trusten by', but not the light of historical reason he had sought.

Silas's failure highlights the internal conflicts in the novel. The tale is no simple endorsement of organicist theories of social development. As the fairy tale elements are balanced by the darker history of Molly or Dunsey, and the stress on moral responsibility by the seemingly uncontrollable nature of Silas's fits, so Silas's growth into psychological continuity is offset by the seeming recalcitrance of social history; its refusal to conform to a pattern of ordered development. The dark vision of the 'great manufacturing town', where the jail hides the sky, suggests that the novel's Edenic conclusion can only be achieved by moving backwards in history to the pre-industrial landscape of Raveloe. Eliot's portrayal of Raveloe, however, is marked by the same duality that characterizes the rest of the tale. On the one hand it appears a land of Edenic bounty, with 'orchards looking lazy with neglected plenty' (ch. II, 21). Protected by nature, 'it was nestled in a snug well-wooded hollow', and centred round 'a fine old church' (ch. I, 7). The peasantry, on the other hand, are described as 'pressed close by primitive wants . . . To them pain and mishap present a far wider range of possibilities than gladness and enjoyment: their imagination is almost barren of the images that feed desire and hope, but is all overgrown by recollections that are a perpetual pasture to fear' (ch. I, 6). The image is a grim one; but, throughout the novel there is no direct representation of this poverty and fear.

The narrative appears torn between an intellectual appreciation of poverty and a desire to celebrate the organic community of the feudal order. Thus the loving details lavished on Miss Nancy's arrival at Squire Cass's, the feast, and the New Year's Eve dance seem to confirm for the reader, as for the assembled community of villagers, the 'fitness of things':

> That was as it should be − that was what everybody had been used to − and the charter of Raveloe seemed to be renewed by the ceremony. (Ch. XI, 156–7)

This ritual of renewal is disrupted, however, by the arrival of Silas with Eppie in his arms. For Godfrey, Silas seemed 'an apparition from that hidden life which lies, like a dark by-street, behind the goodly ornamented façade that meets the sunlight and the gaze of respectable admirers' (ch. XIII, 174). The dark by-streets are not confined to the manufacturing town of Silas's past, but intrude even upon the gay procession in the White Parlour 'where the mistletoe-bough was hung, and multitudinous tallow candles made rather a brilliant effect, gleaming from among the berried holly-boughs, and reflected in the old-fashioned oval mirrors fastened in the panels of the white wainscot' (ch. XI, 156). The villagers' own belief in a harmonious natural order, celebrated here in these images of brilliant festivities, is shown to be founded on an illusion. In place of the villagers' affectionate respect for the gaiety of their superiors' lives, we should perhaps substitute the narrator's bitter vision of our rural forefathers, 'men whose only work was to ride round their land, getting heavier and heavier in their saddles, and who passed the rest of their days in the half-listless gratification of senses dulled by monotony' (ch. III, 44).

The narrative is curiously ambivalent as to the image of rural life it wishes to portray. The vision of the intrinsic negativity and barrenness of the squirearchy's lives is in sharp contrast with the later celebration of the 'order and purity' in the Red House once the 'presiding spirit' of Nancy has entered. No irony is visible in this description, and indeed, an image of essential social order is intrinsically necessary if Eppie and Silas are to be seen at the close as participants in an integrated community, not outcasts separated from the life of a village which was itself riven by internal conflict.

The text of *Silas Marner* is fundamentally divided: it offers both a moral endorsement of the values of organic continuity, and a clear-sighted representation of the social conditions that would undermine their validity. The conclusion seems to confirm the values of consensus that for Comte, Lewes and Spencer underpinned the movement of history. As Comte observes:

> The consensus of the social organism extends to Time as well as Space. Hence the two distinct aspects of social sympathy; the feeling of Solidarity, or union with the Present, and of Continuity, or union with the Past. (1875–7, I, 291)

George Eliot employs the psychological extension of organicist social theory to show how the unchanging physiological structure of Silas's mind allows him to grow into solidarity with his present, and into a sense of union with his past. Physiology seems to vindicate the essential ordered progression of history.

This model of history cannot account, however, for the

abrupt breaks in Silas's social or psychological life signalled by his expulsion from Lantern Yard or his cataleptic fits — occurrences that suggest George Eliot's uneasiness with a uniformitarian theory of development. She clearly does not hold to the model of the rational, self-controlling actor that underpinned contemporary theories of economic and social progress. Like Lewes, whose physiological theory of psychology undermined the theory of organic historical development from which it had been derived, she also turns to physiological theory to explore internal psychological conflict, and the breakdown of individual identity. Her use of physiological psychology thus reflects her contradictory attitudes to organicist theories of history. On the one hand, the unified physiological structure of Silas's mind stands as guarantee of essential social continuity. But on the other, the principles of physiology also reveal a social and psychological world characterized not by unity and continuity, but conflict and disruption. The different functions of physiological psychology highlight the central questions raised by the novel: physiology enables George Eliot to reaffirm her ideological and emotional commitment to theories of ordered development, whilst simultaneously exploring the social and psychological inadequacies of this conception.

APPENDIX

Although catalepsy was a fairly common term in nineteenth-century physiology I have not been able to find a detailed examination of its causes or implications. Owsei Temkin has shown in *The Falling Sickness* (1971) how it was confused with forms of epilepsy from ancient medicine through to the nineteenth century, and the same general confusion as to its nature seems to reign in mid-Victorian discussions. Robert Macnish described it in *The Philosophy of Sleep* as a form of trance during which 'the whole body is cold, rigid and inflexible; the countenance without colour; the eyes fixed and motionless; while breathing and the pulsation of the heart are, to all appearance, at an end. The mental powers, are generally suspended, and participate in the universal torpor which pervades the frame' (1835, 38). Its nature, he adds, is continually unknown and though the suspension of the heart and lungs is more apparent than real, 'consciousness in a great majority of cases, is abolished'. Though the remote causes are obscure, he continues, it has been known to follow a fit of terror, or 'hysteria, epilepsy, or other spasmodic diseases, and is occasionally an accompaniment of menorrhagia and intestinal worms'. This eclectic list is fit demonstration of the confused state of medical understanding at the time. Amongst George Eliot's contemporaries catalepsy was associated with hypnotic trances; Carpenter describes the state of a subject undergoing electro-biology (or mesmerism) as like that of cataleptic subject – his body could be moulded into any position. (Carpenter, 1874, ch. XIV). Spencer in *The Principles of Sociology* (1876) associates catalepsy with 'ideas of swoon, apoplexy, ecstasy and other forms of insensibility' in his study of the responses of the primitive mind to these phenomena. Catalepsy, it seems, was thus a commonly available term in both physiological and social discussions of the mind. Though there was agreement about the physical nature of its manifestations, there appears to have been no adequate discussion of its causes. Macnish supported his discussion by giving details of cases of people who were buried alive, and Lewes concludes *The Physiology of Common Life* with similar stories. These accounts of inexplicable trances, or states of apparent death in life, would clearly have been known by George Eliot, and could furnish a possible source for the catalepsy of Silas.

For a contemporary medical discussion of Silas's malady, which suggests that the inexplicability of catalepsy (or narcolepsy) persists to this day, see Simon, 1966.

ACKNOWLEDGMENT

A different version of some of this material has already appeared in *George Eliot and Nineteenth-Century Science: The Make-Believe of a Beginning*. I am grateful to Cambridge University Press for permission to reprint it.

FURTHER READING

Beer, 1983

Burrow, 1966

Carroll, 1967

Graver, 1984

Levine, 1981

Lewes, 1859–60

McLaverty, 1981

Pinney, 1963

Shuttleworth, 1984

Smith, 1973

Spencer, 1855

Whyte, 1962

Wiesenfarth, 1970

Young, 1970 and 1973

Michelet and the Uses of Natural Reference

ROGER HUSS

EDITOR'S INTRODUCTION

Jules Michelet was primarily a historian, his contact with science and medicine being that of an enthusiastic amateur. Here we encounter the phenomenon of deliberate popularization for the first time in this book, for it is pre-eminently as a popularizer that Michelet is to be remembered. He was a prolific writer on historical, political and domestic subjects as well as on natural history. The large numbers his books sold indicate the growing market in the mid-nineteenth century for accessible scientific works. No doubt Michelet's enthusiasm was perfectly genuine, but the most interesting thing about it is the manner in which it reveals his social and political preoccupations and the tensions that underlay them. As Huss indicates, when Michelet speaks of nature, he simultaneously evokes the human realm. Nature serves as a romanticized, simplified version of human social life, yet even Michelet cannot suppress disturbing elements in nature, and hence conflicts and contradictions arise for him in his writings about nature just as we saw them do for the other writers discussed in the book.

Huss shows how the public/private distinction can usefully be applied to Michelet's work: it was a distinction which stood

at the heart of his social thought. We now recognize the importance of this pair of terms in Western political thought as well
as the strong gender connotations they carry (Elshtain, 1981).
Natural history comes into both domains for Michelet, but in
rather different forms. It pertains to the public through a form
of organicism which is somewhat different, however, from the
notion of 'organic' we have encountered in George Eliot. For
Michelet it is a question of treating nation-states as if they
were organisms, leading to their personification and to an
enhanced sense of nationalism. By contrast in the private,
domestic realm which Michelet so ardently idealized and promoted in mid-nineteenth-century France, nature and nature
study are identified with the feminine and constitute, in Huss's
words, a retreat. It is important to recognize what they were a
retreat from. Michelet, as one of the first historians to write
about the French Revolution of 1789 and to celebrate the role
of 'the people' in it, played an active part in French public life.
(Michelet, 1846). He was committed to the Revolution of
1830 as he was to that of 1848 and was bitterly disappointed
by the failure of the latter. His view of his own society was thus
both highly charged and complicated. Huss points for example to Michelet's complex relationship to 'the people', a complexity which is echoed in the ways in which he writes about
'the masses' in nature. Although Michelet proclaimed himself
a 'man of the people', he came in fact from the skilled artisa-
nate of Paris – his father was a printer – and he was for most
of his life part of the bourgeois intellectual world of the capital.
His writings on domesticity and the family idealize the secure
world of the petty-bourgeoisie where a non-working wife
could build a nest – a far cry from the daily existence of working families in the period. It is this commitment on Michelet's
part to the embourgeoisement of the working class which
accounts for what Huss describes as his individualism, especially in relation to work.

Michelet's concern with domestic life and the nature of familial relations naturally led him to consider sexuality and gender. We have already noted the widespread association of woman with nature, and the variety of inflections the idea has been given. Michelet gave it his own particular stamp – a highly sexualized vision of a sometimes fragile, sometimes pulsating feminine principle needing to be controlled and penetrated by the organizing, paternal male (Michelet, 1859). Here the intertwining of Michelet's ideas about nature, society and the family is particularly evident. Along with this also goes a voyeurism which provides himself and his readers with a vicarious pleasure by invading the private realm, whether of animals or human beings. Precisely because it does reveal the private, such an activity is tinged with prohibitions and hints of titillation, as in the use of the microscope to reveal an intimate, previously hidden world.

Just as we can locate Michelet clearly in his political context, his intellectual debts are equally clear. He admired the great French biologists of the eighteenth and nineteenth centuries and writers imbued with natural theology, such as Bernardin de Saint-Pierre. For both groups nature was a repository of meaning. Among biologists there was a special emphasis on the dynamism of living nature, the interaction between organism and environment and a fascination with the organization of living things, particularly with the transition from 'lower' to 'higher' animals. We find Michelet most interested in the areas of science and medicine which reflect on the phenomenon called 'life', partly because it was the most humanly significant part of the universe. He espoused a form of global animism – everything is alive or as if alive. The general interest in the sciences of life is characteristic of the period covered by this book, and it was fuelled by a vast number of different concerns, some of which have been outlined in the Introduction.

Huss argues that Michelet's treatment of nature served to reinforce the *status quo*. This is true, but not always in the expected ways. To link Michelet with natural theology, for instance, implies a certain religious commitment, since the natural theologian infers God's existence from the design of natural phenomena. In practice Michelet was violently anti-clerical, believing that priests were in league with uneducated women to perpetuate superstition and oppression. On the other hand he had a strong sense of the power, beauty and diversity of nature, and of the creative powers of the universe. His was in this sense a spiritual and moralistic view of the world but he did not espouse a particular creed. Michelet's opposition to traditional, non-republican political systems has already been mentioned. His enduring commitment was to France as an organic whole, that is, as a political unit, and to the middle class as the architects of the nation. No doubt this is connected with his admiration for a centralized state run by a professional elite drawn from or into the bourgeoisie. In this connection Michelet discusses a subject which is one of the best examples of the pervasive power of metaphors – the division of labour. This metaphor, which derived in part from the new, more specialized organization of industrial production, provides an image of a whole which indicates a certain relationship between the constituent parts and which offers individuals an account of their place within society. In a similar vein, we suggested earlier how important the nervous system was in generating models of civil society and the body politic which indicated how the relationships between different social groups could be conceptualized.

The idea of division of labour for Michelet came from physiology and biology and more specifically from attempts to explain changes which became apparent if the whole animal kingdom were reviewed at a glance. Lamarck, whom Michelet greatly admired, had noted, for example, that the flesh of simple animals has greater regenerative powers than that of more complex ones. It is, in other words, more versatile, exhibiting less division of labour, a phenomenon that appeared to be borne out by the fact that vertebrates have a larger number of specialized physiological systems, i.e. greater division of labour, with more different kinds of constituent tissues than invertebrates (Jordanova, 1984, 51). It was this preoccupation with vitality across the whole animal kingdom which fostered the interest of the physiologist Henri Milne-Edwards, to whom Michelet was indebted, in the idea of division of labour. There were, of course, other sources: political economy and psychology being the most important. Nor was this interest confined to France. The most influential example of such thinking in the nineteenth century was certainly Herbert Spencer, a Lamarckian and close friend of George Eliot, who interwove his biological and social ideas with great facility.

Michelet should also be placed in the French literary tradition, which included Buffon, and which produced natural history writings for a large audience. A wide range of works should be included in this group, including Bernardin de Saint-Pierre's writings, with their careful, detailed descriptions of vegetation and of topography. The vogue for natural history was certainly encouraged by the prestige of institutions like the Jardin du Roi, which became the Muséum National d'Histoire Naturelle during the Revolution, a period which saw its expansion and consolidation.

The presence in the Muséum of people like Lamarck and the Geoffroy Saint-Hilaires (father and son) who were committed to a more philosophical view of organisms, certainly encouraged the kind of interest Michelet had in nature, which was pre-eminently 'romantic'. Problematic though such a term might be (Williams, 1983, 274–6), it serves the useful purpose of alerting us to an emotional dimension in Michelet's writings. Huss uses the apt term 'euphoric' to indicate something of the flavour of the natural history books. Michelet above all, in whatever he wrote, sought to draw the reader in to share his own feelings and responses, to create a community of feeling which would change the way people lived. Although it would be simplistic to concentrate on the euphoria alone, it did serve the important function of binding together ideas about nature, human life and society into a moralistic whole.

Huss's essay shows once again the two main themes of the book. First, that views of nature are never unproblematic: however strong the desire is to present nature in a certain way, both it, and the language available for use about it, keep resisting our tidy categorizations. And once slippage between natural and moral domains is embraced, as it is by Michelet, it cannot always be controlled – unwelcome extrapolations keep popping up. The second theme is the ways in which languages of nature serve to mediate social and political concerns. In Michelet the mediations are apparent in his linguistic practices, as when he uses, for example, words like 'city' and 'civil war' with patently political connotations. Although openly didactic, Michelet's natural history writings cannot be set aside as 'merely' popularizations as if they carry no implications about 'real' science, for they capture preoccupations, conflicts and enthusiasms which went to the core of mid-nineteenth-century French science and society. National destiny, the future of the family and the control of sexuality were all negotiated through languages of nature.

*I*n the works of Jules Michelet (1798–1874), whether historical or non-historical, differences of subject are overshadowed by the recurrence of his preferred themes: the virtues of French culture and the Revolution, the people, woman and nature. These themes are themselves frequently interconnected: for example, the progress of the revolutionary spirit is linked to the development of the sciences of nature in eighteenth-century France: the dynamism and complexity of the most humble beings (coral polyps, flowers, insects) teaches a democratic lesson (1866, 441–2) and enables Michelet to present the republic as 'natural' (Viallaneix, 1971, 448). For Michelet 'the *sciences of life*' (his emphasis) 'are the sciences of love and show us that life is identical and that all beings are united in kinship and fraternity' (1858, 46); natural history is 'a branch of politics' (1856, 49). The rehabilitation of the people is conflated with the raising of those other oppressed and misunderstood beings, women, children and animals (1846, 192). The harmony towards which history tends is part of a greater fraternity, 'the great City' in which all living beings will one day be united (1868, xix). Discussion of the functions of natural reference in Michelet's work thus inevitably involves consideration of other realms — political, social, conjugal — for which nature is presented as exemplary.

This essay is divided into two sections. The first uses two early historical texts, the *Introduction to Universal History* (1831) and *Portrait of France* (1833), to show how Michelet exploits the prestige of the life sciences in order to promote a mythology of France as a living organism. In these works nature, in particular human anatomy and physiology, is a source of positive analogies which purport to characterize France as a nation and are used to legitimize the high status claimed for it among other nations. Michelet saw patriotism as a principal factor of social cohesion and an essential element of a future national system of education (1846, 239ff). The sec-

ond section of this essay deals with his popular natural history
books, *The Bird* (1856), *The Insect* (1857), *The Sea* (1861)
and *The Mountain* (1868), works in which reference to nature
is more sustained and direct. Here Michelet's anthropomor-
phis makes nature exemplify, more or less explicitly, social
and personal values. The celebration of nature in these works
shares common features with the celebration of France as a living organism – in both cases the values of solidarity and harmony are emphasized, the mother country and 'the universal
mother', nature, both being characterized by their unity.
Nature is accordingly, together with the history of France, a
fundamental subject of Michelet's ideal national curriculum.
Michelet uses his discourses on nature to edify his readers,
urging upon them the unity of all life and the ideals of fraternity
and sociability, as well as other values, such as those of work,
the conjugal family, maternal love and self-sacrifice. Our
examination of the nature books will point, however, to the
limits of this euphoric discourse and suggest that for Michelet
nature is not simply an exemplary realm but also contains
echoes of social and personal conflicts which are acknowledged only obliquely, emerging metaphorically or symbolically. The way in which Michelet's writing strives to reassure,
to minimize the conflict and difficulty it encounters, will be
demonstrated by a discussion of inadequacies in some of the
analogies he draws between the animal and human worlds.

ANATOMICAL AND PHYSIOLOGICAL ANALOGY IN MICHELET'S REPRESENTATION OF FRANCE

Although Michelet's active interest in natural history as a
study in its own right is not evident until 1840, when he
attended the lectures of Antoine Serres (1786–1868), professor of anatomy and natural history at the Muséum d'Histoire
Naturelle, Paris, by 1831 his awareness of the life sciences
had already been stimulated by his friendship with Dr W. F.
Edwards (1776–1842), polymath elder brother of the

physiologist Henri Milne-Edwards (1800–85). Moreover, at this period the prestige of the Muséum d'Histoire Naturelle stood high, and in 1830 there had been considerable public interest in the dispute of the zoologists Cuvier (1769–1832) and Etienne Geoffroy Saint-Hilaire (1772–1844) over the 'unity of plan' in nature (Cahn, 1962, ch. 20 and 21). It is an indication of the status of the life sciences that the term *physiologie* was being used by writers to lend authority to works of social and psychological observation, as in Brillat-Savarin's *Physiology of Taste* (1825) and Balzac's *Physiology of Marriage* (1829). The novelist Balzac, in particular, was finding in organic nature a potent source of analogy for his conception of Parisian life as a multiple yet coherent entity: in *Ferragus* (1833) the extended metaphor of the lobster conveys the dynamic and articulated unity of the waking city, while *The Human Comedy* as a whole rests on the idea of zoological analogy and the classification of 'social' species (*La Comédie Humaine*, 1829, I, 51). Michelet's use of terminology drawn from the life sciences is part of this broader context.

Michelet saw history as a progressive movement of emancipation by which humanity would overcome local constraints and eventually attain a state which was at once universal and centralized. He makes it clear that France has a special role to play in this movement : by virtue of the universal character of its culture and its centralized institutions, France indicates the direction of history, so much so that Michelet's *Introduction to Universal History* could, he writes, just as well be entitled *Introduction to the History of France* (1831, 277). Michelet supports his conception of France by characterizing it as a living organism, whose relationship to its environment (i.e. surrounding nations) is dynamic:

The sign and guarantee of the living organism, its power of assimilation, is to be found here in the highest degree: French France has been able to attract, absorb and give identity to the English, German and Spanish Frances by which she was surrounded. She has neutralized them one by the other and converted them all into her own substance. (1831, 247)

The metabolic metaphor is used here to naturalize France's ability to assimilate culturally and politically the outlying provinces which were otherwise subject to foreign influence. In this respect Rome, whatever her other imperfections, had prefigured France: 'Rome expands and contracts with the regularity of a living organism; she breathes in, if I may so express myself, the Latin, Sabine and Etruscan peoples and, once they have become Roman, breathes them out into her colonies. Thus was she able to assimilate the whole world' (1831, 234). Similarly, France is supremely capable of taking in and processing foreign ideas so as to give them a more general validity: 'Locke's sensationalism became European only by passing through Voltaire' (1831, 257). The analogy with a living organism not only helps Michelet present France in dynamic terms but also involves the notion of a centralized order based on the solidarity of different functions which can be observed in the higher animals. In the *Introduction* Michelet sees the provincial isolation of Italy and southern Germany as depriving men of the 'powerful assistance of the division of labour' available to the people of France, 'that multiple unity', 'that gigantic person made up of thirty million men' (1831, 248). The economic concept of division of labour had already been imported into natural history by Milne-Edwards, who saw the principle of the division of physiological labour as the criterion of the degree of perfection of each species in the hierarchy of organic nature (Merz, 1965, IV, 559). There would be widespread use of the concept in France during the last quarter of the nineteenth century to support organicist and solidarist theories of society (Zeldin, 1973, I, 656–7) and Michelet's work was itself widely read at that time. Raymond

Williams (1972) has discussed a comparable migration of ideas from the social to the natural sciences and back in a talk on social Darwinism. Michelet does not define in economic terms the division of labour which makes France a 'multiple unity'; he simply allows his readers to be borne along by the recent biological connotations of the concept which place France at the top of the scale of organized creatures. When Michelet develops the theme of centralization at greater length in his *Portrait of France* the immediate context is again one of physiological metaphor. France presents the appearance of a human body with both gastric and cerebro-spinal systems: Normandy, Brittany, Poitou, Auvergne and Guyenne on the one hand; on the other Languedoc, Provence, Burgundy, Champagne, Picardy and Flanders where the two systems are connected. Paris is the 'sensorium'. The strength and beauty of the whole, it is asserted, consist in 'the reciprocity of assistance, . . . the solidarity of the parts, . . . the distribution of functions, . . . the division of social labour' (1833, 381). Here, as elsewhere in Michelet, physiological analogies serve a persuasive rather than an analytical function; specific examples of reciprocity and solidarity in French national life are not given, although it should be remembered that the experience of the 1830 Revolution, 'the lightning flash of July' (1869a, 11), remained exemplary of social cohesion for Michelet, and cast its idealistic light on much of his subsequent work. More immediately recognizable as a reality is the privileged status of Paris, the 'sensorium' in which it can indeed be argued that the representatives of 'provincial originality' (1831, 248) become aware of themelves as part of a national culture, in the particular sense, for example, that the most influential educational institutions draw their students from the whole of France to Paris. The varied spectacle of Michelet's own provincial students at the Ecole Normale Supérieure evoked in the *Introduction* (1831, 290) is perhaps the most concrete example of Paris as nerve-centre that he offers. Otherwise what is striking

is the space which Michelet devotes to the biological second
term of his comparisons at the expense of specific reference to
his main subject: to support his assertion that limitation of
'local life' by centralization raises a society to a higher level,
Michelet quotes at length from the comparative anatomist
Dugès to the effect that in the lower animals 'local life is
strong'. Each segment of a leech has a completeness which
enables it to live separately from the other segments for a time.
As one climbs the scale of animate nature one finds segments
more intimately connected with each other and a greater con-
centration of sensation. The higher the animal in the scale the
more complete its centralization. Since 'nations can be classified like animals' (1833, 383) France is highest in the hierarchy of nations.

   A final example may be offered of the function of physiological reference in Michelet's apology for the dominant position
of Paris in the life of France. In the *Portrait of France*
Michelet presents Paris as surrounded by a belt (*ceinture*) or
circle of cities (Rouen, Orleans, Châlons, Rheims), which are
caught up in the capital's 'movement'. More distant cities
(Nantes, Bordeaux, Clermont, Toulouse, Lyons, Besançon,
Metz and Strasbourg) form a second belt. Paris manages to
reach the excentric Marseilles by *reproducing* itself in Lyons.
The ideas of circles and movement are next neatly combined in
the image of the vortex (*tourbillon*). This image conveniently
supports the myth of France as an animate being, since it is frequently used in the life sciences of the time to evoke an
organism's exchanges with its environment (Milne-Edwards
refers to nutrition as a vortex) and more generally to define life
itself and the dynamic persistence of its forms (Cuvier, 1817,
13). The role of Paris as the centre and most vital part of the
living being that is France is then persuasively established,
on the level of eloquence if not of argument, by a sentence
which both exploits these physiological connotations of the
whirlpool/vortex image and invites us to visualize the circles

reaching out from their northern centre: 'the vortex of the nation's life is at its densest in the north; in the south the circles it describes grow weaker and broader' (1833, 378).

The themes of transformation and centralized organic unity conveyed by Michelet's exploitation of physiological analogy in these two patriotic texts remain leitmotivs of his subsequent works, whether histories, works of social propaganda – *The People* (1846), *The Student* (his 1848 lectures), *Our Sons* (1869) – or the nature books. In the second part of this essay I will concentrate on direct, as opposed to metaphorical, reference to nature, but will still emphasize the persuasive function of this reference, which urges Michelet's conceptions of national, social, conjugal and personal life on the reader.

THE NATURE BOOKS

In the autobiographical essay 'How the Author Was Led to the Study of Nature', which opens his first nature book, *The Bird* (1856), Michelet describes nature as a retreat and source of consolation. Adopting his favourite pose of historian-martyr he recalls himself working, a sick man, amidst the ruins of the Republican hopes of 1848, on his account of the conflicts of 1793 ('the sadness of the past merged with the sadness of the present'), and seeking solace after a day's suffering, in the 'innocent peace' of the accounts of naturalists read to him by his young wife Athénaïs (1856, 6). He claims that *The Bird* avoids 'human analogy' and provides 'an escape (*alibi*) from the world of men, the deep solitude and wilderness of the distant past' (1856, 8). There is certainly a sense in which Michelet's nature books represent a withdrawal to another place, a form of absenteeism (the term *alibi* used by Michelet simply means an elsewhere: modern connotations of bad faith are not intended) and it will be argued below that one function of the books is to constitute nature as refuge by associating nature study with the protected private world of the conjugal home which figures prominently as an ideal in Michelet's prop-

agandist writing. What initially strikes the reader of the nature
books, however, is the fact that, while they appear to present
nature as a retreat from the 'world of men', far from avoiding
human analogy and taking nature on its own terms, they are
shot through with anthropomorphism. Nature is constantly
presented in human terms and at the same time perceived as
containing models and lessons for humanity.

It will be seen that this assimilation of natural and human
realms functions in a way that, ambiguities notwithstanding, is
fundamentally confirmatory of the social *status quo*. This is
consistent with the natural theological framework which gives
the nature books their overt structure: although Michelet's
concept of nature, inspired in part by his reading of Lamarck,
is a dynamic and transformationist one based on the evolution
of species, it is still informed by a providential teleology and
presents the features of harmony and equilibrium to be found
in the classical French natural theologies of Fénelon (*Treatise
on the Existence of God*, 1712), Bernardin de Saint-Pierre
(*Studies of Nature*, 1784) and Chateaubriand (*Genius of
Christianity*, 1802), or of the more vigorous Anglo-Saxon
tradition reflected in Paley's *Natural Theology* (1802) and in
the *Bridgewater Treatises* (Chalmers *et al.*, 1833–6). As such
Michelet's view of nature attempts to minimize conflict and
inequality: a reference to Darwin and the 'struggle for life' is
followed by the remark that the struggle is innocent, creates
the harmony and balance of nature, and is in fact not a struggle
at all but rather peace, exchange, rotation (1868, 183).
Michelet implicitly recommends respect for the larger order in
which particular species or groups have their proper function
and utility. Just as society needs its garbage collectors and
undertakers so in nature 'the essential task of public sanitation'
is discharged by gulls and crustacea, while minute crabs sweep
the beaches clean of dead jelly fish like agile undertakers
(1861, 211). Like his contemporary Charles Kingsley, who
in *The Wonders of the Shore* (1855) remarks of the madre-

pore, 'by profession a scavenger, and a feeder on carrion', that 'he' is 'as useful as he is beautiful' (Kingsley, 1949, 261), Michelet emphasizes the noble or beautiful appearance of creatures who exercise such base functions: vultures resemble Turkish pashas 'draped in a noble cloak of grey' (1856, 170), carrion-beetles carry out their 'sinister trade' in the most beautiful dress, while the dung-beetle 'which disposes of droppings is dressed in sapphire in payment for this service' (1857, 146–7). What such ennoblement implies for the organization of human society is in no sense a disturbance of a rather paternalistic hierarchy: rather it seeks to authorize a more generous attitude towards deserving subordinates. Michelet's pervasive theme of raising the lowly (whether animals, women, children or the people) remains largely an affair of the sympathetic heart.

It would nevertheless be inaccurate to describe Michelet's writing merely as complacently paternalistic. Much of the nature books' interest lies precisely in the anxieties that they attempt to exorcise through language which constantly implies but evades its disturbing subject: writing becomes an unstable mixture of alibi (in the modern sense of the term) and confession. One prominent anxiety concerns Michelet's relation to what he describes as 'the people', an ambiguous relation which appears figuratively in his uneasy attitude to the masses of the insect and marine worlds. Michelet likes to assert that in spite of his success he has been true to his popular origins, remaining a man of the people, sharing its vitality, instinctiveness and simplicity. He sees his role as that of intermediary, both explaining the people in its true dignity to his readers and using a language which will be accessible to the people itself. The dream of a language which is an act, breaking down the barriers between men, is not, however, realized: 'I was born of the people, I carried the people in my heart. . . . But its language, its language was closed to me. I have failed to make the people speak' (1869b, 363). This failure of communication is dramatized metaphorically in *The Insect*. Michelet had already (in *The People*) established equivalences between the people, the child, woman and nature itself (1846, 175 and 186) and it is such equivalences which make for much of the metaphorical density of the nature books. Although an over-view of Michelet's production suggests that each equivalent term provides the subject of a separate work or number of works (nature in *The Bird, The Insect, The Sea* and *The Mountain*, woman in *Love* (1858) and *Woman* (1859), the child in *Our Sons*, and the people in *The People*), in fact Michelet's totalizing tendency, his aspiration to write about all subjects at once, makes such a classification inadequate: the nature books are also metaphorical (and sometimes literal) reflections on the people, woman and the child as well. The identification of the people with nature which concerns us here is most evident in *The Insect* and *The Sea*, and the analyses which follow will be drawn from the first of these books.

In the light of Michelet's anxiety to communicate with the people there is a certain logic in the contrast he establishes between the bird, with whom imaginative communication was easy — 'we exchanged our languages. I spoke for him, he sang for me' (1857, vi) — and who was readily characterized by Michelet as a fellow artist (Michelet as nightingale), and the insect (or people), alien, hidden behind warlike armour, inaccessible to communication. This distance represents a challenge to the writer's empathy, a gulf which he tries to overcome by presenting the insect as a creature which is sensitive and industrious:

> If you work and if you love, insect, whatever your appearance, I cannot shun you. We are in a sense related. And what am I myself, if not a worker. (1857, viii)

In *The People* Michelet had sought to correct an ill-conceived and negative view of the people, to rehabilitate them in the eyes of their critics. In the course of this process, however,

Michelet expresses preferences for certain groups within the people (a term never adequately defined) at the expense of others: he shows particular tenderness for the small proprietor and the peasant while evoking with distaste 'the rabble of the factories' (1846, 90), the industrial proletariat which, he hastens to remind the reader, is untypical of French society at the time (1846, 152). One senses Michelet making an *effort* of sympathy: 'this crowd (of factory workers) is not inherently bad' (1846, 102).

Similarly, a somewhat uneasy rehabilitation of the teeming insect world is the theme of the opening chapter of *The Insect*, entitled 'Terrors and Aversions of a Child'. Here Michelet uses a fragment of his wife's autobiography (a longer section of which is also used to introduce *The Bird*) in which she describes her family's empty country house invaded by spiders, centipedes and woodlice, while the garden's fruits are destroyed by wasps. The immediate interest of the passage lies in Michelet's assertion that we are all, like the young Athénaïs, vulnerable to such fears and repulsion, and his use of the following analogy to support his point:

> How would we react to our workers if they always went around bristling with the steel and metal implements they use in their labours? They would strike us as strange and monstrous; they would frighten us. (1857, 8)

The comparison is preceded by a self-contradictory attempt to explain away the insect's weapons: the insect lives in a world of conflict so his panoply of weapons which seems so threatening to man is only to be expected and, in any case, most of them are not weapons at all, just 'the peaceful implements they use to earn their living, the tools of their trade' (1857, 8).

In the rehabilitation of the insect its social characteristics play a significant role (the social insects, bees, ants and termites, are the subject of a large part of the book). Considered simply in terms of numbers the insects are terrifying: Michelet

writes of them demanding a hearing, addressing to the higher
species, man, a 'claim terrifying because of the number of the
claimants' (1857, iv), but once they are organized in a 'city'
the spectator's terror is exorcized and gives way to admiration. The shift, metaphorically, is from the people as disturbing mass to the people as a republic of citizens. Michelet's first
description of an ant colony (1857, xix–xxii) accordingly
develops in an elevated manner. Furthermore, as will be seen,
it has a temporal dimension which invites the reader to his-
toricize the political analogy contained in the term 'city', and
interpret the passage in terms of republican history.

The description is, typically for Michelet, given the authority of personal experience: in a wood near Lucerne, Athénaïs
Michelet, prodding at a rotten treestump, whose previous
inhabitants, scolytids, had been overthrown by a colony of
ants, breaks down the walls of the city to reveal the galleries
within. While his young wife empathizes excitedly with the
sudden agitation of the colony (an empathy which reinforces
the equivalence between woman, child, nature and, by implication, the people), Michelet reflects that the occupation of
the scolytids was ancient history: they had been eliminated by
some 'great chemical transformation' (the reference is to formic
acid) which had enabled the ants, over a period of generations, to burn out and 'cleanse' (the French uses the verb
assainir, a term evoking the domain of public health) their
edifice, the equal, in its way, of Babylon and Babel (Thebes
and Nineveh are also mentioned), but now, like them, a ruin.
Michelet does not develop his reflection into an explicit allegory of recent French history; instead, after referring to his
familiarity as an historian with the fall of republics and
empires, he quotes a line from Homer on the fall of Troy, but
the pathos attending the fall of the ant republic nevertheless
encourages the reader to identify it with the short-lived Second
Republic, just as the earlier 'great chemical transformation'
which evicted the scolytids may be read as standing for the

Revolution of 1789. Homeric pathos does not simply distance it also lends a recent defeat the dignity of myth.

In a series of rhetorical questions which closes this episode, Michelet presents himself as powerless to reconstruct 'this devasted world', incapable of helping 'this great insect people, industrious and deserving, persecuted, devoured or scorned by all the tribes of animate nature, and which nevertheless provides all of us with the most vivid examples of disinterested love, of civic duty and of sociability'. This melancholy resignation implicity expresses the limits of Michelet's practical activity as a republican, and his acceptance of the *fait accompli* of the Second Empire which had sent his fellow republicans Quinet and Victor Hugo into exile. What Michelet offers is simply an oblique and figurative service to republicanism: 'What can I do for this great people of insects? . . . one thing. Understand it, explain it and, if I can, cast upon it the light of a benevolent interpretation' (1857, xxiii).

While the virtues attributed to the ants can be read as exemplary for human society (Michelet celebrates their altruism, industry and sense of posterity), the imprecision of the analogies implied between the two realms allows the text to legitimize certain assumptions. For example, the idea of the ants constructing their 'city' (the French term *cité* is itself usefully ambiguous indicating both a place to live and a political system, a republic) implies an idealized conflation of the worlds of work and politics. In fact, human workers could not be said to contribute to the construction of the republic simply by continuing their 'persevering work', although such an illusion would appeal to a writer who, like Michelet, excluded violent change as a prelude to a new political system. Furthermore, the ants' struggle to construct their republic is basically a struggle against an environment (Michelet sees this colony finally succumbing to the autumn rains) and thus provides an insufficient analogy for the obstacles which threaten human organization from within. Finally, the distinction between private and public realms is also interestingly obscured by the fact that the ants, while building dwellings for themselves (the terms *demeure* and *appartement* refer to private dwellings), are also constructing a collective habitat. Thus although Michelet finds a metaphor for political disillusion in the natural world, the natural also provides him with a reassuring simplification of the human world.

The simplification is most evident in passages which bring together humans and insects on a literal level. In the forest of Fontainebleau ants and quarrymen (together with woodpeckers) are associated in an edifyingly industrious concert which Michelet contrasts with 'the great sickness of the day, restlessness and pointless agitation' (1857, xxxiii). Rhetorically it is all the easier for Michelet to assimilate men and ants to each other since the contiguous space they occupy justifies a metonymous transference: 'the ants work the sand, the quarrymen work the sandstone. They share the same spirit' (Michelet uses the word *génie*, which has the appropriate secondary meaning of 'engineering'), 'ant-men above the ground, ants which are almost men beneath' (1857, xxxvi). This symmetry of work, described by Michelet in moral terms ('their industrious patience', 'their admirable perseverance') distracts the reader from the distinctions it would be possible to draw between the activity of the quarrymen and that of the ants: the product of the quarrymen's work is not directly enjoyed by the quarrymen themselves but goes to pave the streets of Paris, and their occupation not only brings them into contact with a natural resistance (like that encountered by the ants) but also subjects them to the constraints of a market. These distinctions are evaded and Michelet simply foregrounds the active but modestly contained and unambitious life ('*vie active et recueillie*') of the ants as exemplary for human workers. The suppression of difference is further evidenced in Michelet's assimilation of the work of ants and quarrymen to his own 'tireless labour' as an historian. The paradox is worth noting that in this text Michelet finally uses social insects as a way of focusing on individual effort – the contradiction is an important one to which we shall return later in this essay when discussing the public and private functions of the nature books and their individualistic petty-bourgeois ideology.

Significantly, the most sustained evocation of work in *The Insect* occurs in connection with the solitary spider (included in the book in spite of the zoological distinction between arachnida and insects). Michelet's celebration of the republican virtues of the social insects (bees are republicans too, in spite of appearances) might have suggested a negative appraisal of the reclusive spider. Instead Michelet particularly values the withdrawn self-reliance of the spider, which he assimilates first to a self-employed artisan and next to the small manufacturer: his body is his spinning-mill and the substance he draws from himself to make the web and thus live is described as a personal capital investment (*'une mise de fonds'*). Michelet shows the same sympathy for the vulnerable spider caught up in a vicious circle – 'to spin you must eat, to eat you must spin' (1857, 210) – as he had for the small businessman in the chapter of *The People* entitled 'Servitudes of the Manufacturer': but once again the analogy has obvious shortcomings since it identifies owner, factory and worker in the individual person of the spider and thus simplifies the implications of the term *chômage* (unemployment) which Michelet uses merely to describe an inactivity which would be fatal to the spider. Here unemployment is simply related to individual effort and the analogy contains no term equivalent to the wage-earners who would also suffer unemployment if the mill closed.

Thus far our discussion of the nature books has concentrated on Michelet's exploitation of the natural to exemplify and present as unproblematic certain social and political ideals. The area of human experience referred to has been, ostensibly at least, public ('la cité'). The ideals which will be examined below can be described as domestic or private. Here, as above, the unproblematic surface presented by the nature books is often belied by the content of Michelet's examples.

The nature books and the didactic works, *Love* and *Woman*, which contain Michelet's most literal evocations of the joys of domestic life, are closely interconnected. While *Love* and *Woman* use natural example to support the values of conjugal harmony and the home, the nature books in their turn provide metaphorical celebrations of these values, as well as introducing the conjugal dimension literally in the persons of the Michelet couple, united in nature study.

The ideal home is the 'small detached house' (1858, 59) which the wife adorns (she does not work outside the home) and in which she is safe, like a bird in a nest. This 'delicate, impressionable and penetrable person' must be protected from the miasmas and moral dangers of the outside world, 'the disturbing mixture of a hundred corrupt and corrupting things which rise up to her from the street' (1859, 76–7). In an exemplary passage of *The Mountain* the home appears as a fortress, under assault from without: with their thick walls the old houses of the Engadine give protection against the harshest winter and even contain a refuge within a refuge in the shape of a small chamber hidden above the stove, a 'paradise' reached by a discreet staircase, a 'happy nest' where husband and wife 'take refuge, huddle together and live like marmots'. This retreat Michelet sees both in terms of the cultivation of conjugal harmony and, quoting the sixteenth-century Huguenot naturalist Bernard Palissy, as a contrast to the conflicts of politics and public life: 'How to wrap oneself up, to enclose oneself in a deep repose? Is not the model of a secure shelter the carapace or the shell whose thick whorls are a guarantee of safety?' (1868, 318). The symbolic value of the house closed against the hostile elements is also evident in a section of *The Sea* entitled 'The Storm of October 1859' in which the sounds of the raging sea heard from within a beleaguered cliff-top house are compared to the howling of 'a ghastly mob' and a 'horrible rabble' (1861, 85). Also in *The Sea*, the sea urchin provides a model of defence (186), although it is less admirable than forms which are not only enclosed but are also double, made up of 'two associated halves': the example of certain shellfish implicitly poeticizes the private delights of the protected conjugal home:

Each shell is double, containing both lover and beloved. Just as the palaces of the Orient hide their marvels behind gloomy walls, so here the outside is rough and the interior dazzling. The marriage takes place by the glow of a small sea of mother of pearl which, multiplying its mirrors, gives the house, even though it is closed, the charm of a mysterious enchanted twilight. (1861, 193).

Yet although Michelet asserts that nature provides authority for the state of marriage – 'In natural history, the higher animals tend to married life and attain it at least for a time. And this is, to a great extent, what makes them the higher animals' (1858, v) – and waxes lyrical over animals as homemakers and selfless mothers (1856, 64, 265 *et passim*; 1857, 213, 298, 346 *et passim*; 1861, 244, 253–4 *et passim*), educators of their young (1856, 287) and loving couples (1861, 245), the sexual relationships which he presents in the nature books are in fact most frequently fraught with difficulty. Mating whales (described as 'lovers') present a pathetic and grotesque spectacle, slipping against each other in a union which looks more like a combat (1861, 242). The spider may evoke agreable images of domestic seclusion – one has a 'back-room' hidden behind the end of a funnel, while another constructs a nest with a door – but the male must approach the female with great care lest he be devoured: the human connotations are reinforced here by a reference to cannibalism on the notorious raft of the *Medusa* (1857, 222). When she acknowledges him, even responding ardently, he sometimes panics and flees. The fact that Michelet imagines such sombre courtship taking place on the domestic ceiling introduces a lugubrious note of sexual conflict into the idealized home (1857, 223).

The union of male and female is hardly less problematic in the world of plants, but in this case the theme is that of difficulty overcome and the dominant tone in a highly anthropomorphic text is that of the erotic novel. Michelet attacks the standard botanic nomenclature because French uses feminine nouns to designate the male parts ('stamen' and 'anthera' are feminine in French) and masculine nouns ('*le* pistil' and '*le* stigmate') for the female. Instead he prefers terms like 'lover', 'husband', 'lady', which transform his account into a figurative representation of human sexual intercourse (1868, 247–50). In the blue gentian, observed by Michelet in the peace of his room, the pistil towers above the stamens and makes fertilization seem a hopeless task: 'It is she who totally dominates. Sovereign and colossal in comparison with her tiny lovers, she seems to confront them with an everlasting difficulty.' The scene is 'half tragic'. Michelet sympathizes with the lovers ('I felt pity for these unfortunates') confronted by the virginal whiteness of 'the lady'. A style characterized by exclamation and rhetorical questions strives to generate erotic suspense and empathy as one airborne 'atom', one 'husband' among a thousand candidates, miraculously scales the peak: will she receive him, 'will she, proud, still closed, not relent towards him?' A drop of honey, 'the flower's yes', appears on her threshold and signals his victory. He encounters no further resistance, it is as if she replies, 'I surrender, you are my master!' Now Michelet is surprised to see, with the help of his microscope, the male swelling prodigiously. For a moment he is alarmed and, in a phrase which naively reveals the vicarious nature of the writer's involvement, imagines an exchange of roles between spectator and actor: 'If he had continued thus with his prodigious impetus, our roles would have been reversed and I would have become the atom' (1868, 258).

It can be seen from the above examples that in its implications for the private sphere as for the public, nature is not merely an exemplary realm. It also provides the writer with a language in which he can express sexual frustration and, on occasion, obtain imaginary relief for this frustration.

The frustration or displacement of desire is particularly relevant to the view of marriage expressed in *Woman* and *Love*. In these works it is made clear that male desire has to be tempered to the vulnerable, innocent creature that is woman (1858, 4–10, 69–75; 1859, 273–4, 279–80, 287, 371–2). At the same time a woman's own desire is presented as dangerous to her. For example, in a complex passage in *Woman*, flowers are seen as usefully calming the excitability of the girl child – 'woman, particularly as a child, is totally subject to her nerves' (1859, 129) – and are said to possess a 're-lative innocence'. Yet the 'organ of love' of certain species, seen under the microscope, is surprisingly similar to the sexual organs of the higher life-forms (the style is euphemistic in its indirectness); the flower thus ceases to be innocent. Indeed, its heady perfume might 'penetrate' the child were she not busily engaged in tending the flower like a mother. Thus 'maternal feelings counterbalance and cure love'. The flower ceases to be a 'lover' and is safely transformed into a daughter (not just a child but a female child, to be doubly safe). The 'pernicious and dangerous rapture' is held at bay. A similar pattern of repression is reflected in *The Mountain* in a sustained symbolic representation of female desire. Here the earth is presented as a woman, with cyclical movements, yearning in vain for the sun, her 'adored lover'. Her aspiration subsides 'as if she had reflected and was holding herself back, though not without a sigh' (1868, 131).

Turning now to the function which Michelet claims for nature study and the somewhat different function which, we shall argue, it principally fulfils, we encounter again the divergence between public and private realms which has been

referred to above. Although Michelet refers to nature as an
alibi, a means of escape, he just as often claims a public function for nature. The nature books were conceived as popular
books, as is evident from their style, and indeed reached a
wide audience. In them Michelet sees himself as contributing
to the moralization of his audience (the theme of regeneration
being particularly important in *The Sea* and *The Mountain*).
He even makes certain practical recommendations relating to
public health and recreation: the sea and the mountains provide a hygiene which is both physical and moral (1861, 'Re-
birth through the Sea', 345–408; 1868, 'Can Our Age Rise
Again?', 347–65). Nevertheless, much of the thrust of nature
study as Michelet presents it remains directed away from the
public realm. By placing his own idyll with Athénäis in the
foreground of each of the nature books he explicitly presents
nature study as an intimate conjugal pursuit, and by the association of woman with nature (1857, 399; 1861, 386; 1859,
159) he makes nature study an annex of the private world of
the home with which woman is exclusively identified.

In each of the nature books the domestic context of nature
study is given great prominence. The introductory chapter of
The Bird incorporates Athénäis's autobiographical account
of the country house and garden, with its harmonious community of men and animals, in which she spent her childhood, a
paradise lost on her father's death. Michelet resumes with a
detailed description of the house and garden near Nantes
to which the couple withdrew in 1852 (after Michelet had
refused to sign the oath of allegiance to the Empire) and which
reconstituted the childhood paradise (Athénäis refers to
Michelet as a second father). In *The Insect* their house and
garden again figure prominently (1857, xxiv, 47, 276–89,
362–4). Even where nature is experienced away from home
(as in *The Sea* and *The Mountain*) a domestic context is carefully re-established. For the ailing young wife sent by her husband to spend a restorative summer by the sea, Michelet pre-

scribes with an architect's detail the house she should take: in particular it should have a small garden protected from the wind, and its own sea-water pool 'in which she can place the day's discoveries and small curiosities given her by the fishermen' (1861, 379). The process by which nature is thus domesticated can be clearly traced in *The Sea*, where the ocean appears first as a threatening desert (1861, 3–6) and later as 'God's great swimming-pool' (418). Its life can be observed with impunity in the sheltered confines of rock pools, 'those miniature oceans' (385) which can finally be reproduced more privately at home. In *The Mountain* interiors are frequently evoked (1868, 7–8, 17–18, 110, 318) as are the gardens of Athénaïs's childhood and marriage (224); at Bex, in the Alps, nature is enjoyed from a balcony and flowers are brought by a willing local girl to be studied by the Michelets under the microscope in their room (245–7). The microscope can indeed be regarded as taking the process of domestication or privatization a stage further, as it provides a still more intimate frame for nature than do either the garden or the room which contains the instrument. An ideal representation of nature concentrated on a narrow private space within the larger private space is provided by an earlier visit to the Alps: Michelet stays at an inn near Lucerne and takes as his study 'an exceedingly spacious room which, with its seven windows opening onto the mountains, the lake and the town, and its triple aspect, provided me with a marvellous light at all hours of the day. From morning till evening the sun was my faithful companion and turned around my microscope, placed in the middle of the room' (1857, xii–xiii). Here the seven windows and triple aspect give the scene the mythical quality of fairy tale as if to emphasize its exemplary character.

Another connotation, that of femininity, reinforces Michelet's use of the microscope to symbolize withdrawal from the world. For Michelet the qualities demanded by microscopic study are specifically feminine: 'one must become something of a woman in order to succeed with it' (1857, xi). The instrument requires patience, dexterity and, above all, time, the freedom to repeat over and over again the same observation. In short, to use the microscope one must be 'out of the world, outside time' (1857, xi). This, for Michelet, feminine connotation supports the other recurrent themes of woman as mediator of nature and woman as nature herself.

The microscope, then, evokes a composed world in which the hours pass with no sense of urgency and external reality is not allowed to intrude. Such is the tender familiarity the instrument inspires that it is even personified as 'my little copper man' (1857, 113). Of course, the peaceful context in which the observer scrutinizes the object beneath the lens might conceivably be troubled by the character of the observer's discoveries. Indeed, when Michelet introduces the microscope by means of a vivid, hagiographical excursus on the Dutch naturalist Swammerdam (1637–80) he stresses the horror of 'the living infinite' (1857, 91–2) and imagines the inventor recoiling from 'the abyss of nature in conflict, devouring itself.' He goes on to compare the effect on Swammerdam of his discoveries to the reactions of a man in a boat being carried calmly but inexorably towards the Niagara falls (106–7). Yet Michelet modulates from this starting point in a typically reassuring fashion: above all the microscope offers wonderful transformations of reality, revealing the unexpected beauty of humble objects (113–15, 191). This theme is a commonplace of popular scientific writing in the nineteenth century and similar passages can be found in, for example, the *Household Words* of Charles Dickens.

The attractions of home nature study as it is presented by Michelet do not, however, depend merely on the beauty of the objects examined (nor even on the morally edifying lessons which, as has been seen, Michelet attempts to draw from the scrutiny of nature). There is in the control and manipulation of living things, in the spectacle of their conflicts, of their sexual activity and even of their death, a satisfaction which overrides the disturbing effect of what is observed. Contained by the Michelets within their garden or on the table in their study, nature, in its smaller representatives the insects, can provide a miniature theatre of human affect in disguise. Even when anthropomorphism is most rampant in Michelet's description of such performances the result for the spectator is still a diverting one, just as literary fictions may give pleasure and reassurance even when calling upon the reader to identify with human suffering. Recurrent terms from the world of spectacle – 'prodigious drama' (1861, 133), 'phantasmagoria' (1861, 142), 'mime' (1857, 123), 'coup de théâtre' (1857, xix) – show nature functioning as entertainment. To conclude this section two passages from *The Insect* in which the 'spectacular' element is prominent will be discussed in some detail, since they demonstrate the way in which potentially disturbing material can be dramatized, contained and distanced. In both cases Michelet presents his wife and himself as experimenters and spectators, witnessing and to some extent provoking spectacles of violence, sex and death.

The first scene takes place during a stay in Switzerland where Michelet and Athénaïs begin to study insects seriously. No longer satisfied with the external view offered by entomological collections, they decide to 'penetrate the internal organs with scalpel and microscope' (1857, 20) and are thus forced to 'commit our first crimes' (the conjugal harmony which is one desired effect of nature study is given a lugubrious yet comic twist by this picture of two accomplices). Michelet stresses the intensity of their feeling in a way which unwittingly points up its literary component: 'this preoccupation, this emotion, more *dramatic* than might be imagined, spoilt our trip' (20, my emphasis). The spectacle of 'suffering life (and life on which we had to inflict suffering)' is presented as spoiling their enjoyment of the mountains: 'the eternal epic of the infinitely great hardly competed with the *drama* of our infinitely small'.

Yet there is in the following elaboration of this antithesis between the vast and the diminutive an aestheticizing elegance
which devalues the emotion it seeks to reinforce: 'A fly concealed the Alps from us. The agonies of a coleopter which
took ten days to die cast a veil over Mont Blanc; the anatomy
of an ant caused us to forget the Jungfrau' (20). The victim
whose sufferings Michelet chooses to relate in detail is a stag-
beetle discovered by Athénaïs during a solitary walk and
brought back by her to be etherized. The insect is presented in
her first-person account as a horrifying apparition: locked in
combat with a smaller beetle, it destroys the harmony of the
peaceful landscape Athénaïs had been enjoying. The
anthropomorphism of her account is negative and stigmatizes
the beetles as feudal lords used to devouring their vassals and
thus not deserving of pity. Nevertheless, with the tip of her
parasol she instinctively interrupts the struggle without harm-
ing either beetle. In the rest of the account, continued by
Michelet, the couple's sympathy is shown shifting to the stag-
beetle. Although the observations, and worse, to which the
beetle is subjected are at first presented as a punishment for its
'fratricidal voraciousness' the suffering of the insect when
etherized becomes an occasion for the Michelets to empathize
with it. Ether usually provides 'a faster and seemingly sweeter
death' but the 'prisoner' after an hour or two revives, attempts
to walk, and falls as if drunk. A further dose is no more effective. The Michelets are surprised to see that although the beetle's powers of locomotion are impaired the ether has excited
'what one might call its amorous faculties' (the formulation
conveys coy reticence and perhaps also the awareness that the
interpretation is questionable). The beetle painfully approaches a dead female of its own species (which *happens* to
be lying on the same table), groping at her in an apparent
attempt to resuscitate her (the theme of resuscitation is, it may
be recalled, at the centre of Michelet's picture of his relationship, as historian, to the dead past). We are directed to inter-

pret this 'strange, funereal spectacle' in human terms, as 'touching for anyone who knows (with the knowledge of the heart) that all nature is identical' (25). Michelet and Athénaïs try to separate 'this Juliet from this Romeo' but he still refuses to succumb to the ether: 'the indomitable male mocked all poisons'. Eventually they shut the beetle in a box (shades of premature burial) where it is subjected to further massive doses of ether and takes a fortnight to 'consummate its torture' and die. Michelet claims that its tender-hearted executioners shared this ordeal, reflecting all the while on the strange persistence of love and comparing their own role to that of the Fates cutting the thread just before the victim's moment of fulfilment.

In this sombre tale the distancing and aestheticizing of the themes of sex and death is achieved by a variety of means: there is the intrinsic distance of the experimental context – the protagonist is manipulated, his reactions observed; there are the aestheticizing analogies from the world of dramatic fiction (Romeo and Juliet) and of mythology (the Fates); and there is reflection and comment from the experimenters in their somewhat disingenuous role as epic witnesses. This distancing framework contains and domesticates the sometimes disturbing elements which work in the opposite direction to establish identity not distance: nature is one, therefore the indomitable urge of the stag-beetle is that of the human male; the beetles are Romeo and Juliet, admittedly characters in fiction but still a *human* couple, like the only other couple present, Michelet and Athénaïs who, it is claimed, experience the beetle's torture themselves. Like the stag-beetle, Michelet, the historian, was concerned to resuscitate the dead. A further identity, supported by the autobiographical evidence of Michelet's *Journal*, published posthumously between 1959 and 1976, as well as by the symbolic content of much of his other writing, involves an implied assimilation of Athénaïs to the dead Juliet: If Michelet = Romeo = the stag-beetle = the persistent male,

Athénaïs is the frigid female, the corpse he tries unsuccessfully to resuscitate. Similarly, if Michelet and Athénaïs execute the stag-beetle before it can achieve sexual fulfilment this can be read as an attempt to present censorship of male sexuality as a joint decision taken by the story-book Michelet couple, perfectly united in their murderous work ('our crimes').

A second example of nature's home theatre is provided by Michelet's account of conflict between two species of ant witnessed in his garden at Fontainebleau (1857, 276–89). The main difference displayed by this episode, entitled 'Civil War', is that its implications, albeit undeveloped, are political as well as private. As before, the events observed are provoked by the fascinated spectators themselves for it is they who bring one species of ant (carpenter ants) from the forest into the garden and onto the territory of the other species, the smaller mason ants. In effect, the Michelets stage-manage the destruction of the carpenter ant republic, for the ant society introduced into the garden has already been diminished by the process of transplantation and is now overwhelmed by the more enterprising smaller ants. The Michelets' initial sympathy for the mason ants (who have been invaded) gives way to indignation as they watch them tear the nymphs (pupae) of the interloper ants out of their protective covering in a scene graphically described as a collective rape. Typically, Michelet exploits the episode's dramatic possibilities, adopting an epic style to trace the peripeteia of the conflict, and leaving the implications of the title, with its potential reference to the civil conflict of 1848, unworked out. The most specific of his anthropomorphic analogies, which assimilates the virulent mason ants to savage Iroquois or Hurons, is remarkably distancing and defuses any implied reference to the civil conflicts which preceded the fall of the Second Republic. The destruction of the ant republic certainly generates pathos as Michelet pictures a sole survivor bearing a cradle away into the shadows, but the pathos remains unfocused. In spite of the episode's title, sexual implications emerge more strongly than do political ones. The brutal scene of the rape of the nymphs is linked with Michelet's account of his own painful extraction of a nymph from its casing (1857, 284). Thus once more the analogy between the observer (Michelet) and the actors (the violent mason ants) in the drama observed indicates a displacement of desire (censorship by diversion) and foregrounds the vicarious use to which the scrutiny of nature is so often put in the works we have been discussing.

This essay has attempted to show that in Michelet's work nature supports a discourse which is both euphoric and problematic. An exemplary nature, figuring as the second or principal term of analogies with humanity, is used by Michelet to legitimize certain values, but the analogies lack rigour and imply simplifications of national, social, economic and conjugal reality. Even when the euphoric surface of Michelet's writing is troubled by the apprehension of conflict, death and sexuality in nature, this disturbance, presented through the eyes of the amateur naturalist and his wife, takes on a spectacular and aesthetic quality. Nature is thus not only a source of value and a vehicle of idelology but also a theatre in which realities at odds with this ideology can still be contemplated, even enjoyed, at a distance. The hesitation between ideological and diversionary uses of nature combines with the tension between public and private values, which has been another theme of this essay, to make the nature books unresolved and challenging texts, in spite of the gestures of resolution they contain.

FURTHER READING

Barthes, 1954

Borie, 1984

Europe, 1973

Gossmann, 1974

Orr, 1976

Revue d' Histoire Littéraire
de la France, 1974

Viallaneix, 1975

Bibliography

Except where otherwise stated, the place of publication is London.

Aarsleff, H. (1967), *The Study of Language in England, 1780–1860*, Princeton.

Aarsleff, H. (1982), *From Locke to Saussure: Essays on the Study of Intellectual History*.

Abrams, M.H. (1971), *The Mirror and the Lamp* (first published 1953).

Addison, J. (1854), 'On Pleasures of the Imagination', in *The Spectator with a Biographical and Critical Preface and Explanatory Notes*, vol. 3, 269–303.

Akenside, M. (1744), *The Pleasures of Imagination. A Poem in Three Books*.

Alison, A. (1790), *Essays on the Nature and Principles of Taste*.

Anderson, W.C. (1985), *Between the Library and the Laboratory: The Language of Chemistry in Eighteenth-Century France*, Baltimore.

Anon. (1744), *Hermippus Revivified: or, The Sage's Triumph over Old Age and the Grave*.

Anon. (1758), *Tabes Dorsalis, or, The Cause of Consumption in Young Men . . .*

Ariès, P. (1973), *Centuries of Childhood*, Harmondsworth.

Ashton, J. (1882), *Chapbooks of the Eighteenth Century*.

Ault, D.D. (1974), *Visionary Physics: Blake's Response to Newton*.

Bain, A. (1876), *The Emotions and the Will*, 3rd edn, New York, (first published 1859).

Balzac, H. de (1829), *Physiologie du Mariage* (vol. 7 of *La Comédie Humaine*, Paris, 1965) (first published 1829).

Balzac, H. de (1833), *Ferragus* (vol. 4 of *La Comédie Humaine*, Paris, 1965) (first published 1833).

Balzac, H. de (1965), *La Comédie Humaine*, 7 vols, Paris.

Barrell, J. (1983), *English Literature in History 1730–1780: An Equal, Wide Survey*.

Barrett, P.H. (ed.) (1977), *The Collected Papers of Charles Darwin*, 2 vols, Chicago.

Barthes, R. (1954), *Michelet par Lui-Même*, Paris.

Barthez, P.J. (1858), *Nouveaux Eléments de la Science de l'Homme*, 3rd edn, Paris.

Baudelaire, C. (1975), *Oeuvres Complètes*, 2 vols, Paris.

Beer, G. de (ed.) (1958), *Evolution by Natural Selection: Darwin and Wallace*, Cambridge, (contains the *Sketch* of 1842 and the *Essay* of 1844).

Beer, Gillian (1983), *Darwin's Plots: Evolutionary Narrative in Darwin, George Eliot and Nineteenth-Century Fiction*.

Beer, J. (1969), *Blake's Visionary Universe*, Manchester.

Berger, J. (1972), *Ways of Seeing*, Harmondsworth.

Berger, J. (1980), *About Looking*.

Bernard, C. (1957), *An Introduction to the Study of Experimental Medicine*, New York (first published 1865).

Bernard, Sir T. (ed.) (1805), *The Reports of the Society for Bettering the Condition and Increasing the Comforts of the Poor*, 2 vols.

Bernardin de Saint-Pierre, J.-H. (1784), *Etudes de la Nature*, Paris.

Bernardin de Saint-Pierre, J.-H. (1966), *Paul et Virginie*, Paris (first published 1788).

Bernardin de Saint-Pierre, J.-H. (1982), *Paul and Virginia*, ed. and trans. J. Donovan.

Bichat, M.-F.-X. (1800), *Recherches Physiologiques sur la Vie et la Mort*, Paris.

Black, M. (1962), *Models and Metaphors*, Ithaca, New York.

Blake, W. (1972), *The Complete Writings of William Blake; with Variant Readings*, ed. G. Keynes.

Borie, J. (1984), 'Une Gynécologie Passionnée', in *Misérable et Glorieuse, la Femme du XIXᵉ Siècle*, 2nd edn, Brussels.

Boucé, P.-G. (ed.) (1982), *Sexuality in Eighteenth-Century Britain*, Manchester.

Bowler, P.J. (1983), *The Eclipse of Darwinism: Anti-Darwinian Evolution Theories in the Decades around 1900*, Baltimore.

Brady, F. (1970), '*Tristram Shandy*: Sexuality, Morality, and Sensibility', *Eighteenth-Century Studies* 4, 41–56.

Bredvold, L.I. (1961), *The Brave New World of the Enlightenment*, Ann Arbor.

Brillat-Savarin, J.A. (1825), *Physiologie du Goût*, Paris.

Brissenden, R.F. (1968), ' "Sentiment": Some Uses of the Word in the Writings of David Hume', in R.F. Brissenden (ed.), *Studies in the Eighteenth Century*, Canberra, 89–107.

Brissenden, R.F. (1974), *Virtue in Distress: Studies in the Novel of Sentiment from Richardson to Sade*.

Brooke, H. (1788), *A Collection of the Pieces*.

Brookner, A. (1972), *Greuze: The Rise and Fall of an Eighteenth-Century Phenomenon*.

Brooks, P. (1984), *Reading for the Plot: Design and Invention in Narrative*, Oxford.

Brumfitt, J.H. (1972), *The French Enlightenment*.

Bryson, G. (1968), *Man and Society: The Scottish Inquiry of the Eighteenth Century*, New York.

Bryson, N. (1981), *Word and Image: French Painting of the Ancien Régime*, Cambridge.

Buck, P. (1982), 'People Who Counted: Political Arithmetic in the Eighteenth Century', *Isis* 73, 28–45.

Buckle, H.T. (1857–61), *History of Civilisation in England*, 2 vols.

Burke, E. (1803), *A Philosophical Inquiry into the Origin of our Ideas of the Sublime and the Beautiful*, Montrose (first published 1757).

Burrow, J.W. (1966), *Evolution and Society: A Study in Victorian Social Theory*, Cambridge.

Butler, M. (1981), *Romantics, Rebels and Reactionaries: English Literature and its Background 1760–1830*, Oxford.

Cabanis, P.J.G. (1956), *Oeuvres Philosophiques*, 2 vols, Paris.

Cadogan, W. (1748), *An Essay Upon Nursing and the Management of Children from their Birth to Three Years of Age*.

Cahn, T. (1962), *La Vie et L'Oeuvre d'Etienne Geoffroy Saint-Hilaire*, Paris.

Canguilhem, G. (1971), *La Connaissance de la Vie*, 2nd edn, Paris.

Carpenter, W.B. (1874), *Principles of Mental Physiology*.

Carroll, D.R. (1967), '*Silas Marner*: Reversing the Oracles of Religion', *Literary Monographs* 1.

Carroll, D.R. (ed.) (1971), *George Eliot: The Critical Heritage*, New York.

Carter, A. (1979), *The Sadeian Woman: An Exercise in Cultural History*.

Cassirer, E. (1951), *The Philosophy of the Enlightenment*, Princeton.

Centenaire de la Fondation du Muséum d'Histoire Naturelle (1893), Paris.

Chalmers, T., Kidd, J., Whewell, W., *et al.* (1833–6), *Bridgewater Treatises*.

Chambers, E. (1741, 1783), *Cyclopaedia: or, An Universal Dictionary of the Arts and Sciences* (first published 1728).

Charlton, D.G. (1984), *New Images of the Natural in France: A Study in European Cultural History 1750–1800*, Cambridge.

Chateaubriand, F.-R. de (1802), *Le Génie du Christianisme*, Paris.

Cheyne, G. (1733), *The English Malady*.

Clough, A.H. (1968), *The Poetry of Arthur Hugh Clough*, ed. A.L.P. Norrington.

Cobbett, W. (1824), 'To Landowners. On the Evils of Collecting Manufacturers into Great Masses', *Cobbett's Political Register* 52 (Oct.–Dec.), 448–81.

Cohen, R. (1964), *The Art of Discrimination*, Berkeley.

Coleman, W. (1977), 'L'Hygiène et L'Etat selon Montyon', *Dix-Huitième Siècle* 9, 101–8.

Coleman, W. (1982), *Death is a Social Disease: Public Health and Political Economy in Early Industrial France*, Madison, Wisconsin.

Coleridge, S.T. (1817), *Biographia Literaria; or, Biographical Sketches of My Literary Life and Opinions*, 2 vols.

Collignon, C. (1764), *An Enquiry into the Structure of the Human Body, Relative to its Supposed Influence on the Morals of Mankind*, Cambridge.

Colp, R. (1979), 'Charles Darwin's Vision of Organic Nature', *New York State Journal of Medicine* 79, 1622–9.

Comte, A. (1853), *The Positive Philosophy of Auguste Comte*, trans. and ed. H. Martineau, 2 vols.

Comte, A. (1875–7), *System of Positive Polity or Treatise on Sociology Instituting the Religion of Humanity*, trans. J.H. Bridges, F. Harrison, E.S. Beesly and R. Congreve, 4 vols.

Cooter, R.J. (1976), 'Phrenology: The Provocation of Progress', *History of Science* 14.

Cooter, R.J. (1985), *The Cultural Meaning of Popular Science: Phrenology and the Organisation of Consent in Nineteenth-Century Britain*, Cambridge.

Copley, S. (1982), 'The Natural Economy: A Note On Some Rhetorical Strategies in Political Economy – Adam Smith and Malthus', in F. Barker *et al.* (eds), *1789 Reading Writing Revolution* (Proceedings of the Essex Conference on the Sociology of Literature, July 1981) Colchester, 160–9.

Cowper, W. (1782), *Poems*.

Crocker, L.G. (1959), *An Age of Crisis: Man and World in Eighteenth-Century French Thought*, Baltimore.

Crocker, L.G. (1963), *Nature and Culture: Ethical Thought in the French Enlightenment*, Baltimore.

Cross, W.L. (ed.) (1904), *The Works of Laurence Sterne*, New York.

Cullen, M.J. (1975), *The Statistical Movement in Early Victorian Britain*, Hassocks.

Cuvier, G. (1817), *Le Règne Animal*, 4 vols, Paris.

Darwin, C. (1959), *On the Origin of Species*, A Variorum Edition, ed. M. Peckham, Philadelphia.

Darwin, C. (1968), *On The Origin of Species by Means of Natural Selection, or the Preservation of Favoured Races in the Struggle for Life*, ed. J. Burrow from the first edition (1859), Harmondsworth.

Darwin, C. (1975), *Charles Darwin's Natural Selection being the Second Part of his Big Species Book written from 1856 to 1858*, ed. R. Stauffer.

Darwin, E. (1799), *The Botanic Garden: a Poem in Two Parts. Part I, The Economy of Vegetation*, 4th edn, *Part II, The Loves of the Plants*, 5th edn.

Darwin, E. (1801), *Zoonomia; or, The Laws of Organic Life*, 3rd edn, 4 vols.

Darwin, E. (1803), *The Temple of Nature; or, The Origin of Society*.

Darwin, F. (ed.) (1887), *The Life and Letters of Charles Darwin, including an Autobiographical Chapter*, 3 vols.

Delaporte, F. (1982), *Nature's Second Kingdom*, Cambridge, Mass.

De Porte, M. V. (1974), *Nightmares and Hobbyhorses: Swift, Sterne, and Augustan Ideas of Madness*, San Marino, Cal.

Derrida, J. (1970), 'Structure, Sign, and Play', in R. Macksey and E. Donato (eds), *The Languages of Criticism and the Sciences of Man: The Structuralist Controversy*, Baltimore.

Derrida, J. (1976), *Of Grammatology*, trans. G. Spivak, Baltimore.

Dickens, C. (ed.) (1973), *Household Words* (1850–9), re-edited with an introduction by Anne Lohrh, Toronto.

Diderot, D. (1953), *Supplément au Voyage de Bougainville* and *Le Rêve de d'Alembert*, in *Selected Philosphical Writings*, ed. J. Lough, Cambridge.

Diderot, D. (1972), *Le Neveu de Rameau*, ed. R. Desné, Paris.

Donzelot, D. (1980), *The Policing of Families: Welfare versus the State*.

Douglas, M. (1966), *Purity and Danger: An Analysis of Concepts of Pollution and Taboo*.

Douglas, M. (1970), *Natural Symbols: Explorations in Cosmology*.

Douglas, M. (1975), *Implicit Meanings: Essays in Anthropology*.

Dowden, E. (1878), *Studies in Literature:* 1789–1877.

Drake, J. (1707), *Anthropologia Nova, or A New System of Anatomy*.

Duncan, C. (1973), 'Happy Mothers and Other New Ideas in French Art', *Art Bulletin* 55, 570–83.

Duncan, C. (1981), 'Fallen Fathers: Images of Authority in Pre-Revolutionary French Art', *Art History* 4, 186–202.

Eagleton, T. (1982), *The Rape of Clarissa*, Oxford.

Easlea, B. (1983), *Fathering the Unthinkable: Masculinity, Scientists and The Nuclear Arms Race*.

Ehrard, J. (1963), *L'Idée de Nature en France dans la Première Moitié du XVIIIᵉ Siècle*, Paris.

Eliot, G. (n.d.), *Silas Marner, The Lifted Veil, Brother Jacob*, Edinburgh.

Ellegård, A. (1958), *Darwin and the General Reader: The Reception of Darwin's Theory of Evolution in the British Periodical Press*, 1859–72, Goteburg.

Elshtain, J.B. (1981), *Public Man, Private Woman: Women in Social and Political Thought*, Oxford.

Elshtain, J.B. (ed.) (1982), *The Family in Political Thought*, Brighton.

Erdman, D.V. (1977), *Blake: Prophet Against Empire*, 3rd edn, Princeton.

Europe (1973), 51 (Nov.–Dec.) (special issue on Michelet)

Fairchilds, C. (1978), 'Female Sexual Attitudes and the Rise of Illegitimacy: A Case Study', *Journal of Interdisciplinary History* 8, 627–67.

Fénelon, F. (1712), *Traité de l'Existence de Dieu*, Paris.

Feuerbach, L. (1854), *The Essence of Christianity*, trans. from the second German edn by Marian Evans.

Figlio, K.M. (1975), 'Theories of Perception and the Physiology of Mind in the Late Eighteenth Century', *History of Science* 13, 177–212.

Figlio, K.M. (1976), 'The Metaphor of Organisation: An Historiographical Perspective on the Bio-Medical Sciences of the Early Nineteenth Century', *History of Science* 14, 17–53.

Fitton, R.S. and Wadsworth, A.P. (1958), *The Strutts and the Arkwrights 1758-1830: A Study of the Early Factory System*, Manchester.

Flandrin, J.-L. (1979), *Families in Former Times: Kinship, Household and Sexuality*, Cambridge.

Flew, A. (1970), 'Introduction' to T.R. Malthus, *An Essay on the Principle of Population*, Harmondsworth.

Forster, R. and Ranum, O. (eds) (1976), *Family and Society*, Baltimore.

Forster, R. and Ranum, O. (eds) (1980), *Medicine and Society in France*, Baltimore.

Foster, M. (1924), *Lectures on the History of Physiology*, Cambridge (first published 1901).

Foucault, M. (1970), *The Order of Things: An Archaeology of the Human Sciences*.

Foucault, M. (1979), *The History of Sexuality*, vol. 1 Introduction.

Fox Keller, E. (1985), *Reflections on Gender and Science*, New Haven.

French, R.K. (1969), *Robert Whytt, the Soul, and Medicine*.

Frye, N. (ed.) (1966), *Blake: A Collection of Critical Essays*, Englewood Cliffs, New Jersey.

Furst, D.C. (1974), 'Sterne and Physic: Images of Health and Disease in *Tristram Shandy*', Columbia University dissertation.

Galilei, G. (1967), *Dialogue Concerning the Two Chief World Systems*, trans. Stillman Drake, Berkeley and Los Angeles.

Gélis, J. *et al* (eds) (1978), *Entrer dans la Vie*, Paris.

Gerard, A. (1780), *An Essay on Taste*, 3rd edn, Edinburgh (first published 1759).

Gillespie, N.C. (1979), *Charles Darwin and the Problem of Creation*, Chicago.

Gillis, J.R. (1974), *Youth and History: Tradition and Change in European Age Relations, 1770–present*, New York.

Gillispie, C.C. (1951), *Genesis and Geology: A study in the Relations of Scientific Thought, Natural Theology, and Social Opinion in Great Britain, 1790–1850*, Cambridge, Mass.

Gilpin, W. (1792), *Three Essays: On Picturesque Beauty; On Picturesque Travel; and on Sketching Landscape*.

Gisborne, T. (1796), *Walks in a Forest*.

Glacken, C. (1967), *Traces on the Rhodian Shore: Nature and Culture in Western Thought from Ancient Times to the End of the Eighteenth Century*, Berkeley.

Glass, D. (1978), *Numbering the People: The Eighteenth-Century Population Controversy and the Development of Census and Vital Statistics in Britain*.

Goldberg, R. (1984), *Sex and Enlightenment: Women in Richardson and Diderot*, Cambridge.

Gonnard, R. (1923), *Histoire des Doctrines de la Population*, Paris.

Gossman, L. (1974), 'The Go-Between: Jules Michelet 1798–1874', *Modern Language Notes* 89, 503–41.

Graham, J. (1973), 'Ut Pictura Poesis', *Dictionary of the History of Ideas*, vol. 4, New York, 465–76.

Graver, S. (1984), *George Eliot and Community: A Study in Social Theory and Fictional Form*, Berkeley.

Gray, T., Collins, W., and Goldsmith, O. (1969), *The Poems of Thomas Gray, William Collins, Oliver Goldsmith*, ed. R. Lonsdale.

Greene, D.J. (1953), 'Smart, Berkeley, the Scientists and the Poets: A Note on Eighteenth Century Anti-Newtonianism', *Journal of the History of Ideas* 14, 327–52.

Grimsley, R. (ed.) (1979), *The Age of Enlightenment 1715–1789*, Harmondsworth.

Gruber, H.E. (1980), 'The Evolving Systems Approach to Creative Scientific Work: Charles Darwin's Early Thought', in T. Nickles (ed.), *Scientific Discovery: Case Histories*, Dordrecht, 113–30.

Gruber, H. and Barrett, P. (eds) (1974), *Darwin on Man: A Psychological Study of Scientific Creativity together with Darwin's Early and Unpublished Notebooks*.

Hagstrum, J.H. (1958), *The Sister Arts: The Tradition of Literary Pictorialism from Dryden to Gray*, Chicago.

Hagstrum, J.H. (1980), *Sex and Sensibility: Ideal and Erotic Love from Milton to Mozart*, Chicago.

Haight, G.S. (ed.) (1954–78) *The George Eliot Letters*, 9 vols, New Haven.

Haller, A. von (1754), *Dr. Albert Haller's Physiology*.

Haller, A. von (1755), A Dissertation on the Sensible and Irritable Parts of Animals, in *Bulletin of the History of Medicine*, Supplement 4 (1936), 651–99.

Hampson, N. (1968), *The Enlightenment*, Harmondsworth.

Harris, R.W. (1968), *Reason and Nature in Eighteenth-Century Thought*.

Hartmann, E. von (1893), *Philosophy of the Unconscious: Speculative Results According to the Inductive Method of Physical Science*, trans. W.C. Coupland, 2nd edn, 3 vols.

Hazard, P. (1946), *La Pensée Européenne au XVIIIᵉ Siècle; de Montesquieu à Lessing*, Paris.

Herwig, H.M. (1700), *The Art of Curing Sympathetically or Magnetically*.

Hesse, M.B. (1966), *Models and Analogies in Science*, Notre Dame, Indiana.

Hesse, M.B. (1979), *The Structure of Scientific Inference*.

Hine, E.N. (1973), 'Condillac and the Problem of Language', *Studies on Voltaire and the Eighteenth Century* 106, 21–61.

Hipple, W.J. (1957), *The Beautiful, the Sublime and the Picturesque in Eighteenth-Century British Aesthetic Theory*, Carbondale, Illinois.

Holbach, P.H.D., Baron d' (1770), *Le Système de la Nature*, Amsterdam.

Hopkins, G.M. (1967), *The Poems of Gerard Manley Hopkins*, ed. W.H. Gardner and N.H. Mackenzie, 4th edn, Oxford.

Hooykaas, R. (1963), *The Principle of Uniformity in Geology, Biology and Theology*, Leiden.

Hume, D. (1888), *A Treatise of Human Nature*, ed. L.Selby-Bigge, Oxford.

Hunter, J. (1794), *A Treatise on the Blood, Inflammation, and Gun-shot Wounds*.

Hutcheson, F., the elder (1726), *An Inquiry into the Original of Our Ideas of Beauty and Virtue; in Two Treatises*, 2nd edn (first published 1725).

Jacob, F. (1973), *The Logic of Life: A History of Heredity*, trans. B.E. Spellman, New York.

Jacobs, E. *et al.* (eds) (1979), *Woman and Society in Eighteenth-Century France.*

Johnson, J. (1968), *Disorders of Sexual Potency in the Male,* Oxford.

Johnson, S. (1755), *A Dictionary of the English Language,* 2 vols.

Jones, C. (1978), 'Prostitution and the Ruling Class in Eighteenth-Century Montpellier', *History Workshop Journal* 6, 7–28.

Jones, G. (1980), *Social Darwinism and English Thought: The Interaction Between Biological and Social Theory,* Brighton.

Jones, W.P. (1961), 'The Ideas of the Limitations of Science Prior to Blake', *Studies in English Literature* 1, 97–114.

Jordanova, L.J. (1980a), 'Natural Facts: A Historical Perspective on Science and Sexuality', in C. MacCormack and M. Strathern (eds), *Nature, Culture and Gender,* Cambridge.

Jordanova, L.J. (1980b), 'Romantic Science? Michelet, Morals and Nature', *British Journal for the History of Science* 13, 44–50.

Jordanova, L.J. (1982), 'Guarding the Body Politic: Volney's Catechism of 1793', in F. Barker *et al.* (eds), 1789 *Reading Writing Revolution* (Proceedings of the Essex Conference on the Sociology of Literature, July 1981), Colchester, 12–21.

Jordanova, L.J. (1984), *Lamarck,* Oxford.

Jordanova, L.J. (1985), 'Gender, Generation and Science: William Hunter's Obstetrical Atlas', in W.F. Bynum and Roy Porter (eds), *William Hunter and the Eighteenth-Century Medical World,* Cambridge, 385–412.

Jordanova, L.J. and Porter, Roy (eds) (1979), *Images of the Earth: Essays in the History of the Environmental Sciences,* Chalfont St Giles.

Kaplan, E.K. (1977), *Michelet's Poetic Vision: A Romantic Philosophy of Nature, Man and Woman,* Amherst, Mass.

Keele, K.D. (1957), *Anatomies of Pain,* Oxford.

Keynes, G. (1971), *Blake Studies: Essays on His Life and Work,* 2nd edn.

King-Hele, D. (1977), *Doctor of Revolution: The Life and Genius of Erasmus Darwin.*

King-Hele, D. (ed.) (1981), *The Letters of Erasmus Darwin*, Cambridge.

Kingsley, C. (1863), *The Water-Babies*.

Kingsley, C. (1949), *The Wonders of the Shore* in *The Water-Babies and Glaucus; or, The Wonders of the Shore* (first published 1855).

Klingender, F.D. (1975), *Art and the Industrial Revolution*, St Albans (first published 1947).

Knibiehler, Y. (1976), 'Les Médecins et la "Nature Feminine" au Temps du Code Civil', *Annales E.S.C.* 31, 824–45.

Knight, R.P. (1796), *The Progress of Civil Society: A Didactic Poem, in Six Books*.

Kolakowski, L. (1972), *Positivist Philosophy from Hume to the Vienna Circle*, Harmondsworth.

Laclos, P.A.F.C. de (1979a), *Oeuvres Complètes*, Paris.

Laclos, P.A.F.C. de (1979b), *Les Liaisons Dangereuses*, Harmondsworth.

Lamarck, J.B. (1809), *Philosophie Zoologique*, 2 vols, Paris.

La Mettrie, J.O. de (1748), *L'Homme Machine*, Amsterdam.

Larrissey, E. (1982), 'A Description of Blake: Ideology, Form, Influence', in F. Barker *et al.* (eds), *1789 Reading Writing Revolution* (Proceedings of the Essex Conference on the Sociology of Literature, July 1981), Colchester, 101–9.

Larson, J. (1971), *Reason and Experience: The Representation of Natural Order in the Work of Carl von Linné*, Berkeley and Los Angeles.

Lavater, J.-G. (n.d.), *La Physiognomie ou L'Art de Connaître les Hommes d'après les Traits de Leur Physiognomie*, Paris (first published 1775–8).

Lawrence, C. (1979), 'The Nervous System and Society in the Scottish Enlightenment', in B. Barnes and S. Shapin (eds), *Natural Order. Historical Studies of Scientific Culture*, Beverly Hills.

Le Doeuff, M. (1981–2), 'Pierre Rousel's Chiasmas: From Imaginary Knowledge to the Learned Imagination', *Ideology and Consciousness* 9, 39–70.

Levine, G. (1981), *The Realistic Imagination: English Fiction from Frankenstein to Lady Chatterley*, Chicago.

Lewes, G.H. (1853), *Comte's Philosophy of the Sciences*.

Lewes, G.H. (1858), *Sea-side Studies*, Edinburgh.

Lewes, G.H. (1859–60), *The Physiology of Common Life*, 2 vols.

Lewes, G.H. (1874–5), *Problems of Life and Mind, First Series: The Foundations of a Creed*, 2 vols.

Locke, J. (1706), *An Essay Concerning Human Understanding*, 5th edn (first published 1690).

Logan, J.V. (1936), *The Poetry and Aesthetics of Erasmus Darwin*, Princeton.

Lonsdale, R. (ed.) (1984), *The New Oxford Book of Eighteenth Century Verse*, Oxford.

Lovejoy, A.O. (1927), ' "Nature" as Aesthetic Norm', *Modern Language Notes*, 444–50 (reprinted in *Essays in the History of Ideas*, Baltimore, 1948, 69–77).

Lovejoy, A.O. (1961), *The Great Chain of Being: A Study of the History of an Idea*, Cambridge, Mass. (first published 1936).

Lyell, C. (1830–3), *Principles of Geology*, 3 vols.

MacCormack, C.P. and Strathern, M. (eds) (1980), *Nature, Culture and Gender*, Cambridge.

McKendrick, N. (1961), 'Josiah Wedgwood and Factory Discipline', *Historical Journal* 4, 30–55.

McLaren, A. (1973–4), 'Some Secular Attitudes towards Sexual Behaviour in France: 1760–1860', *French Historical Studies* 8, 604–25.

McLaverty, J. (1981), 'Comtean Fetishism in *Silas Marner*', *Nineteenth-Century Fiction* 36.

Maclean, I. (1980), *The Renaissance Notion of Woman*, Cambridge.

Maclean, K. (1949), 'Imagination and Sympathy: Sterne and Adam Smith', *Journal of The History of Ideas* 10, 399–410.

McManners, J. (1981), *Death and the Enlightenment: Changing Attitudes to Death among Christians and Unbelievers in Eighteenth Century France*, Oxford.

McNeil, M. (1986), *'Under the Banner of Science': Erasmus Darwin and his Age*, Manchester.

Macnish, R. (1835), *The Philosophy of Sleep*, 2nd edn, New York.

Macherey, P. (1978), *Towards a Theory of Literary Production* (first published in Paris 1966 as *Pour une Théorie de la Production Littéraire*).

Malthus, T.R. (1803), *An Essay on the Principle of Population; or, A View of its Past and Present Effects on Human Happiness; with an Inquiry into Our Prospects Respecting the Future Removal or Mitigation of the Evils which it Occasions*, 2nd edn of *An Essay on the Principle of Population* (1798).

Mandeville, B. (1924), *The Fable of the Bees*, ed. F.B. Kaye, 2 vols, Oxford.

Manier, E. (1978), *The Young Darwin and his Cultural Circle: A Study of the Influences Which Helped Shape the Language and Logic of the First Drafts of the Theory of Natural Selection*, Dordrecht.

Manuel, F. (1972), *Freedom from History and Other Untimely Essays*.

Marivaux, P.C. de C. de (1949a), *Romans*, Paris.

Marivaux, P.C. de C. de (1949b), *Théâtre Complet*, Paris.

Marx, K. (1973), *Grundrisse: Foundations of the Critique of Political Economy (Rough Draft) 1857–8*, trans. M. Nicolaus, Harmondsworth.

Marx, K. (1976), *Capital: A Critique of Politcal Economy*, vol. 1 (1867), trans. B. Fowkes, introduced by E. Mandel, Harmondsworth.

Marx, K. (1977), *Selected Writings*, ed. D. McLellan, Oxford.

Marx, K. and Engels, F. (1965), *Selected Correspondence*, ed. S.W. Ryanyanskaya, Moscow.

Mauzi, R. (1960), *L'Idée de Bonheur au XVIIIᵉ Siècle*, Paris.

Mead, R. (1762), *Medical Works*.

Merchant, C. (1980), *The Death of Nature: Women, Ecology and the Scientific Revolution*, New York.

Mercier, R. (1960), *La Réhabilitation de la Nature Humaine (1700–1750)*, Villemoble.

Merz, J.T. (1965), *A History of European Thought in the Nineteenth Century*, 4 vols, New York (first published 1904–12).

Michelet, J. (1831), *Introduction à l'Histoire Universelle*, in *Oeuvres Complètes*, vol. II, Paris, 1972 (first published 1831).

Michelet, J. (1833), *Tableau de France*, in *Oeuvres Complètes*, vol. IV, Paris, 1974 (first published 1833).

Michelet, J. (1846), *Le Peuple*, Paris, 1974 (first published 1846).

Michelet, J. (1848), *L'Etudiant*, Paris, 1974 (lectures given in 1848, first published under this title in 1877).

Michelet, J. (1856), *L'Oiseau*, Paris, n.d. (part of the 1898–1903 edition of his *Oeuvres Complètes*, first published 1856).

Michelet, J. (1857), *L'Insecte*, Paris, 1859 (first published 1857).

Michelet, J. (1858), *L'Amour*, Paris.

Michelet, J. (1859), *La Femme*, Paris, n.d. (part of the 1898–1903 edition of his *Oeuvres Complètes*, first published in 1859).

Michelet, J. (1861), *La Mer*, Paris, n.d. (part of the 1898–1903 edition of his *Oeuvres Complètes*, first published 1861).

Michelet, J. (1866), *Histoire de France au Dix-Huitième Siècle (Louis XV)*, Paris.

Michelet, J. (1868), *La Montagne*, Paris, n.d. (part of the 1898–1903 edition of his *Oeuvres Complètes*, first published 1868).

Michelet, J. (1869a), *Préface à l'Histoire de France*, in *Oeuvres Complètes*, Paris, 1974 (first published (1869).

Michelet, J. (1869b), *Nos Fils*, Paris, 2nd edn, 1870.

Michelet, J. (1959–76), *Journal*, 4 vols, Paris.

Miles, J. (1965), *Pathetic Fallacy in the Nineteenth Century: A Study of a Changing Relation between Object and Emotion*, New York.

Mill, J.S. (1854), *Three Essays on Religion: Nature; The Utility of Religion; and Theism*, 2nd edn.

Miller, J. Hillis (1963), *The Disappearance of God: Five Nineteenth Century Writers*, Cambridge, Mass.

Mivart, St George (1875), 'Instinct and Reason', *Contemporary Review* 25.

Montesquieu, C. de S., Baron de la Brède et de (1949–51), *Oeuvres Complètes*, 2 vols, Paris.

Moravia, S. (1978), 'From *Homme Machine* to *Homme Sensible*: Changing Eighteenth-Century Models of Man's Image', *Journal of the History of Ideas* 39, 45–60.

Morgan, T. (1735), *The Mechanical Practice of Physic*.

Mornet, D. (1932), *La Pensée Française au XVIIIe Siècle*, Paris.

Morrell, J., and Thackray, A. (1981), *Gentlemen of Science: Early Years of the British Association for the Advancement of Science*, Oxford.

Muirhead, J.P. (1859), *The Life of James Watt, with Selections from his Correspondence*, 2nd edn, (first published 1858).

Müller, F.M. (1861–4), *Lectures on the Science of Language*, 1st and 2nd series.

Nicolson, M.H. (1946), *Newton Demands the Muse: Newton's Opticks and the Eighteenth Century Poets*, Princeton.

Okin, S.M. (1980), *Women in Western Political Thought*.

Orr, L. (1976), *Jules Michelet: Nature, History and Language*, Ithaca, New York.

Paley, W. (1830), *Natural Theology: or, Evidences of the Existence and Attributes of the Deity, Collected from the Appearances of Nature*, new edition (first published 1802).

Passmore, J. (1970), *The Perfectibility of Man*.

Paulson, R. (1971), 'The Pictorial Circuit and Related Structures in Eighteenth Century England', in P. Hughes and D. Williams (eds), *The Varied Pattern: Studies in the Eighteenth Century*, Toronto, 165–87.

Paulson, R. (1979), *Popular and Polite Art in the Age of Hogarth and Fielding*, Notre Dame, Indiana.

Petit, H. (1963), 'The Limits of Reason as a Literary Theme in the English Enlightenment', *Studies on Voltaire and the Eighteenth Century* 24, 1307–19.

Phillipson, N. (1981), 'The Scottish Enlightenment', in R. Porter and M. Teich (eds), *The Enlightenment in National Context*, Cambridge, 19–40.

Picavet, F. (1891), *Les Idéologues*, Paris.

Pinney, T. (ed.) (1963), *Essays on George Eliot*, New York.

Politi, J. (1977), *The Novel and its Presuppositions: Changes in the Conceptual Structure of Novels in the Eighteenth and Nineteenth Centuries*, Amsterdam.

Pope, A. (1753), *An Essay on Man* (first published 1733–4).

Pope, A. (1966), *Poetical Works*, ed. Herbert Davis.

Praz, M. (1970), *Mnemosyne: The Parallel Between Literature and the Visual Arts*, Princeton.

Prévost, Abbé (A.F. Prévost d'Exiles) (1942), *Histoire du Chevalier des Grieux et de Manon Lescaut*, Cambridge (first published 1731).

Priestley, J. (1777), *A Course of Lectures in Oratory and Criticism*.

Radner, J.B. (1979), 'The Art of Sympathy in Eighteenth-Century British Moral Thought', in R. Runte (ed.), *Studies in Eighteenth Century Culture*, 8, 189–210.

Randall, J.H. (1962), *The Career of Philosophy*, 2 vols, New York.

Rather, L.J. (1965), *Mind and Body in Eighteenth Century Medicine: A Study Based on Jerome Gaub's De Regimine Mentis*.

Revue d'Histoire Littéraire de la France (1974), 74 (Sept.–Oct.) (special issue on Michelet).

Roberts, T.A. (1973), *The Concept of Benevolence: Aspects of Eighteenth-Century Moral Philosophy*.

Robinson, P. (1982), 'Virginie's Fatal Modesty: Some Thoughts on Bernardin de Saint-Pierre and Rousseau', *British Journal for Eighteenth-Century Studies* 5, 35–48.

Rodgers, J. (1978), 'Ideas of Life: *Tristram Shandy* and Contemporary Medicine and Physiology', University of East Anglia PhD dissertation.

Rodgers, J. (1980), ' "Life" in the Novel: *Tristram Shandy* and Some Aspects of Eighteenth-Century Physiology', *Eighteenth-Century Life* 6 (n.s. 1), 1–20.

Roger, J. (1963), *Les Sciences de la Vie dans la Pensée Française du XVIIIᵉ Siècle*, Paris.

Roger, J. (1980), 'The Living World', in G.S. Rousseau and R. Porter (eds), *The Ferment of Knowledge: Studies in the Historiography of Eighteenth-Century Science*, Cambridge, 255–83.

Rosen, G. (1974), *From Medical Police to Social Medicine*, New York.

Rosen, G. (1976), 'A Slaughter of Innocents: Aspects of Child Health in the Eighteenth-Century City', *Studies in Eighteenth Century Culture* 5, 293–316.

Rousseau, G.S. (1976), 'Nerves, Spirits and Fibres: Towards Defining the Origins of Sensibility', in R.F. Brissenden and J.C. Eade (eds), *Studies in the Eighteenth Century III*, Toronto, 137–57.

Rousseau, G.S. (1980), 'Psychology', in G.S. Rousseau and R. Porter (eds), *The Ferment of Knowledge: Studies in the Historiography of Eighteenth-Century Science*, Cambridge, 143–210.

Rousseau, G.S. and Porter, R. (eds) (1980), *The Ferment of Knowledge: Studies in the Historiography of Eighteenth-Century Science*, Cambridge.

Rousseau, J.-J. (1964), *Julie ou la Nouvelle Héloïse* in *Oeuvres Complètes*, vol. 2, Paris (first published 1761).

Rousseau, J.-J. (1974), *Emile*, trans. B. Foxley, introduced by P.D. Jimack (first published 1762).

Roussel, P. (1777), *Système Physique et Moral de la Femme*, Paris.

Rudwick, M.J.S. (1972), *The Meaning of Fossils: Episodes in the History of Paleontology*.

Ruskin, J. (1873), *Love's Meinie*, Keston, Kent.

Sade, D.A.F. de (1966), *Justine, Philosophy in the Bedroom and Other Writings*, New York.

Sade, D.A.F. de (1972), *La Philosophie dans le Boudoir*, Paris.

Schofield, R.E. (1963), *The Lunar Society of Birmingham: A Social History of Provincial Science and Industry in Eighteenth Century England*, Oxford.

Seylaz, J.-L. (1968), *'Les Liaisons Dangereuses' et La Création Romanesque chez Laclos*, Geneva.

Shaftesbury, A.A.C., 3rd Earl of (1900), *Characteristicks of Men, Manners, Opinions, Times*, ed. J.M. Robertson, 2 vols.

Shorter, E. (1976), *The Making of the Modern Family*.

Shuttleworth, S. (1984), *George Eliot and Nineteenth-Century Science: The Make-Believe of a Beginning*, Cambridge.

Simon, R. (1966), 'Narcolepsy and the Strange Malady of *Silas Marner*', *American Journal of Psychiatry* 123.

Simson, T. (1752), *An Enquiry How Far the Vital and Animal Actions of the More Perfect Animals Can Be Accounted for Independent of the Brain*, Edinburgh.

Smiles, S. (1865), *Lives of Boulton and Watt*.

Smiles, S. (1894), *Josiah Wedgwood, F.R.S.: His Personal History*.

Smith, B. (1960), *European Vision and the South Pacific, 1768–1850: A Study in the History of Art and Ideas*, Oxford (revised edition, New Haven, 1985).

Smith, O. (1984), *The Politics of Language, 1791–1819*, Oxford.

Smith, R. (1970), 'Physiological Psychology and the Philosophy of Nature in Mid-Nineteenth-Century Britain', University of Cambridge PhD dissertation.

Smith, R. (1973), 'The Background of Physiological Psychology in Natural Philosophy', *History of Science* 11, 75–123.

Sommerville, J. (1982), *The Rise and Fall of Childhood*, Beverly Hills.

Spacks, P.M. (1967), *The Poetry of Vision: Five Eighteenth-Century Poets*, Cambridge, Mass.

Spacks, P.M. (1978), 'The Dangerous Age', *Eighteenth-Century Studies* 11, 417–38.

Spencer, H. (1855), *The Principles of Psychology*.

Spencer, H. (1876), *The Principles of Sociology*, New York.

Stauffer, R.C. (1975), *Charles Darwin's Natural Selection, being the Second Part of his Big Species Book written from 1856 to 1858*.

Staum, M.S. (1974), 'Cabanis and the Science of Man', *Journal of the History of Behavioural Sciences* 10, 135–43.

Staum, M.S. (1980), *Cabanis: Enlightenment and Medical Philosophy in the French Revolution*, Princeton.

Sterne, L. (1904), *The Works of Laurence Sterne*, ed. W.L. Cross, New York.

Sterne, L. (1940), *The Life and Opinions of Tristram Shandy, Gentleman*, ed. J.A. Work, New York (first published 1759–67).

Strauss, D.F. (1846), *The Life of Jesus, Critically Examined*, trans. from the 4th German edn by Marian Evans, 3 vols.

Sussman, G. (1982), *Selling Mothers' Milk: The Wet-Nursing Business in France, 1715–1914*, Urbana, Illinois.

Temkin, O. (1971), *The Falling Sickness: A History of Epilepsy from the Greeks to the Beginnings of Modern Neurology*, 2nd rev. edn, Baltimore.

Thody, P. (1975), *Laclos: Les Liaisons Dangereuses*, 2nd edn.

Thomson, J. (1901), *The Complete Poetical Works of James Thomson*, ed. J.L. Robertson.

Tissot, S.A.A.D. (1772), *Onanism, or a Treatise upon the Disorders Produced by Masturbation*, Dublin.

Traer, J.F. (1980), *Marriage and the Family in Eighteenth-Century France, Ithaca*, New York.

Tuveson, E.L. (1960), *The Imagination as a Means of Grace: Locke and the Aesthetics of Romanticism*, Berkeley.

Tuveson, E. (1967), 'Shaftesbury and the Age of Sensibility', in H. Anderson and J.S. Shea (eds), *Studies in Criticism and Aesthetics, 1660–1800*, Minneapolis, 73–93.

van Duzer, C.H. (1935), *The Contribution of the Idéologues to French Revolutionary Thought*, Baltimore.

Vartanian, A. (1960), *La Mettrie's L'Homme Machine: A Study in the Origins of an Idea*, Princeton.

Viallaneix, P. (1971), *La Voie Royale. Essai sur l'Idée de Peuple dans L'Oeuvre de Michelet*, Paris.

Viallaneix, P. (ed.) (1975), *Michelet Cent Ans Après*, Grenoble (part of *Romantisme, Etudes Romantiques* series).

Volney, C.-F. (1934), *La Loi Naturelle, ou Catéchisme du Citoyen Français*, Paris (first published 1793).

Voltaire, F.-M. A. de (1937), *Traité de Métaphysique* ed. H. Temple Patterson, Manchester.

Wasserman, E.R. (1950), 'The Inherent Values of Eighteenth-Century Personification', *Publications of the Modern Language Association of America* 65, 435–63.

Watt, I. (1963), *The Rise of the Novel: Studies in Defoe, Richardson and Fielding*, Harmondsworth (first published 1957).

Webster, C. (1975), *The Great Instauration: Science, Medicine and Reform 1626–1660*.

Wedgwood, J. (1783), *An Address to the Young Inhabitants of the Pottery*, Newcastle.

Whyte, L.L. (1962), *The Unconscious Before Freud*.

Whytt, R. (1751), *An Essay on the Vital and Other Involuntary Motions of Animals*, Edinburgh.

Whytt, R. (1755), *Physiological Essays*, Edinburgh.

Whytt, R. (1765), *Observations on the Nature, Causes, and Cure of those Disorders Which Have Been Called Nervous, Hypochondriac, or Hysteric*, Edinburgh.

Wiesenfarth, J. (1970), 'Demythologising *Silas Marner*', *English Literary History* 37.

Willey, B. (1940), *The Eighteenth-Century Background*.

Williams, R. (1963), *Culture and Society 1780–1950*, Harmondsworth (first published 1958).

Williams, R. (1972), 'Social Darwinism', *The Listener*, 23 November, 696.

Williams, R. (1975), *The Country and the City*, St Albans.

Williams, R. (1983), *Keywords: A Vocabulary of Culture and Society* (first published 1976).

Wilson, C. (1958), *Mercantilism*.

Wollstonecraft, M. (1975), *A Vindication of the Rights of Woman*, Harmondsworth (first published 1792).

Wood, J.G. (1877), *Nature's Teachings: Human Invention Anticipated by Nature*.

Young, R.M. (1969), 'Malthus and the Evolutionists: The Common Context of Biological and Social Theory', *Past and Present*, no. 43, 109–45.

Young, R.M. (1970), *Mind, Brain and Adaptation in the Nineteenth Century: Cerebral Localization and the Biological Context from Gall to Ferrier*, Oxford.

Young, R.M. (1973), 'The Role of Psychology in the Nineteenth-Century Evolutionary Debate', in M. Henle *et al.* (eds), *Historical Conceptions of Psychology*, New York.

Zeldin, T. (1973), *France 1848–1945* Vol I: *Ambition, Love and Politics*, Oxford.

INDEX

This first edition of
Languages of Nature
was finished in April 1986.

It was typeset in 11/13½ pt Cheltenham
on a CRTronic 300 and printed by
Harris cold-set web offset
onto Publishers Antique Wove
80g/m^2, vol. 18 paper

The book was commissioned by Robert M. Young,
copy edited by Elaine Donaldson,
designed by Carlos Sapochnik,
and produced by Free Association Books.